10.00

P9-DTL-935

Your Boat's
Electrical System

Volumes in the Motor Boating & Sailing Guide Series, of which this is one, deal in close detail with separate areas of the maintenance and repair of today's pleasure boats and their associated equipment. Each book is written by an expert in the field, fully illustrated with necessary drawings, photos and diagrams, and update as required. The Guides are designed for the skipper interested in both the economies and pleasures of personal boat maintenance, and for the owner who cannot do the work himself, but who wants to be aware of what's done aboard his vessel.

From Motor Boating & Sailing Books—publishers of Chapman's **Piloting, Seamanship, and Small Boat Handling**

Your Boat's Electrical System

BY CONRAD MILLER

MOTOR BOATING & SAILING BOOKS

224 West 57th Street, New York, N.Y. 10019

Copyright © 1973 by The Hearst Corporation

959 Eighth Avenue, New York, N.Y. 10019

Library of Congress catalog card number: 73-88057

ISBN 0-910990-17-4

All rights reserved. This book or parts thereof
may not be reproduced in any form without
permission.

This book was designed by WILLIAM BOSSERT

Illustrations by RICHARD MEYER

Composition, printing and binding by
THE HADDON CRAFTSMEN, INC., SCRANTON, PA.

Contents

CONTENTS

Author's Preface

THIS BOOK is about pleasure boat electricity, the circuits carrying it from its source, and those distributing it throughout the boat. Both alternating and direct current systems are covered in a way that attempts to help the yachtsman understand and care for his boat's electrical systems.

Emphasis is on safety and the practical, the book being aimed at the boat owner who enjoys his own boatkeeping. To help him in maintenance, trouble-shooting, tune-up, and possible modification work, circuits are first described, then workable approaches to maintenance or rework are suggested.

The text spills over into engine mechanics simply because the most vital parts of the engine are electrical. Consequently, ignition, starting and starting circuits, although strictly engine components, become part of this work on marine electricity.

Both author and publisher hope that this book will fill a void in boating literature, while helping boatkeepers do a better job of electrical maintenance and trouble-shooting.

C. M.

The Author

ALWAYS keenly interested in electrical and mechanical things, Conrad Miller was sparked on by his father who gave him transformers, electric motors, batteries, and spark coils instead of mundane toys when Miller was in the first grade. By the age of eight he was on the air with a spark gap transmitter; but a few months later he was put off the air when local radio listeners found what was wrecking reception of *Amos 'n Andy*.

An avid boatman and boating writer, Miller started sailing on Barnegat Bay at the age of six, raced sneakboxes all of his boyhood, wrote his first boating magazine article at seventeen, and had his first book "Small Boat Engines" published when he was nineteen. That was back in the early nineteen forties, and he has been writing about boats and engineering ever since.

His schooling included studies at Rutgers, Cornell, G.M. Technical Institute, The Command & General Staff School, and several U.S. Army technical schools.

During World War II, Miller taught for two years at the U.S. Army Ordnance School, then went to North Africa and finally to China-Burma-India where he dropped supplies to allied troops, organized maintenance companies in Burma, and managed to escape a flaming air crash where everything else was totalled. Immediately after the hostilities, he served in the Ballistic Research Laboratory at Aberdeen Proving Ground. He was discharged from the service with the rank of major.

After the army, Miller joined Woods Hole Oceanographic Institution, training as an oceanographic observer at Scripps Institute of Oceanography. Following this, he was assigned to the first Bikini Atom Bomb Test expedition as an oceanographer. There he spent the better part of a year watching the bombs detonate, calibrating instruments, and chasing around the Pacific in small boats making measurements of radioactivity. Much to his surprise, the day after one of the blasts, he found his picture on the front page of the New York papers, fishing up a Nansen bottle of radioactive water.

Fun and adventure being over, Miller went home from the Bikini expedition, settled down in New Jersey, and with a friend started an electronic manufacturing company which they operated together for some eighteen years. Fates smiled on the enterprise and it prospered swimmingly, Miller selling out in 1962 to become editor of *Rudder* magazine.

During the years in the electronic manufacturing business, Miller continued boating and writing, mixing the two in hundreds of magazine articles plus a second book on marine engines published by Sheridan House.

Currently, the author is on the engineering staff of Tenney Engineering Company, Union, N.J., is Technical Editor of *Motor Boating & Sailing*, consultant to NAEBM Westlawn School of Yacht Design, member of American Boat & Yacht Council, and member of Institute of Electrical and Electronic Engineers. He is a celestial navigation buff and for years has written a monthly column carrying a celestial navigation problem.

Miller lives in Edison, N.J. with his wife Marian and sons Win, "Digger," and Keith. Favorite part of the house is the excellent workshop used by the four men, including the youngest, Keith, who gets transformers, electric motors, batteries, and spark coils for Christmas, and who, at the tender age of five, can make a respectable soldered joint.

~~~~~~

CHAPTER I

Fundamentals

Electricity—What Is It?

IT FLOWS through wires. It operates all maner of lights and machines aboard the boat, sparks the engine into action, bothers the compass, starts fires, causes corrosion, can be a blessing or curse, depending upon whether it is corroding hardware or energizing a bilge pump.

But what is electricity? The dictionary says: "Electricity is one of the fundamental quantities in nature, giving rise to a magnetic field of force." But those words leave a lot untold.

Even the great Lord Kelvin had difficulty in teaching his students what electricity really is. There is a story that the famous scientist once lectured a university class on electricity and magnetism. Finishing his dissertation, he turned from the blackboard to question the students about the subject.

"Well," he asked, scanning the upturned faces, "what is electricity?"

A dozing young man at the back of the class raised his hand; then, alarmed at his own involuntary action, quickly pulled it down again. But alas, Kelvin's keen eye had sighted him.

"Ah!" said Lord Kelvin," Mr. Smith knows what electricity is; and he is going to tell us."

The hapless young student rose, gulped, looked at his feet, and stammered, "I am sorry, sir, I have forgotten."

In the dreadful silence that followed, Kelvin drew himself up, adjusted his glasses, and glared down at the class for what seemed an eternity. Then he said: "Gentlemen, you have just witnessed one of the major tragedies of our century. Only two people know what electricity is: God and Mr. Smith. God will not tell us; and Mr. Smith has forgotten." And with that, he gathered his gown about him and swept out of the room.

We may not know all of what electricity is, but we do know that it's a force (Electromotive Force—EMF or E) which pushes a current (I) through a load (Resistance—R). Electromotive Force is measured in terms of *volts,* and it is analogous to the water pressure in a pipe. Current is measured in terms of *amperes,* and is analogous to the rate of water flow through a pipe. Resistance is measured in terms of *ohms,* and is analogous to the friction offered to the flow of water through plumbing by valves or other restrictions within the pipe.

Electrical power is measured in terms of *watts,* and is analogous to the water flow rate through a pipe against a given pressure head. How to handle volts, amps, ohms and watts as units of measurement is dealt with a bit later in this chapter.

Sources of Electricity

Aboard the boat, electricity flows from a variety of sources. Among these are:

1. **Storage batteries:** In the storage battery, energy is held in chemical form, being converted to electricity when an external circuit is made across its terminals. The conventional lead-acid storage battery cell puts out about two volts regardless of its physical size. To force a storage battery to give more than two volts, cells are cascaded in series, each adding its voltage to the prior one. Thus, a 12 volt storage battery has six cells. As shown

CELLS IN SERIES

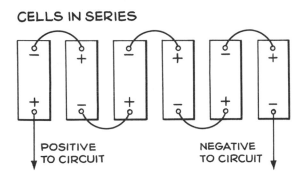

POSITIVE
TO CIRCUIT

NEGATIVE
TO CIRCUIT

Fig. 1-1 When battery cells are strung in series, each adds its voltage to the one it follows. The six two-volt cells shown will deliver 12 volts to the external circuit.

in Figure 1-1, the negative terminal of each cell is connected to the positive of the next.

Current capability, not voltage, depends upon the battery's physical heft. Thus, a powerful diesel engine starting battery is bigger and heavier than one used to crank an outboard motor. But their voltages may be identical. As one wag put it, looking at a motorcycle battery and comparing it to a 300-pound diesel starting battery: "That monster may offer only 12 volts, same as the tiny one; but they sure are damn big volts!"

2. **Dry Cells:** Flashlight batteries and the cells powering portable radios are called *dry cells* even though there is a wet paste inside the case. The common zinc-carbon cell generates about 1.5 volts regardless of its size, the tiny penlight cell having identical voltage to the quart bottle size doorbell battery. When more than 1.5 volts are required, the cells are placed in series. However, when heavier current is to be furnished, cells are wired in parallel. Now, *voltage* of the combination is the same as for one cell, but *current capability* equals that of one cell multiplied by the number of cells. This is shown in Figure 1-2.

3. **Capacitors:** Sometimes called *Condensers,* capacitors store electrical charges fed to them. They don't generate electricity in

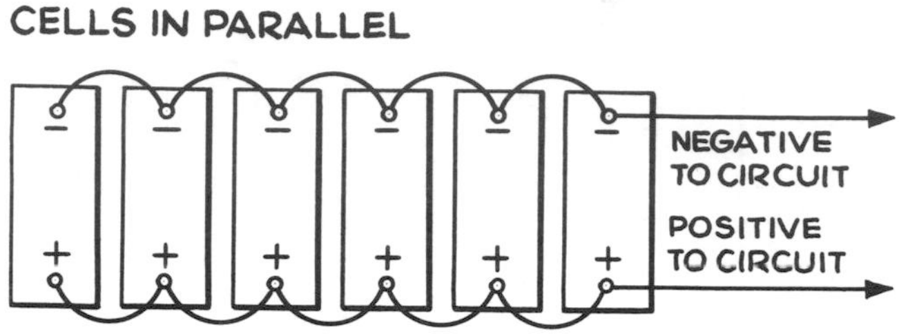

CELLS IN PARALLEL

Fig. 1-2 Voltage from a battery of cells connected in parallel is the same as for one cell. However, six cells, each capable of two amperes, will deliver 12 amperes to the external circuit, when wired as shown.

the sense that batteries do, but they take a charge equal to the voltage impressed on them, and store it.

The storage capability of a condenser is utilized in capacitor discharge ignition. Here, the capacitor is charged to several hundred volts, then discharged rapidly into the ignition circuit. Compared to dry or wet cells on a size or weight basis, capacitors store but little energy. However, they accept a full charge almost instantly, can store high voltage, and can release their entire reserve of energy in mere thousandths of a second.

4. **Generator and Alternator:** Dynamic machines, these: motor-driven generators and alternators convert mechanical power to electricity, forcing it into the boat's electrical system. Both voltage and current are a function of machine design, the scope being almost unlimited. Typical machines for marine battery systems are six, 12, and 24 volts, while most alternators serving the boat's housepower needs are 115 or 230 volts. Current capability depends upon size, and upon how hard the rotating machine is driven.

5. **Magnetos:** Many outboards and some inboard engines derive ignition electricity from an engine-driven magneto. Sometimes a separate accessory, but often a part of the flywheel, the magneto is a special purpose generator, converting engine power to electric current specifically tailored to ignition requirements.

14

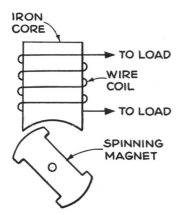

IRON
CORE

TO LOAD

WIRE
COIL

TO LOAD

SPINNING
MAGNET

Fig. 1-3 Generators, alternators, and magnetos create electricity by spinning a magnet close to a coil wound on an iron core.

6. **Shore Power Cord:** A common power source for boats berthed in marinas and yards, the power cord is more a link than a source of electricity. Through it flows household type alternating current; and its power handling capability depends upon its size, fittings, and the circuits feeding it.

7. **Electrochemical Reactions:** Frequently refered to by boatmen as electrolysis, electrochemical reaction between underwater hardware of different metals generates electricity. Such current is an unwelcome intruder aboard the boat. It performs no useful function, and can destroy otherwise sound hardware through electrolytic corrosion.

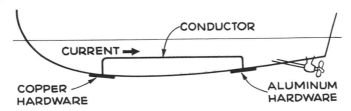

CONDUCTOR

CURRENT ➡

COPPER
HARDWARE

ALUMINUM
HARDWARE

Fig. 1-4 Dissimilar metals placed under the floating hull generate electricity which flows from one to the other through any conductive path between the metals.

15

DIRECT CURRENT

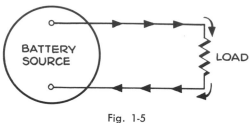

Fig. 1-5

Kinds of Current

Direct current (d.c.) is the kind of electricity which flows from a battery, through its associated circuit, and back to the battery. While the circuit is energized, current flows constantly in one direction, like water flowing through a pipe.

Alternating current (a.c.) is the variety which comes from receptacles on the pier and from a.c. motor-generators aboard the boat. So far, no one has invented an a.c. battery. Alternating current pulsates through its wires, flowing in one direction for a fraction of a second, then reversing itself and flowing in the opposite direction. In the United States, a.c. pulses back and forth 60 times a second, at a frequency defined as 60 Hertz. An especially useful characteristic of a.c. is that it can be easily transformed from one voltage to another with little energy loss, whereas with d.c., transformation involves complicated converters or high losses or both.

ALTERNATING CURRENT

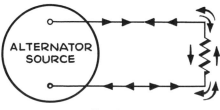

Fig. 1-6

Units of Measurement

Earlier, we introduced the terms volt, ampere, ohm, and watt. As you recall, these terms define electric parameters—for both d.c. and a.c. Let's review the terms again:

  * **Volt** expresses the pressure forcing electricity through a conductor, and is analogous to the water pressure in a pipe.

  * **Ampere** describes the current, or rate of flow, through the conductor and is analogous to the rate of water flow through a pipe.

  * **Ohm** defines the resistance to current flow, and is analogous to friction offered the flow of water through a pipe.

  * **Watt** is a measure of electric power, just as horsepower is a measure of mechanical power. It is analogous to the water flow rate through a pipe against a given pressure head.

Ohm's Law

An electrical law originated by Georg Simon Ohm over a hundred years ago defines the relationship of voltage, current, and resistance in a circuit. Knowing any two elements, you can calculate the third. Said Georg, "Let **E** equal voltage, **I** equal current, and **R** equal resistance."

Then:

$$I = \frac{E}{R}; R = \frac{E}{I}, \text{ and } E = IR$$

Assume that you know the voltage (**E**) is 12 volts and current (**I**) is six amperes. You can determine resistance from the second equation $R = \frac{12}{6} = 2$. Thus, the circuit has two ohms resistance.

Another example is where voltage is 115, resistance of a heater element is 23 ohms. How much current does the heater draw? $I = \frac{E}{R} = \frac{115}{23} = 5$. The heater draws five amps.

Calculating Watts

We saw that wattage is a measure of power. To find the watts

17

being dissipated by a circuit, multiply volts times amperes (**EI**). Thus, if five amps flows in a 115 volt circuit, wattage is $5 \times 115 = 575$ watts.

Another way to compute wattage, where current and resistance are known, is to multiply current squared times resistance (**I²R**). Thus, where current is 5 amps and resistance 23 ohms, $I^2R = 25 \times 23 = 575$ watts.

Measuring the units

To design electrical circuits, control their function, and trouble-shoot, we must be able to measure what's going on in the conductors. The basic measuring tools are the voltmeter, ammeter, and ohmmeter.

VOLTMETER

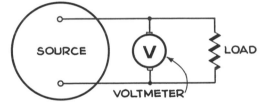

Fig. 1-7 The voltmeter is connected across the line in parallel with the load. Having high resistance, it demands little power.

* The **voltmeter** is an instrument of high resistance, connected directly across the conductors or line. Because of its high resistance, it draws little current, placing a negligible load on the circuit. The meter movement senses circuit voltage, magnetically deflecting a pointer in proportion to measured voltage.

* The **ammeter** is an instrument of low resistance, connected in series between the power source and load. A good ammeter has

AMMETER

Fig. 1-8 An ammeter is wired in series with the load. Offering little resistance, it causes negligible voltage drop.

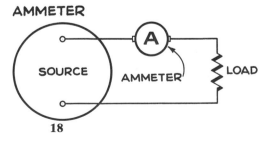

such low resistance that the power loss through it is of no consequence. Its internal movement senses circuit current, magnetically deflecting a pointer in proportion to measured current.

* The **ohmmeter** incorporates a penlight or flashlight battery, providing its own current for resistance measurements; and it is always connected to a deenergized or "dead" circuit element. The instrument comprises a cell of known voltage in series with an internal known resistance and a sensitive ammeter, called a milliammeter.

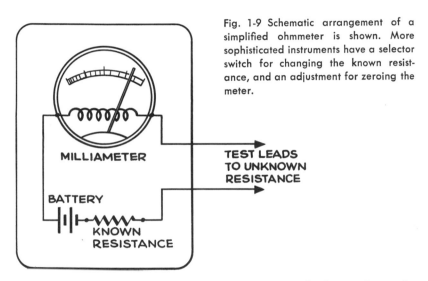

Fig. 1-9 Schematic arrangement of a simplified ohmmeter is shown. More sophisticated instruments have a selector switch for changing the known resistance, and an adjustment for zeroing the meter.

When the ohmmeter's test leads are touched together, the meter swings to zero ohms, indicating no external resistance in series with the leads. When the test leads are separated, the meter falls to infinity, indicating substantially infinite external resistance. When the leads are placed in series with an external resistance, such as a light bulb, the meter deflects in proportion to that resistance. For example, if the instrument's internal resistance is 60 ohms and the test leads are touched in series with 60 ohms, the meter will indicate half scale, pointing to "60."

The Multimeter

A most useful electrician's trouble-shooting tool is the **multimeter**, a portable, sometimes pocket size, instrument incorporating all three popular meters. An inexpensive multimeter might have the following scales: Ohms center scale deflection: 6, 60, 600, 6,000, and 60,000. Volts full scale: 3, 15, 60, 300, 600, and 1,200. Current full scale, in amperes: 0.003, 0.03, 0.3, 3.0, and 10.

Most multimeters measure both a.c. and d.c. voltage. However, they only measure direct current amperes. For alternating current ampere measurements, the snap-on ammeter is used by trouble shooters.

The A.C. Snap-On Ammeter

The hand-held a.c. snap-on ammeter measures alternating current flowing through a conductor without metal-to-metal contact with the conductor. It does so by magnetically "feeling" the current flow; and its use and operation are described later in this book.

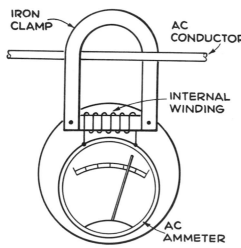

Fig. 1-10 Clipped around an insulated conductor, the alternating current ammeter measures current by detecting the pulsating magnetic field around one wire.

Wire Size vs. Gauge

As emphasized many times throughout the book, larger diameter wires offer less resistance than smaller ones, and voltage drop through them is less. Consequently, large diameter wires create less power loss than skinny ones. The reader is asked to keep in mind that American Wire Gauge (AWG) sizes are like shotgun bores: the higher the number, the smaller the conductor. For example, size #12 AWG wire measures about 0.081 inch diameter, and offers approximately 1.6 ohms resistance per thousand feet. Contrast this to #22 AWG wire which measures 0.025 inch diameter, and has over 16 ohms resistance per thousand feet.

Basic Circuits

Most electrical circuits fall into two categories: parallel and series. Of the two, parallel circuits are most popular in boating electricity.

* All loads are connected between the two conductors in a parallel circuit. Each load has available the same voltage as the others; and each draws current as determined by its resistance.

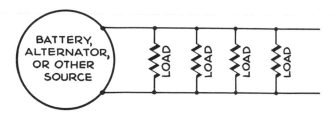

Fig. 1-11 In a parallel circuit, the loads such as lights, motors, or heaters, are wired across the power lines like ladder rungs.

* Loads are connected end-to-end, "series strung," in a series circuit. Each load sees the same current as the others. If all loads have the same resistance, each load sees voltage equal to source voltage divided by the number of loads. Thus, 10 equal light bulbs in series with a 100 volt feed will each see 10 volts.

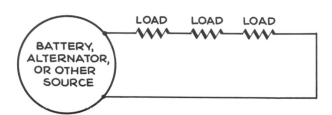

Fig. 1-12 In a series circuit, loads follow along one after the other like a string of cars on a train.

Temperature vs. Resistance

Common conductors increase in resistance as temperature increases. Keep this in mind when trouble shooting with an ohmmeter. For example, a 115 volt 100 watt light bulb offers 132 ohms resistance when burning. But its cold resistance, measured with an ohmmeter, is only 15 ohms.

Grounded Circuits

One side of a circuit, whether a.c. or d.c., is frequently connected to ground, usually as a safety measure. In a few instances where "ground" is the frame of a metal machine, ground is used as one of the current-carrying conductors. This arrangement is used on cars and trucks, but seldom on boats. The many aspects of grounds and grounding are covered extensively in chapters that follow.

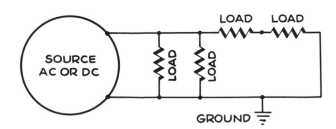

Fig. 1-13 One conductor in this series-parallel system is grounded.

DEFINING OUR TERMS

The definitions that follow take minor liberties that the scientist or electrical engineer may grouse about; but with them, the author tries to make clear the meaning of electrical and related words the way they are used in this book. Purists are invited to keelhaul the author if they deem the analogies a little salty in spots.

alternating current (a.c.): Electricity that flows first in one direction, then in the reverse direction through its conductors. Each wire becomes positive, then negative, reversing polarity typically 60 times a second. Analogous to water oscillating back and forth inside a pipe.

alternator: A machine that generates alternating current. In battery charging alternators, the generated a.c. is internally changed to direct current before reaching the terminals.

ampacity: Current carrying capacity of a conductor expressed in amperes. Analogous to the diameter of a water pipe.

ampere: The amount of electricity flowing. Analogous to the quantity of water flowing through a pipe. One ampere flowing through one ohm gives a voltage drop of one volt.

amphoteric: Capable of reacting chemically either as an acid or base. Aluminum is amphoteric, requiring special protection as a marine metal.

anode: The positive terminal of an electrolytic system, the one at which oxidizing reactions occur. When zinc is fastened to bronze on under-water hardware, the zinc is *anodic*.

arc: Flash of electricity across a gap, usually seen as a blue or yellow spit of flame.

armature: The spinning rotor of a d.c. motor or generator. Also the fixed coils (stator) in an automotive type alternator.

autotransformer: A transformer in which there is a connection between primary and secondary windings. Some have one simple winding with a tap, one terminal being common to primary and secondary. Variac and Powerstat are trade names for variable autotransformers.

binnacle: The box, stand, or housing carrying the boat's compass.

brush: A carbon or copper spring-loaded sliding contact, bearing on a commutator or rotor, carrying current to or from the rotating member in a motor or generator.

capacitance: The size of a capacitor, its capacity, usually expressed in microfarads (MFD) for boat electricity. Typical distributor capacitor (condenser) is 0.1 MFD, typical motor starting capacitor: 100 MFD.

capacitor: Also condenser. Component that stores electric charges. In effect, will conduct a.c. but block d.c. Analogous to a stretchable membrane across a water pipe, allowing water to oscillate, but not flow unidirectionally.

capacity shield: In an isolation transformer, a faraday screen preventing energy transmission from shore to the boat except by desired electromagnetic means of coupling. The shield knocks out the capacitive coupling between shore and boat windings.

capacitive coupling: Transfer of energy from one component to another due to capacitance between the two.

cathode: The negative terminal of an electrolytic system, the one at which reducing reactions occur. The protected one. When zinc is fastened to bronze underwater hardware, the bronze becomes cathodic.

charger: An electrical appliance to convert alternating current to direct current of lower voltage, used to charge the boat's batteries.

circuit breaker: An automatic switch that opens its circuit upon detecting excess current. Analogous to an automatic safety valve on a pressurized water tank.

clip-on ammeter: An a.c. ammeter which measures current in a conductor by proximity, there being no connection other than magnetic.

conductive: Something that conducts electricity such as metals and salt water.

conductor: Material that allows electricity to flow through easily. Copper is a good conductor.

corona: A faint blue glow near the surface of an electrical conductor at high potential.

corrosion: Deterioration of hardware and other metals because of reaction with the environment.

commutator: Radial copper segments on the rotor of an electric motor or generator, conducting current from the brushes to the spinning windings.

cross fire: The undesired firing of one spark plug caused by voltage transfer from the wire serving another plug.

current sensing relay (CSR): A relay which responds to current flowing through a circuit, rather than to voltage across the circuit.

dead-front switchboard: One with no exposed live parts on the front.

deviate: To deflect the needle of a compass by local influence, as through the effect of a current-carrying conductor.

dielectric: A non-conductor. Special dielectrics are used for elements inside capacitors. Oil impregnated paper is an example.

diode: A two terminal component, vacuum tube or semi-conductor, which passes current in one direction, blocking it in the other. Analogous to a check valve in a water pipe.

direct current (d.c.): Electricity that flows in one direction through a conductor. Analogous to water flowing through a pipe.

electrode: A conductor used to make electrical contact with a non-metallic surface, as with seawater or other electrolyte.

electrolysis: Passage of electricity through a liquid, such as seawater.

electrolyte: A liquid conductor of electricity, such as salt water or battery acid solution.

electrolytic corrosion: Destruction of metals through electrolysis.

eliminator, battery: A power pack or battery charger with filtered output, suitable for operating direct current accessories from the alternating current line.

ferrite: A molded, kiln fired, magnetic transformer core material usually used for high frequency or pulse transformers.

full-wave rectifier: A circuit that changes alternating current to pulsating direct current, rectifying both halves of each cycle. Output is smoother than that of the half wave rectifier.

fuse: A thin ribbon of metal that melts or burns, opening its associated circuit on detecting excess current. Analogous to a freeze-out or blow-out plug on a pressure vessel.

galvanic anode: A "low noble" metal that protects, frequently zinc or magnesium.

galvanic corrosion: Corrosion resulting from electric current between dissimilar metals in an electrolyte.

galvanic series: A list of metals and alloys arranged according to their relative potentials in seawater. Metals close to each other on the list "fight" the least.

ganged: Switches or switch functions are ganged when the throwing of one transfers all at the same time. Circuit breakers can be ganged.

gauge: Wire diameter. High gauge number designates small wire.

generator: A machine to generate electricity. Analogous to a water pump.

grounded: A conductor which is normally current-carrying, when at earth potential.

grounding: A conductor at earth potential which is normally non-current-carrying. Typical of safety conductors which ground equipment frames.

hot: A conductor not at ground potential. Also, one that can give a shock.

housepower: Euphemism describing 115/230 volt, single phase, 60 Hertz, alternating current used domestically, at dockside, and on board boats. The word is not in standard dictionaries.

half-wave rectifier: A circuit that changes alternating current to pulsating direct current, rectifying only half of each cycle. Output is rougher than that of the full wave rectifier.

insulator: A material that will not allow electricity to flow through. Nylon and ceramics are good insulators.

induction motor: An a.c. motor without brushes or commutator wherein the rotor is energized by transformer action. (Note: A *very* few induction motors, repulsion-start type, have a commutator. They are seldom seen on modern appliances.)

inductive load: An electrical load, as given by induction motor or transformer. May draw much more current from the line than is indicated by its wattage.

isolation transformer: A power transformer, located on the boat, which furnishes a.c. to the boat's system, coupling to shore power magnetically, but severing all connections by direct conductor.

loading coil: A wire-wound coil in the transmitter or receiver circuit which makes the antenna seem electrically longer than its physical length. Often a part of the whip antenna.

locked rotor current: The amperes which a' motor draws when its shaft is locked. This is the current the motor can demand for the first split second after it is turned on, but has not yet accelerated.

microfarad (MFD): The usual measure of a capacitor's electrical size or capacitance. A 2 MFD unit stores twice the energy of a 1 MFD unit at the same voltage.

27

Micro-Switch: A miniature switch, easily actuated, and of high current handling ability, considering its small size.

negative: The polarity of a boat's battery which is usually grounded. Polarity of the bottom of a flashlight battery. Polarity of a cathode. The electrode from which electrons flow to the anode. Symbol is $-$. Color code on battery charger terminals is often black.

noble: When a more noble and less noble metal are electrically connected and placed in an electrolyte, as salt water, the less noble corrodes; the more noble is protected.

ohm: Measure of resistance. Analogous to pressure drop in a water pipe when water flows. 1 ohm causes 1 volt drop when 1 ampere flows.

pinion: A small gear designed to mesh with a large gear, such as the small gear on a starter drive mechanism.

polarity: The distinction between positive and negative conductors, and also between north and south magnetic poles in a machine.

pole: Referring to a switch or relay, the number of conductors which the device can switch on and off, or transfer from one circuit to another. Single and double pole devices are most common on the boat.

polyphase: A power system with more than one phase. (See *three-phase*.)

positive: The polarity of a boat's conductors which are usually hot. Polarity of the top button on a flashlight battery. Polarity of an anode. The electrode to which electrons flow from the cathode. Symbol is $+$. Color code on battery chargers is usually red.

potential: Voltage.

power center: A dockside enclosure having power receptacles, fuses or circuit breakers, and sometimes a light on top.

power factor: The ratio of watts to volt-amperes in an a.c.

circuit. At low power factor, there can be considerable current, but few watts dissipated. Analogous to a lot of water oscillating to and fro inside a pipe against a spring load, but with little water flowing from source to faucet.

Powerstat: Trade name for a variable autotransformer.

rectifier: A device or network to convert a.c. to d.c. The word is sometimes used to describe a complete battery charger or power supply.

relay: A switch activated by a small current in its coil. Heavy duty power relays are called *contactors*.

resistance: Measured in ohms. The degree to which current is retarded from flowing. Small diameter copper wire has higher resistance than large diameter wire. Analogous to a small water pipe having greater resistance to flow than a large one.

resistive load: An electrical load of pure or almost pure resistance such as a light bulb or toaster.

rheostat: A variable resistance. Analogous to a throttling valve in a water pipe.

root mean square (RMS): Housepower voltage varies throughout each cycle; and the value we measure is ordinarily the RMS value. It is equal to 0.707 of the peak voltage. Thus, if RMS voltage is 115, potential at the crest of each 60 cycle wave is about 163 volts.

rotor: The spinning part of a motor, generator, or alternator.

salinity: The percentage of salts dissolved in water. Seawater has a salinity of about 3.5% in the open ocean. Brackish water has lower salinity than seawater.

short circuit: Condition where the circuit's two conductors touch together at a point between the source (such as a battery) and the termination (such as a light).

shunt: A conductor connecting two points in a circuit in parallel with another conductor. A resistor across ammeter terminals is called a shunt. Sharing the current, it will allow an ammeter of, say, 1 ampere full deflection, to measure 10 amperes.

silicon controlled rectifier (SCR): A transistor type device which acts like a high speed relay. When a small current is passed through its trigger circuit, it "fires," allowing heavy current to flow through its main terminals.

single phase: The standard housepower electrical system where one set of waves represents the voltage.

solenoid: Wire wound as a helix. Also a term applied to plunger relays used in engine starting circuits.

stator: The fixed, stationary poles and windings in a generator or motor.

stray current corrosion: Corrosion of underwater parts caused by flow of battery current, or other current, between submerged hardware. Corrosion occurs at the electrically positive part where current flows from the metal part to the seawater.

sweat: To solder.

synchronous speed: As applied to a motor, the rpm of the rotor where the speed is locked in step with the power line frequency. A four-pole synchronous machine rotates 1,800 rpm on a 60 Hz line. Analogous to a surfboard catching a wave and riding it without ever falling behind.

tap: As applied to a motor, transformer, or coil winding: a wire connected to the winding turns somewhere between the start and finish turns.

thermal protector: A temperature sensitive device inside a motor which shuts down the machine upon detecting that its windings are over-heated. When the motor cools, the protector resets, starting the motor again.

three phase: A power system where three sets of waves represent the voltage; and crests of the waves are displaced 120 degrees apart. It is a three or four wire system found in factories, but is almost unknown on the pier.

throw: As applied to a switch: the number of selections it can make. A single throw switch offers on-off. A double throw switch can connect its incoming wire or wires to two different circuits alternately, and frequently has a "center off" position. The term is applied to describe relays, also.

transformer: An a.c. device to magnetically couple one circuit to another. It can raise or lower the output voltage relative to the input. See also *autotransformer* and *isolation transformer*.

trip-free: A circuit breaker which will function to interrupt the current even though the reset handle is manually held against the trip.

universal motor: An electric motor with armature and brushes which will operate on a.c. or d.c. Commonly used in hand drills and vacuum cleaners.

volt: The pressure or push behind the electricity in a circuit. Analogous to the pressure in a water pipe. One volt can push one ampere through one ohm.

vector: A line segment whose length represents magnitude and whose orientation in space represents direction. Useful for finding the resulting force when two separate forces act on a point.

watt: Measure of electrical power. In direct current, volts times amperes equals watts. In alternating current, volts times amps times power factor equals watts. Theoretically, 746 watts equals 1 horsepower. Electric meters measure the number of watts used per hour.

zener diode: A semiconductor that suddenly starts to conduct at one particular voltage. Used as a stable, accurate reference voltage, somewhat like a standard cell.

CHAPTER II

Understanding the Battery

STORAGE BATTERIES are the very heart and center of the boat's direct-current electrical system. They not only provide the enormous current (hundreds of amperes) required to start the engine, but they also contribute a moderating effect, smoothing voltage fluctuations while the charging circuits are operative.

Batteries act not only as gigantic "springs" to wind the engines into action, they also serve as electrical fly-wheels, soaking up power when the generator pushes it into the system; returning power when the generator cannot keep up with demands.

Battery Function

Storing hundreds of watt-hours of energy while being charged, the batteries force that work back into the electrical system during discharge. Lacking the battery's moderating effect, the boat's electrical system would show wide voltage variations with which the conventional charging systems would be completely unable to cope.

Lead-Acid

By far the most popular kind of battery aboard the modern cruiser or work boat is the lead-acid type. It is the same as the

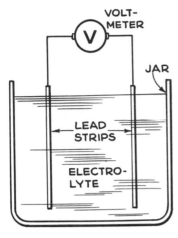

Fig. 2-1 Two strips of lead immersed in a glass of lead acid electrolyte form a basic kitchen sink experimental battery. When charged, one strip becomes positive, the other negative.

popular battery on cars, trucks, and buses, most commonly in 12 volt configuration.

Understanding what makes it tick will help the intelligent boatkeeper do a good job of battery maintenance. A simple "cellar shop" experiment is interesting and demonstrates the principle behind the lead-acid battery. The reader may like to try it:

Hang up two strips of lead, such as two flattened lengths of solder, inside a jar on opposite sides, and keep the strips from touching. Fill the jar with dilute sulphuric acid, available from a battery shop in plastic containers. Careful! The acid will burn your hands or clothes. If you splash it, wash immediately with plenty of soap and water.

To the lead strips in the jar connect a source of direct current at about three volts, and you will then be charging your miniature cell. Bubbles will rise to the surface of the acid and one strip will turn brown, while the other strip will remain lead colored. After a period of charging, the brown strip is covered with a layer of lead peroxide and becomes the cell's positive plate. The clear lead plate becomes negative; and the two plates plus the acid now comprise a small electric cell.

After detaching the charging source, touch a pair of voltmeter probes to the dry part of the strips: You should see a potential between them of about two volts. That is the approximate *voltage* of any lead-acid cell, regardless of its size. Bigger cells generate more *current*, but *voltage* remains the same. Remember: when higher voltage is required, cells are connected in series. Repeated charge and discharge of your small cell will increase the thickness of lead peroxide film on the positive electrode; and this will increase the cell's capacity. However, voltage will remain at about the two-volt level.

The miniature experimental cell described above works the same in principle as the big, heavy batteries on a boat. In practice, current is amplified hundreds of times because the effective area of the plates is increased in proportion. Voltage is raised to 12, 24, or more as desired, through stringing of the cells in a series to form a "battery" of cells, from whence cometh the name. Surface, upon which current depends, is multiplied not only through the incorporation of many large plates, but also by corrugating, grooving, and sponging of the lead. In a high-capacity cell, sponging is important: Electrolyte can then flow through the lead's pores contacting active material many times greater in area than presented by the apparent outer surface.

The Inside Story

Engineers with Exide Power Systems Division of ESB, one of the largest battery manufacturers in the world, describe the electro-chemical action in a lead-acid battery cell in the following words:

$$\text{Discharge}$$
$$\longrightarrow$$
$$PbO_2 + Pb + 2H_2SO_4 = 2PbSO_4 + 2H_2O$$
$$\longleftarrow$$
$$\text{Charge}$$

"In a fully charged battery all the active material of the posi-

34

tive plate is lead peroxide. That of the negative plate is pure sponge lead. All the acid is in the electrolyte, and the specific gravity is at maximum. As the battery discharges, some of the acid separates from the electrolyte which is in the pores of the plates. It forms a chemical combination with the active material, changing it to lead sulphate, and producing water.

"As discharge continues, additional acid is drawn from the electrolyte, while further sulphate and water is formed. As this process progresses, the specific gravity of the electrolyte gradually falls. The proportion of acid is decreasing and that of water is increasing.

"When a battery is on charge, reverse action takes place. Acid in the sulphated active material of the plates is driven out and returns to the electrolyte. Return of the acid to the electrolyte reduces sulphate in the plates and increases specific gravity of the electrolyte. Gravity continues to rise until all the acid is driven from the plates, back into the electrolyte. The plates are then free of sulphate.

"As the cells approach full charge, they cannot absorb all of the energy from the charging current. The excess current breaks

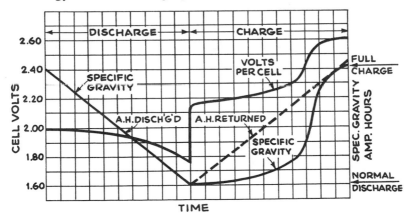

Fig. 2-2 Voltage and specific gravity characteristics during constant rate discharge and charge. Voltage rises immediately as charging starts, but specific gravity lags far behind ampere hours charged until full charge is reached.

up water from the electrolyte into its two components, hydrogen and oxygen, which are liberated from the cell as gases. This is the primary reason for the required addition of water to battery cells."

Charge and Discharge are Different

Rare is the boatkeeper who has not tested a battery's condition or state-of-charge with a hydrometer. Battery experts at ESB point out that decrease in specific gravity on *discharge* is proportional to the ampere-hours discharged. However, as discussed below, the rise in specific gravity indicated by a hydrometer during recharge is not uniform or proportional to the charge in ampere-hours. There is a lag.

Here's what accounts for the delay:

During the early part of the charge there is no effect to mix or stir the electrolyte. Some of the heavier acid forced from the plates fails to rise to the top of the cell and cannot be reached by the testing hydrometer. Later in the charge, when gassing is active, all of the electrolyte becomes a homogenous liquid. As gassing starts, the gravity determined at the cell's top surface, rises rapidly to full-charge level. The lag in measured specific gravity of electrolyte at the top of the cell does not mean that the battery is rejecting the charge. The effect is perfectly normal and the boatkeeper must keep the lag effect in mind when testing batteries being charged after considerable discharge.

What Voltage?

We saw that a single lead-acid cell generates nominal potential very close to two volts. However, exact voltages varies with the specific gravity of electrolyte, and to a great extent on whether the cell is *delivering* current on discharge or *receiving* current on charge. In all batteries, six, 12, or 24 volt, for example, open circuit no load voltage is a direct function of the electrolytes's specific gravity. Within close limits, cell voltage equals specific gravity plus 0.84. This means the open circuit voltage of a cell with electrolyte specific gravity of 1.210 will be 2.05 volts. A battery with six of these cells in series will develop a potential, unloaded, of 12.3 volts; and that theoretical value is very close to the voltage one will find on everyday batteries aboard the boat.

Effect of Load

The last paragraph describes the situation when the cells are unloaded. But assume now that a small electric motor is turned on, throwing a moderate load on the battery. Cell voltage will immediately drop due to internal resistance. As the motor runs for a while, voltage will fall still more as the motor's load discharges the battery. Finally, after continued discharge when the battery nears exhaustion, voltage drops below a value that is useful.

Effect of Charging

It was shown that when a depleted battery is placed on charge its voltage goes up, the extent of the rise increasing with charge rate. At commonly used charging rates on a six-cell 12 volt battery, voltage quickly rises to 12.6 or 12.9, then increases gradually until the charge is about 75% complete. Voltage then rises sharply, finally leveling off to maximum potential at full charge. At that point, voltage in a six-cell battery will be about 15.6 at the finish rate of charge. Because voltage varies with state-of-charge, an accurate, narrow-range voltmeter, properly interpreted, will give the battery-keeper a fair idea of the cell's charging progress.

Specific Gravity

Electrolyte nominal specific gravity varies slightly in different makes and designs of marine batteries. However, most manufacturers specify about 1.260 as the value for a fully charged cell.

Specific gravity decreases as the battery discharges, increases as it charges; Consequently, its value is an approximte indicator of the battery's state. Between full charge and discharge state, a typical battery will evidence a gravity drop of 125 points: Full charge gravity is 1.260, half charge 1.197, and discharged 1.135.

Temperature Effect

Standard electrolyte temperature for hydrometer readings of specific gravity is 77°F, made when electrolyte level is above the plates. In order to get accurate gravity readings, the hydrometer float indication must be corrected for temperature and electrolyte level. The corrections are applied as follows:

1. Add one gravity point for each 3°F above 77°F; alternately, subtract one point of gravity for each 3°F below 77°F.
2. Subtract 15 points for each ½″ below normal level; alternately, add 15 points for each ½″ above normal.

From the above, it is apparent that a battery having electrolyte level ½″ above normal, and with temperature 107°F, will require plus 25 points correction. Thus, if the hydrometer reads 1.235, corrected value is 1.260, indicating the battery is fully charged.

Altered Readings

Specific gravity is never tested immediately after water is added to the cells because the fresh water on top of the cells will make the reading much too low. Time must be allowed, and the battery used, to thoroughly mix the liquids. Battery manufacturers also say that age alters the normal gravity reading, pointing out that a decrease of several points a year is normal.

How Powerful?

"The capacity of a storage battery," say Exide engineers, "is usually expressed in ampere-hours. This is simply the product of the discharge in amperes times the number of hours [the battery can sustain that discharge rate.] However, a single figure of, say, 200 ampere-hours has little significance unless qualified by the many factors influencing a battery's capacity."

Principal factors influencing total capacity are discharge rate, temperature, specific gravity, and final voltage.

Discharge Rate

The higher the amperes of the discharge rate, the less total ampere-hours a battery will deliver under otherwise like conditions. Commonly used as a standard is the eight hour rate, which, for example, would represent 12.5 amperes for eight hours, delivered by a 100 ampere-hour battery. Another common rating applied to boat batteries is the 20 hour rate. A 100 AH battery, so specified, will furnish five amperes for 20 hours before its voltage drops lower than a useable level. It is apparent that a battery of given AH capacity can do more useful work operating a small light bulb than in cranking a heavy engine.

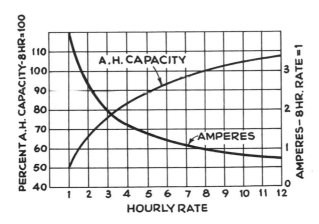

Fig. 2-3 The curves show that a battery's ampere hour capacity increases as discharge rate decreases.

Temperature Effect

Higher temperatures than 77°F increase a battery's capacity, and lower temperatures decrease it. Since engine room temperatures in powerboats frequently reach or exceed 120°F, boat battery capacity is increased as much as 15% above normal.

Gravity Influence

A new battery, originally filled with electrolyte of higher specific gravity will have greater ampere-hour capacity than one filled with fluid of lower gravity. The reader may ask the question: "Then why not fill all batteries with high gravity electrolyte?" The reason is that "high gravity" batteries enjoy a shorter useful life, and lose charge faster when standing idle.

Final Voltage

The minimum useful voltage at various rates of discharge is termed final voltage. It is accepted as lower with high rates of discharge, as when cranking a balky engine. For engine starting currents, final voltage per cell may be as low as one volt. But for low discharge rates, it may be as high as 1.85 volts. Nominal standard rating for batteries is about 1.75 volts per cell, or 10.5 volts for an ordinary 12-volt battery.

Discharge Rate

Battery engineers say that most batteries can be safety discharged at the fastest rate of current they can muster. However, the discharge must not be continued beyond the point where the cells approach exhaustion or where the voltage falls below useful value. In short, fast discharge does not hurt the unit, but overdischarge may.

Overdischarge Hurts

Severe overdischarging can be harmful to a battery, particularly if the battery is not immediately recharged. During normal discharge a moderate amount of lead sulphate is found on the plates, and this is ok. Lead sulphate occupies more space than the sponge lead of the negative plate, so that during discharge the plate material expands slightly. However, if discharge is carried too far, the material may expand to the point where portions of it separate, losing contact with the grid, and remaining permanently as sulphate. Mechanics then refer to the battery as "sulphated".

To some extent, sulphating will occur when a battery is normally discharged and allowed to remain in that state for a long time. A typical case would be when the boat is laid up. That is one of the reasons why a battery should be kept well charged when the boat is laid away.

Fast vs. Slow Charging

Accurately controlled, "fast" charging will not damage a battery. But the key to protecting the battery is *control*. An acceptable rule is that a battery may be charged at any rate in amperes that will not produce excessive gassing or raise electrolyte temperature above 125°F for short periods. Another rule, say Exide engineers, is that any rate is safe which does not force cell voltage to more than 2.4 volts per cell while the current is above the normal or finish rate of charge. Current may be continued at the finish rate whenever charging is required, regardless of cell voltage.

Completely or partially discharged conventional 12-volt batteries can safely absorb charging currents as high as 50 to 80 amperes for a short time. But as the state-of-charge rises, the rate must be promptly reduced. As charge approaches "full," current must be reduced evenly or in steps to the normal or finish rate.

Normal Charging

Battery manufacturers specify a normal or finish rate of charge for each battery. This rate is the amperes of current which can safely be applied any time charging is required and which can be continued to completion of charge without causing excessive gassing or damaging temperatures.

Typical finish rates fall between four and 10 amperes per 100 ampere-hours of battery capacity at the eight hour rate. A safe rate for almost any boat battery in the 100 AH class is six amperes. Charging at that current, you will never hurt a 100 ampere-hour battery: Even though the charge is continued slightly past "full," the only damage will be some lost water due to gassing.

Overcharging

Like excessive discharging, continued overcharging is harmful. It tends to corrode positive plate grids, weakening them physically, while increasing their electrical resistance. In addition, overcharging at high rates creates violent gassing, washing active material from the plates, and shortening cell life. If a battery's electrolyte gravity remains at full value, but the battery demands excessive make-up water, the unit is being overcharged, and the rate should be reduced. This requires lowering generator charging voltage through adjustment of the regulator. Frequently, voltage reduction as little as 5% will improve the situation greatly.

Trickle Charging

Sometimes it would seem convenient to simply plug into dockside power and leave the battery on a constant trickle charge of perhaps three quarters of an amp. Seemingly, this should maintain the battery topped up without further attention.

The method is simple; but battery manufacturers don't particularly like it: Slow, constant trickle charging is not good for conventional boat batteries. It is better to hook up the charger manually, as needed, or to rig a timer to charge the batteries once a day for a short period at the finish rate. Another good plan is to install one of the modern marine power packs which turn off and on automatically in response to battery state-of-charge.

Dry-Charged

Some batteries are manufactured by a special process and are sold as "dry-charged." Before assembly, the plates are dried in an atmosphere free of air or oxygen. Then the cells are assembled and sealed to block out all traces of moisture. When stored in a cool, dry location, dry charged batteries will retain most of their charge for two years, or even longer.

Before being placed in service, a dry-charged battery is filled with electrolyte having specific gravity about 10 points lower than the normal full charge gravity. It is then given a moderate charge and placed in service. The dry-charged battery may be used immediately, although for the first few hours it may not have full capacity depending upon its length of time and condition of storage.

Distilled Water Required?

Among battery mechanics there is always a little discussion as to whether distilled or demineralized water is better for batteries than tap water. It is the opinion of Exide engineers that the vast majority of public water sources are satisfactory for marine battery use. However, the experts also say that water containing large amounts of iron and chlorine is bad for lead-acid storage batteries. Consequently, if the reader is in doubt about his local source, or about the water he may encounter while cruising, he'll find it cheap enough to buy a gallon of distilled water from the local automobile parts store; and he can carry it on board for the season.

Layup

Before a battery is stored for several months, as during the boat's seasonal layup, it should first be given a good, full charge, then stored in a cool place. It must not be allowed to freeze; and, indeed, it will not freeze if it is kept charged. During layup, gravity is checked about once each six weeks, and the cells recharged when gravity dips to around 1.220. Electrolyte is never dumped from a battery during storage; the cells cannot be stored "dry"; and dumping will ruin the plates.

Safety Requirements

Both the American Boat & Yacht Council and the National Fire Protection Association have standards applying to batteries and their installation aboard boats. Important points cited in these standards apply to location, installation and wiring methods.

Location

In a first-class installation, batteries are located so that gas given off during charging will be quickly dissipated by natural and mechanical ventilation. Naturally, they are located high enough that bilge water, even when above normal, will not reach the battery caps and terminals; and they are protected against rain and spray.

Engine starting batteries should be located as close to the starter as practicable to keep the cable lengths short and voltage drop to a minimum. Batteries must be arranged where they are easy to get at for inspection and adding of make-up water.

Installation

Batteries must be secured against shifting and pounding when the boat is in the roughest water; and those in trailered boats must be fastened tightly enough for rough road trailering. The case should be chocked on all sides and supported at the bottom by nonabsorbent insulating supports of a material not affected by acid.

In "code" installations, made in Bristol fashion, the batteries are covered by a nonconductive, ventilated cover to prevent accidental shorting of the terminals. Also, where the hull or compartment material under the battery is aluminum, steel, or other material liable to attack by acid, a tray of lead or fiberglass is fitted under the unit.

Wiring

Batteries are never tapped for voltages other than the total voltage of all the cells comprising the complete battery. Thus, a 12-volt battery, having 6 cells, is never center-tapped between the third and fourth to energize a separate six-volt circuit. If six volts is required aboard, it should be furnished by a separate six-volt battery.

An emergency switch capable of carrying starter current and all other currents must be wired in the "hot" battery lead as close to the battery as possible. There must be no switch in the ground strap lead.

Connections to battery posts must be husky, permanent solder-lug type clamps. Spring clips and temporary clamps are frowned upon.

Maintenance

Based upon principles laid down in this chapter, battery maintenance becomes pretty much a matter of common sense. The following are suggested maintenance procedures:

- The battery's top should be maintained as clean and dry as possible. Water and electrolyte conduct electricity from one binding post to the other, and the resulting electric leak discharges the battery. Baking soda is a good cleaning agent for battery tops; but it must be kept out of the cells at all costs. After the battery top is cleaned, it must be rinsed and then dried off bone dry.
- Voltage regulator controlling the generator or alternator is checked at least once a season. Most nominal 12-volt regulators are designed to maintain the charging circuit at about 14 volts. Higher voltage leads to over-charging on most conventionally operated boats. Lower potential, on the other hand, may allow the

battery to run down. However, on sailboat auxiliary engines, ordinarily used for short intervals, the regulator may be stepped up until charging potential is about 15 volts. This will speed the charging process; and gassing should pose no problem since the engine is not run long enough to overcharge the cells substantially.

• Both cable clamps and binding posts must be brightly burnished before a connection is made. Either a stainless steel brush or coarse sandpaper will do the job.

• Battery cables, both hot and ground, must be replaced when they show signs of corrosion or fraying. Deteriorated cables cause a terrible voltage loss when high currents are drawn, as for starting engines.

• Cells are kept topped up to correct level with clean water, and are checked for state-of-charge with a hydrometer from time to time.

SYNOPSIS

Through its electrochemical process, the lead-acid battery stores a great deal of energy and can release the energy quickly. Charging takes longer than discharging. Battery potential is roughly 2 volts per cell, but is higher when the battery is charging than when discharging. Battery capacity is measured in ampere-hours. Severe overdischarge hurts lead-acid cells, but overcharging does, too. Batteries must be well secured in the boat, must be kept clean, dry, watered, and adequately charged.

CHAPTER III

The Modern Boat's
D.C. Systems

THIS CHAPTER comprises a guide on what to look for in checking over the qualities of an existing direct-current electrical system. It is also a guide on how to inspect the d.c. electrical installation on a new boat under consideration for purchase, and will be an aid to the owner who is expanding his existing circuits or wiring a new boat.

Material in this chapter is guided by two standards: *Safety Standards for Small Craft*, compiled by the American Boat and Yacht Council, and *Fire Protection Standards for Motor Craft, NFPA 302*, authorized by the National Fire Protection Association. What is written here applies to popular direct-current system of six, 12, and 24 volts, or any system up to 50 volts, but not higher.

Wiring Arrangements

How often have you looked at an otherwise neat boat, perhaps one having a workmanlike shoreside a.c. system, and beheld a messy, haphazard looking six, 12, or 24 direct-current system? And how frequently the owner will say, "Oh well, it's only battery voltage; it can't do much harm if it does go haywire."

Such opinions are dangerous. Low-voltage d.c. wiring when short circuited or grounded can cause fire, corrosion, and breakdown of the boat. In fact, the National Fire Protection Association states flatly: "It is to be recognized that low voltage installations do not warrant the use of substandard materials or workmanship, particularly in motorcraft where the possible presence of flammable or explosive vapors render a spark or incandescence liable to serious consequnces."

A good wiring system is simple, straightforward, easy to trace and trouble-shoot. Its switching arrangements prevent improper operation by the inexperienced; and all switches are marked to indicate their purpose. An exception to the labeling of switches is where function is obvious, as in the case of a lamp with integral switch.

Separate Systems

On a cruiser or auxiliary, in fact aboard any boat which operates in "offshore" water, and where reliability is important, the engine starting and ignition system should be entirely separate from the boat's lightning and accessory circuits. Best practice is for each engine to have its own battery and charging circuit, while separate batteries and generators are provided for lighting, bilge pumps, d.c. machinery and the like. A boat equipped in this way should also carry good jumper cables or have a cross-over switching arrangement so that one system can aid the other in emergency. But the basic wiring of the individual systems should be independent so that trouble in one is not reflected in the others.

Appropriate Voltage

Six-volt systems were formerly used for most pleasure craft but in the past 15 years they have given way almost exclusively to 12 and 24 volt arrangements. Six-volt starting motors are more sluggish than those of 12 or 24, and the voltage drop through the boat, even on light loads, is excessive on six volts.

On an older boat in otherwise fine condition, it is frequently worth while altering an old six volt system to 12 or 24 volts.

The job is particularly easy if the engines are being replaced, because then the starters and generators will be of higher voltage. Provided the wiring is neat and trim, the six volt conductors can be retained, with fuses, bulbs, and small motors being replaced as indicated by the change in current and voltage.

Polarity

When a new d.c. system is installed, or an old one reworked and modernized, it should be installed with the negative polarity grounded. Negative ground is now standard throughout the industry; and it is difficult to buy appliances and electronic gear for positive grounded boats.

Extra Circuits

A new d.c. electrical system, or one which is being upgraded, should be wired with fuses or circuit breakers and terminal strips for future additional circuits. Providing for the future in this way helps assure that when new circuits are added they will be neatly, safely hooked up, and not haywired on the tail end of existing circuits, a practice which leads to overloading and possible subsequent fires.

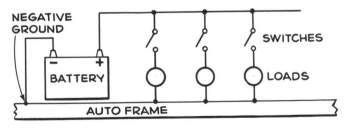

Fig. 3-1 These diagrams delineate the difference between automobile and boat direct current battery systems. The car uses its frame for the negative return.

The Two-Wire System

Perhaps the greatest difference between automotive wiring and marine wiring is that land vehicles almost always use a one-wire system, while boats must use a two-wire arrangement. In car or truck, the positive wire is hot, feeding the lights and appliances; the chassis, frame and body are negative, acting as ground return conductor.

The boat is different. In it the hot wire, usually black or red, is positive, feeding the lights and appliances as in the automobile;

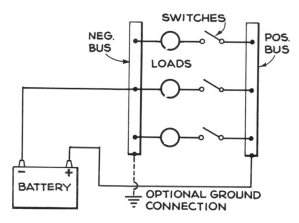

Fig. 3-2 The boat has individual bus bars and connectors. Negative is usually grounded, but a few boats use an ungrounded system where both polarities float free of ground.

but the negative return is not via the hull, but rather by insulated wires, usually coded yellow. Note that the boat's grounded bonding system, described in Chapter Five, is never used as a common current-carrying ground, in the manner of an automobile frame.

Grounded and Ungrounded Systems

Two varieties of low-voltage d.c. systems are used aboard modern boats, *grounded* and *ungrounded*. But the reader is asked to keep in mind that even with the grounded type, the hull or bonding is never used as a current-carrying ground. The systems are connected as follows:

The Ungrounded System

A highly recommended system, but one difficult to use in practice, especially on small boats, is the completely ungrounded system where the entire d.c. circuitry "floats" absolutely without ground as if it were free in space. It comprises a two-wire system in which all current-carrying conductors, including the source of power and all accessories, are completely insulated from ground or "earth" throughout the system.

The two-wire ungrounded system is recommended *provided* the entire system can be guaranteed free of grounds. That guarantee is difficult on a small boat with but one d.c. system. It is difficult because the use of any electrical equipment, including starters and generators, in which current-carrying conductors are connected to metallic frames, will automatically require that the system be grounded. However, all ground potential (negative) conductors must be insulated from ground right up to the point where a common ground point is provided, usually close to the propulsion engine.

The Grounded System

A two-wire system, the grounded circuitry utilizes the boat's common ground point to maintain the negative conductors at ground potential. Except for engine-mounted accessories, which may use the engine block as a common ground return, all electrical circuits must be the two-wire type, having insulated conductors to and from the power source.

Common Ground

In boats using grounded electrical systems, there should be but one common ground point. This should be located at a point well above bilge water level, and as close to the boat's batteries as possible. Only one such point should be established for each system because, among other things, more than one ground point can generate stray currents, inviting corrosion.

The following conductors may be connected directly to the common ground point, once that point is established:

- Engine starter ground return lead and ground lead of the battery.
- Main switchboard ground-return conductor.
- Bonding system conductor.
- Radio ground plate lead.
- Auxiliary generator ground.

The common ground point must not be used as the common return point for individual branch circuits. As shown in Figures 3-2 and 3-3, the return point for branch circuits is the ground bus or ground strip in the main switchboard. This bus, in turn, is then connected by heavy conductor to the common ground point.

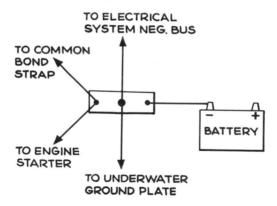

Fig. 3-3 The common ground point, located close to the battery, is the center point of a grounded system.

The majority of d.c. systems are of the grounded type because the engine starter ground return is the engine ground strap, and grounding is inevitable. In this arrangement, the bonding system is connected to the common ground point. However, in the ungrounded d.c. system, where the starter is insulated, the bonding system is not connected to the common ground point and although the point is called "ground," it actually floats at its own potential, not necessarily that of Mother Earth.

Details on the all-important bonding system are found in Chapter 5.

DC Receptacles

Common sense dictates that outlets in the direct current, low-voltage system be distinctly different from the standard 115 volt housepower variety of receptacle, assuming a boat has both systems.

Wiring near the Compass

Direct-current wiring should always be strung as far from the compass as possible because of the flow of current which deviates the instrument in proportion to the amperage. Where wires must be closer than 3 or 4 feet from the binnacle, they must be run in twisted pairs to eliminate or minimize the effect of current on the compass heading. Interesting details on electricity and its effect on the compass are found in Chapter 21.

Switchboards

In a good, safe installation, switchboards and distribution panels are accessibly located in well ventilated places, preferably outside of engine and fuel tank compartments. Where applicable, they are protected from rain, spray or drip from the overhead. Totally enclosed switchboards and distribution panels of the deadfront type are recommended. Deadfront means that the enclosure has no live parts exposed on the front of the panel. Metal enclosures are recommended for switchboards and panels. However, wood or fiberglass may be used, providing all terminal strips, fuse blocks, and the like are mounted on nonabsorbent, noncombustible, high quality insulating materials. The safest enclosures are lined with asbestos or other fire resistant sheeting.

Switches

Cheap landlubbery switches corrode and cause no end of trouble aboard the boat, those intended for household and automobile use often being troublemakers. A good switch for marine use should be intended for that purpose, preferably being approved by Underwriters Laboratories. If a switch is being installed in fuel tank compartment or engine space, it definitely must be approved for marine use.

Every switch should have a little plate fixed to it, or near it, indicating "on" and "off." Naturally, each switch must be rated for the amperes it is to handle. It is best to avoid switches which are not clearly marked with their current rating; and where there is doubt as to the maximum switched current, select a switch of the next higher capacity.

Terminals

Good terminals and connectors are particularly important on a boat's d.c. wiring system because, despite vibration and corrosive environment, they must offer continuity and low resistance to current flow. Terminal lugs recommended most highly are the swaged, or crimped, solderless, tinned copper or brass variety with ring ends. These are better than those with spade or forked ends because they will stay in place even if the stud or nut loosens. A prefered type is shown in Figure 3-4.

Fig. 3-4 Lugs with closed ends are best for marine work.

If you plan a wiring job using the approved kind of lugs, be sure to crimp the lug around the wire with the hand tool made by the manufacturer for crimping his lugs. One popular series of lugs is manufactured by Thomas & Betts, and that company also furnishes a combination crimper-cutter that does a workmanlike job of swaging. Avoid crimping with an ordinary pair of pliers; the connection so made will be mechanically and electrically weak.

A good job requires that the holes in ring type terminals be a nice fit to the stud, and that the terminal also match the size wire to which it is crimped. For extra security, it is recommended that a short length of insulating sleeving be slid over the wire at each terminal connection.

Normal Stud Size	Minimum Stud Diameter	Conductor Size*
6	.138	not recommended
8	.164	16 Awg
10	.190	14, 12 Awg
¼	.250	8, 10 Awg
⁵⁄₁₆	.3125	6 Awg
⅜	.375	4 Awg

* Based on the use of 4 conductors to each terminal stud.

Fig. 3-5 Table specifies minimum stud sizes for terminal studs, as specified by the National Fire Protection Association.

Studs

The studs to which terminals are screwed must be of the minimum size indicated in the accompanying table. In addition, good wiring practice dictates the following:

- No more than four conductors should ever be attached to one terminal stud.
- Connections must be made so there is no strain on the terminal.

Battery Terminals

Heavy noncorroding lugs must be used as storage battery connectors, and the connections to the cables should be soldered, not merely clamped. A perfect fit must mate the clamp to the binding post to assure minimum voltage drop. Terrific current is transmitted through the connection, resulting in unacceptable voltage drop unless the connection is perfect. Hard engine starting is frequently caused by imperfect connections between battery posts and cable clamp. Details on this and other aspects of the battery are found in Chapter 2.

Wiring Installation

A prime rule in good d.c. wiring practice is to keep all wires routed as far above the bilge as possible. It is not hard to imagine what happens to the wiring when it gets soaked with water, oil, and the other varieties of gunk which swash around in the typical bilge.

In addition to being well above the bilge, wiring in a workman-like installation will show many of the following qualities:

1. Conductors protected against physical damage as by being struck, walked on, or pinched by doors and hatch covers.

2. All wiring secured throughout its length each 14 inches or as otherwise required to keep it from flapping loose. Good means of security are noncorroding metal clips with anti-chafing material.

3. Exposed surface wiring, subject to damage, protected by loom, conduit, neat tape wrap, or other workmanlike means.

4. Wire splices conspicuous by their scarcity. Where seen, they are neat, strong, and relieved of strain.

5. Where wiring passes through bulkheads or panels, it is protected against wear by nonchafing ferrules or soft grommets.

Wire Insulation

The purpose of insulation on d.c. wires is, of course, to prevent short circuits and stray current leakage to the hull or machinery. Even though voltage is low, insulation must be of high quality, enabling it to cope with the severe marine environment.

Wire for marine and general use is manufactured with various types of insulation designated *RW, TW, RHW,* and so on. Applications for the various types of insulation are suggested in this table prepared by the National Fire Protection Association.

Wire Conductors

Nothing contributes more to an efficient direct-current network aboard a boat than good, adequate sized conductors. Wires

Type	Insulation	Maximum Operating Temperature	Use
RW	Moisture Resistant Rubber with Oil Resistant Neoprene Jacket	60°C 140°F	General use except machinery spaces
RH-RW	Moisture and Heat Resistant Rubber with Oil Resistant Neoprene Jacket	60°C 140°F	General use except machinery spaces
		75°C 167°F	General use General use
RHW	Moisture and Heat Resistant Rubber with Oil Resistant Neoprene Jacket	75°C 167°F	General use
TW	Moisture Resistant Thermoplastic Flame Retardant	60°C 140°F	General use except machinery spaces
THW	Moisture and Heat Resistant Thermoplastic Flame Retardant	75°C 167°F	General use

Fig. 3-6 Shown are conductor insulation and application specified by NFPA. Lengths of insulated wire may be purchased by type and gauge specification.

which are too small for the current cause inefficiency due to voltage drop and generate heat because of excessive resistance. For a given current, wire size must increase as the distance from source to load becomes greater. Likewise, wire size must grow proportionately to current; otherwise resistance and voltage drop will be excessive.

The most common cause of sluggish performance in electric bilge pumps, pressure water systems, winches, refrigerators, windshield wipers and the like is undersized conductors. Remember that for a given power output, these appliances on 12 volts draw almost ten times as much current as equivalent 115 volt items.

AWG WIRE SIZES BASED ON A 10 PER CENT VOLTAGE DROP

Total Current on Circuit in Amps.	Feet															
	20	30	40	50	60	70	80	90	100	110	120	130	140	150	160	170
6 Volts																
5	14	14	14	12	12	12										
10	14	12	10	10	8	8										
15	12	10	8	8	8	6										
20	10	8	8	8	6	6										
25	10	8	6	6	4	4										
12 Volts																
5	14	14	14	14	14	14	14	14	12	12	12					
10	14	14	14	12	12	12	10	10	10	10	8					
15	14	14	12	10	10	10	8	8	8	8	8					
20	12	12	10	10	8	8	8	6	6	6	6					
25	10	10	10	8	8	8	6	6	6	6	4					
32 Volts																
5	14	14	14	14	14	14	14	14	14	14	14	14	14	14	14	14
10	14	14	14	14	14	14	14	14	14	14	14	12	12	12	12	12
15	14	14	14	14	14	14	14	12	12	12	12	10	10	10	10	10
20	14	14	14	14	14	12	12	12	10	10	10	10	10	10	8	8
25	14	14	14	12	12	12	10	10	10	10	10	8	8	8	8	8
30	14	14	14	12	12	10	10	10	10	8	8	8	8	8	8	6

Fig. 3-7 Length of conductor in feet from source of current to most distant fixture and return is shown for 10% voltage drop.

Rules for Choosing Size

Conductor sizes used for cabin lighting and other circuits where voltage drop is not too critical, may be determined according to Figure 3-7, which is based on a 10% voltage drop.

Conductors used in more critical circuits, where voltage drop must be kept to a minimum (navigation lights, electronic gear, etc.) must not have more than 3% voltage drop. Here, wire size may be determined from Figure 3-8.

If the reader has a special problem and wants to calculate his own conductor size, he may use a formula to give circular

AWG WIRE SIZES BASED ON A 3 PER CENT VOLTAGE DROP

Total Current on Circuit in Amps.	Feet															
	20	30	40	50	60	70	80	90	100	110	120	130	140	150	160	170
6 Volts																
5	12	10	8	8	6	6										
10	8	6	6	5	4	3										
15	6	5	4	3	2	2										
20	6	4	3	2	1	1										
25	5	3	2	1	0	0										
12 Volts																
5	14	12	12	10	10	8	8	8	8	8	6					
10	12	10	8	8	6	6	6	5	5	5	4					
15	10	8	6	6	5	5	4	4	3	3	2					
20	8	6	6	5	4	3	2	2	2	2	1					
25	8	6	5	4	3	3	2	1	1	1	0					
32 Volts																
5	18	16	16	14	14	14	12	12	12	12	10	10	10	10	10	10
10	16	14	12	12	10	10	10	10	8	8	8	8	8	6	6	6
15	14	12	10	10	10	8	8	8	6	6	6	6	6	6	5	5
20	12	10	10	8	8	8	6	6	6	6	5	5	5	4	4	4
25	12	10	8	8	6	6	6	6	5	5	4	4	4	3	3	3

Fig. 3-8 Length of conductor in feet from source of current to most distant fixture and return is shown for 3% voltage drop.

mil area of wire. Once knowing the circular mil dimensions, he may refer to Figure 3-9 to find equivalent wire size. The National Fire Protection Association states that when the calculated circular mil area is less than a given value of wire gauge, the next gauge of conductor is to be used.

Formula for Conductor Size

Assuming that circular mils (cm) are desired, the formula is:

$$cm = \frac{K \times I \times L}{E}$$

where: cm = circular mils of conductor
K = 10.8 a constant representing resistance of copper
I = load current in amperes
L = conductor length from source to fixture and return
E = voltage drop at lead, in volts

Example Calculation

Suppose an electric winch is installed 40 feet from a 12-volt battery. Conductor length is 80 feet. The installer will accept a voltage drop of 1 volt to the winch, which draws 40 amperes at full load. What wire size shall he select?

$$cm = \frac{10.8 \times 40 \times 80}{1} = 34,560$$

Figure 3-9 shows that the wire size next larger than 34,560 circular mils is #4 AWG. That is the size conductor which should be selected for the winch, a pair of number fours running from the source to winch and return.

Conductor Size, AWG	Nominal CM Area	Number of Strands	Resistance OHMS Per 1000 Ft. at 25°C
16	2,583	19	4.09
14	4,107	19	2.58
12	6,530	19	1.62
10	10,380	19	1.02
8	16,510	19	0.641
6	26,250	37	0.410
4	41,740	61	0.253
2	66,370	127	0.162
1	83,690	127	0.129
1/0	105,500	127	0.102
2/0	133,100	127	0.0811
3/0	167,800	259	0.0642
4/0	211,600	418	0.0509

Fig. 3-9 Relationship is shown between size in wire gauge and circular mil area.

Advantage of Higher Voltage

The calculation points up the advantage of higher d.c. voltage in the boat's system, highlighting the reason that the six-volt system was abandoned some years ago. In the winch example, if a 32-volt system were used, current would be reduced to 15 amperes, and a 3-volt drop would be reasonable. Now, the calculation becomes:

$$cm = \frac{10.8 \times 15 \times 80}{3} = 4,320$$

This indicates that a pair of #12 AWG wires would handle the winch if it operated on a nominal 32-volt system. But, consider the ridiculous situation on the old six-volt system, where current would be 80 amperes, voltage drop should not exceed 0.6 volts, and calculations show that a pair of heavy #2/0 AWG cables would be required to do an adequate job.

Fuses and Breakers

Trip-free circuit breakers and fuses are both approved for protecting the boat's circuits against overload. However, from a practical standpoint, circuit breakers are better because they need no replacement after being overloaded. There's little more frustrating than being out on the water with a blown fuse, and no replacement on board.

Two kinds of circuit breakers are available: trip-free and nontrip-free. Only the trip-free should be used. These are magnetically or thermally actuated by overload; and they cannot be bypassed manually during overload or by manual holding of the control button or handle.

Each circuit breaker or fuse should be marked, showing what circuit it serves; and each should be marked with its current rating. Where a circuit is wired with two sizes of conductor, such as #12 and #14, the protective device must be rated to protect the smaller conductor: in this case, the #14 wire.

Some devices, particularly motors, have an internal thermal circuit breaker without manual reset. This protects the device, but not the circuit wiring, and the circuit energizing such a device must still incorporate a fuse or trip-free circuit breaker.

Points to Protect

A well designed electrical system finds a correctly sized fuse or trip-free circuit breaker in the following circuit locations:

1. At the main switchboard, the heavy ungrounded conductor from the master battery switch is load protected. The fuse or breaker is rated not more than 125% of the total switchboard load. Thus, if all the circuits attached to the switchboard can draw 40 amperes total, the main fuse or breaker can be of 50 amperes rating.

2. On larger installations having distribution panels in addition to the main switchboard, there is protection at the main board in ungrounded power feeds to the panels.

3. Each ungrounded conductor comprising a branch circuit is fused or protected by breaker.

4. Circuits which energize d.c. motors have a breaker or fuse in the "hot" lead; and the protection is rated not more than 125% of the motor's full load current.

5. Direct-current generators and alternators are protected against current exceeding their maximum rated capacity. A special precaution is taken here, however, because most battery-charging alternators are damaged if operated with an open circuit while the rotor is excited. To prevent damage, a dual circuit breaker is used. On detecting excess current in the output circuit, the breaker trips, simultaneously opening both the output circuit and exciting circuit, and rendering the alternator completely inert. Conventional generators are protected in the same way, the breaker opening the circuit to the field lead as well as output lead.

Master Battery Switch

A high quality master-battery disconnect switch provides important protection to the boat, electrical system, and battery. Proper location for the master switch is very close to the batteries, wired in each ungrounded lead.

Most battery switches serving more than one battery, double as selector switches, connecting one battery bank or the other to the system. Where this kind of device is used, it must be the make-before break type, connecting the second battery before disconnecting the first. This type of switch assures that at least one battery is always in the circuit. When its handle is turned, the circuit does not open; and the generator or alternator never looks into an open circuit, a situation which might cause damage.

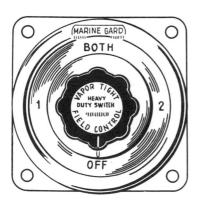

Fig. 3-10 This heavy duty battery disconnect switch incorporates an auxiliary contact to open the generator or alternator control circuit.

The best battery disconnect switches incorporate an auxiliary contact which opens the field circuit of the alternator or generator when the disconnect is open. This protects the generator. Battery switches not incorporating an auxiliary field contact must be marked with a caution saying: "Do not open this switch when generator is running."

SYNOPSIS

For highest reliability, engine and lighting circuits should be independent. Modern d.c. circuits have negative ground, and the

two-wire system is always used for marine work. A common
ground point ties all circuits together, avoiding stray currents.
Switches, terminals and other components should be designed for
marine use, and battery hardware must be especially rugged.
Wires should be kept well above the bilges, and should always be
of more than adequate gauge. Circuit breakers must be the trip
free type; and battery switches should be make-before-break.

CHAPTER IV

~~~~~~

Living With
"Housepower" Aboard

NOT TOO MANY years ago, when there were yacht clubs but few marinas, the majority of cruisers lay at moorings off shore rather than being tied to a pier. They had no umbilical electric cord, and their electrical systems were simple battery-energized affairs of limited capacity.

Then the marina proliferated, cruisers joined runabouts at dockside, the power cord was plugged into a shoreside receptacle, and the age of "housepower" afloat blossomed. On board went a stream of appliances, as families took to spending weekends aboard at the marina: toasters, heaters, irons, refrigerators, washers, driers, deep freezers and, naturally, the TV set. As the appliances multiplied, voltage dropped, the power cord to the pier got hotter, and so did the wiring inside the boat. These are common problems today; and we shall see what to do about them shortly.

The Basic "Housepower" System

Four wires comprise the standard combination 115/230 volt a.c. system that you plug into at the marina. It is the same system used in towns throughout the United States and many other countries. Coded black, red, white, and green or bare, the wires function as follows:

Black wire is hot, carrying a.c. voltage 115 volts above ground. If you touch this wire you may get a shock.

Red wire is also hot, carrying a.c. voltage 115 volts above ground. As with the black wire, if you touch this conductor, you may get a shock.

White wire is the neutral conductor. It is grounded, so if you touch it you will not get a shock unless you are also touching the red or black. The white wire, however, carries full current, just as the black and red do. Sometimes this wire is color coded gray instead of white.

Green or bare wire is purely a safety conductor. Maintained at ground potential, it is not intended to carry working current, but only to act as a protective ground for equipment frames and metal parts which may be touched by humans. On older electrical appliances the green safety wire may be missing, but on modern gear, made in accordance with best practice, the green wire is seen, connected to the appliance frame.

What is Ground?

In describing "housepower" we use the word *ground* several times; and throughout this book, as in other electrical works, the word will appear many times. Just what is ground?

In the electrical world, ground means many things to many people, so many things, in fact, that its significance is lost unless it is defined as specifically applied. Aerospace engineers talk of ground in an airplane 35,000 feet aloft. Marine architects use the word while referring to a yacht floating in a hundred feet of water. How can this be?

These are the facts:

Our earth's moist, conductive soil and the conductive waters of her seas, lakes, and rivers are the real basic ground referred to in building and marina wiring nomenclature. Here, a wire connected to ground is truly "earthed" and is at the earth's ground potential or voltage: The grounded conductor is connected to a water pipe or large-area metal plate buried deep in wet earth. Such a conductor, even though carrying current (as from a source to a motor), will not shock you if you touch it while standing on wet terrain. As mentioned earlier, the white and green wires in the standard a.c. system are grounded.

Note that a good connection to Mother Earth's ground is essential. Simply touching a wire to dry earth or pushing a metal rod into arid sand will not create an effective electrical ground. The conductor must be in contact with wet earth over a considerable area before constituting a good ground.

It is standard practice to connect one current-carrying conductor to ground in a pair carrying alternating current. Even though the wires alternately are driven positive and negative many times a second, one is always at ground potential. Voltage polarity between them changes constantly; but voltage between the grounded one and earth remains close to zero. This is true all the way from the source to the load.

It's a little hard to visualize how the white wire in a pair of 115 volt current-carrying conductors can remain at ground voltage. What happens is that, with the white wire "tied" to ground, the black wire alternately surges above, then below, ground

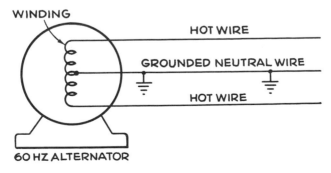

Fig. 4-1 Schematic shows how one wire in an alternating current system can be connected to ground while the other conductors are hot.

potential. In short, the black wire is first 115 volts positive, then 115 volts negative with respect to the grounded white wire. (Technically, it swings even farther high and low than 115 volts. But in practical electricity, the nominal, or root mean square— RMS—value is referred to.)

In electronics, aircraft, and automotive work, a chassis or frame, where all wires of one polarity are connected, is often called "ground." Strangely enough, this pseudo ground may be floating at some potential other than the earth's. Indeed, it does so in an automobile or airplane where the frame may float at any voltage to which it is driven by outside forces—the most extreme example being during a lightning strike, when the whole thing floats at a million volts above earth ground.

Electronic gear usually has a common ground point, which may or may not be tied to true earth. Obviously that point cannot be earthed in an airplane; but it can be in a boat. Seas, lakes, and rivers are, after all, a part of Mother Earth's ground system.

In this book, unless otherwise specified, the word "ground" refers to a real earth ground of the waterpipe and ground plate variety.

How the A.C. System Works

In an a.c. system, such as the one at most marinas, alternating voltage from the black to the white neutral wire is nominally 115

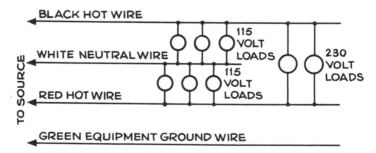

Fig. 4-2 The standard four-wire housepower system has three wires which are current-carrying conductors, and one equipment grounding safety wire.

volts. Voltage from the red to the white is also 115. However, voltage from red to black is 230 volts. The higher voltage is often used for on-board stoves, high capacity air-conditioners, and other heavy appliances; but it is not used for hand-held equipment.

Common practice is to run three-wire feeder circuits comprising black, red, and white conductors. Half the branch circuits to receptacles are wired black-to-white, the other half are wired red-to-white. This arrangement approximately balances the load on the feeder circuit.

Receptacles or power centers along the pier commonly furnish 115 volt power and some also supply 230 volt service. However, physical configuration of the 115 and 230 volt receptacles is different, making it impossible for the boatman to plug into the wrong service. Acceptable types of 115 and 230 volt dock receptacles are shown in the accompanying illustrations.

Dockside Receptacles

Up to the present, there has been confusion concerning pier receptacles and their standardization. Because of this, many cruisers carry an assortment of plugs, adapters, cords, and electrical jury rigs to bring power aboard. Unfortunately, some of these lashups are made from cheap, dime-store fittings coupled to undersized wire; they result in heating of the conductors and loss of voltage aboard the boat.

At this writing, the receptacle picture is improving, and the need for odd-ball plug arrangements should decrease in the future. The latest edition of the National Electrical Code, guide for the electrical industry, pins down what is acceptable. Says the N.E.C.:

"Receptacles which provide shore power for boats shall be rated not less than 20 amperes and shall be single and of the locking and grounding types . . ." This means that for the future, ordinary duplex plug household outlets are ruled out.

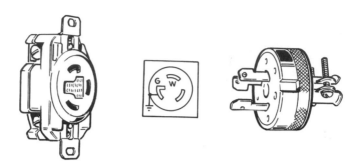

Fig. 4-3 Hubbell Twist-Lock three-wire grounding receptacle rated at 30 amps is suited for use on the pier. Also shown is the type of plug the receptacle accepts. This hardware is for 115 volt service.

Single outlet locking types are the rule. The two kinds are shown in figures 4-3 and 4-4.

Hopefully, more adequate power is on the way, because the new code specifies: "The ampacity for feeder and service conductors supplying power for boats shall be calculated on the basis of a minimum of 25 watts per lineal foot of slip or dock space for boat outlet circuits, plus lighting and other loads." This means that a slip 40 feet long, having a 100 watt light, for example, is required to be wired for 1,100 watts minimum. The feeder for ten such slips must be rated for 11,000 watts; and since it is highly unlikely that the boats in all ten slips will be drawing maximum power at the same time, the supply is ample.

Specific Improvements

The dim lights aboard your docked boat should get brighter as the new standards are compiled with, and as marinas install wiring and receptacles meeting modern requirements. Several electrical hardware companies are now manufacturing 30 amp, 125 volt, two-pole, three-wire grounding, locking receptacles and plugs. Also now available are 50 amp, 125/250 volt, three-pole, four-wire ground locking devices. This husky, high capacity

Fig. 4-4 Locking type four-wire, 50 amp, 115/230 volt receptacle is shown. The three radial slots are for the two hot wires and neutral, while the metal shell is the equipment safety ground connection.

hardware will appear with increased frequency as marinas switch to the modern equipment.

Where possible, you should always steer clear of the old fashioned two-blade, non-grounding plugs and receptacles. They are "unsafe at any current" because they bring the hot black wire and the white neutral wire aboard your boat; but they leave out the green equipment grounding wire, terminating it ashore, thereby creating a serious shock hazard. Remember, that green wire is a safety grounding wire intended to protect you. Around boats and marinas, it should always be attached to appliances at one end and to a grounding receptacle at the other.

Power Centers

A new convenient method of distributing dockside power is through factory-engineered power centers. These are compact fiberglass or metal enclosures having weatherproof outlets, each individual outlet protected by its own circuit breaker. An advantage to this system is that circuit troubles, overloads or short circuits on one boat will trip the breaker on its own power center only. Other boats on the pier will not be affected. Since the tripped circuit breaker is immediately at dockside, the skipper

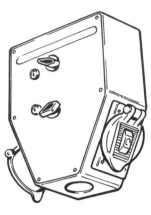

Fig. 4-5

can easily reset it and reenergize his boat's system without hailing the marina operator.

Power centers are appearing on marina piers with increasing frequency, and should do a lot toward providing adequate power to the cruiser having extensive "household" appliances aboard.

That Power Cord

The importance of a good power cord from boat to pier is hard to overemphasize. The best shoreside power source does the boat little good if the connection is a stringy, undersized shore cable terminated at an inadequate on-board receptacle.

Urging the use of husky shore-to-boat equipment, the American Boat and Yacht Council states in *Safety Standards for Small Craft*: "A shore power cable should match the boat shore power inlet and extend at least 10 feet beyond the bow or stern. Type ST-3 conductor cable is recommended, using slightly heavier gauge wire than the system otherwise demands." This means that if 15 amperes is carried, and ordinary considerations indicate #14 gauge wire, the shore power cord should be #12 gauge wire, twelve gauge being heavier than fourteen.

ABYC, in its small craft safety Bible, states the following regarding the on-board power cord receptacle:

"The boat should be fitted with a fixed male shore power inlet receptacle having a suitable watertight protective cover. Receptacles should conform to the standard configuration for the maximum current carrying capacity of the boat's shore power system." Boat owners are urged to use high quality, corrosion resistant, marine type plugs and receptacles. Ordinary, housecat hardware is inadequate: Through corrosion of its metal and deterioration of the plastic, it will cause unwanted voltage drop as it ages, and will become dangerous to handle. Worse, it may fail completely after a few months of use.

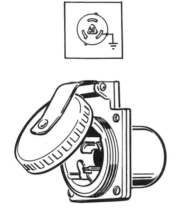

Fig. 4-6 An approved type shore power inlet receptacle has watertight cap, and a blade for equipment ground.

A.C. Wiring Aboard the Boat

The wiring arrangement aboard your boat should meet three principal requirements. To be satisfactory, it must:

1. Present minimum shock hazard.
2. Cause no electrolytic corrosion.
3. Be useful and efficient, offering minimum voltage drop between shoreside receptacle and the appliance it feeds.

To meet the three primary requirements, the on-board a.c. electrical system must be adequately insulated and correctly grounded. Coded wires must be connected to specified terminals; protective devices and switches must be circuited correctly; and above all, the wiring must be workmanlike.

Grounding of A.C. Wiring

Because grounding technique is important in a.c. wiring,

73

ABYC defines exactly what it means by the elusive word *ground,* as follows:

"Ground applies to the potential of the earth's surface . . . including any conductive part of the wetted surface of a hull." This definition eliminates any thought of a "pseudo-ground," floating above earth potential, as found on an automobile frame.

Note carefully ABYC's defined difference between the white or gray coded *grounded* conductor, and the green coded equipment grounding wire. "Grounded conductor is a current-carrying conductor connected to the side of the source which is intentionally maintained at ground potential. Grounding conductor (on the other hand) is a normally *non-current-carrying* conductor provided to connect the exposed metallic enclosures of electrical equipment to ground. Its purpose is to minimize shock hazard to personnel."

ABYC, the safety agency, insists that all the boat's a.c. system be constructed and installed so that it can cope with vibration, shock, and a corrosive atmosphere. The entire system must be permanently installed and designed to provide maximum protection against shock for:

- The crew aboard the boat.
- Swimmers or people in a dinghy or other boat who touch the boat.
- People transferring from boat to shore, touching both simultaneously.

Furthermore, your boat's a.c. system must be designed so that on-board a.c. generators and shore power cannot simultaneously feed the same circuit.

One feature required by ABYC, but frequently omitted from on-board electrical systems, is a monitoring voltmeter. Says the agency: "A system voltmeter installed to read input voltage from shore and/or the output voltage of on-board generators shall be provided and mounted in a readily visible location, except that a voltmeter need not be provided for a simple system with straight resistive loads (lighting, heating, etc.)."

It is recommended that the voltmeter be marked with upper and lower voltage limit marks. These would be at the high and low ten percent points on each side of the system's nominal center. On the standard 115 volt system, the low mark is at 103.5 volts, and the high mark at 126.5 volts. Just as a double check, system frequency and nominal voltage should be clearly written on the main a.c. switchboard. Typical marking would be 115 volts, 60 Hz. The plate is to help prevent the boat from being plugged into the wrong power.

Standard power in the United States, Canada, and most of Mexico, alternates at 60 Hertz (cycles per second). However, almost half the world uses 50 Hz power. If at some distant place in the world, such as Bridgetown, Barbados, you plug into 50 Hz power, some of your on-board appliances will operate the same as on 60 Hz: Toasters, heaters, light bulbs and other resistive appliances will operate ok. But induction motors will run almost 20% slower than at home. Induction motors are the kind used in refrigerators, electric clocks, deep freezers, washing machines, and the like.

Many induction motors designed for 60 Hz, 115 volt power will run satisfactorily on 50 Hz, 115 volts without overheating. However, others will overheat unless, on 50 Hz power, the voltage is reduced to 95 or 100 volts. But as one engineer laughingly put it, "You're lucky to get as much as 95 volts on the stringy end of the line in many 'developing' countries."

If you are lucky enough to be planning an extended cruise away from United States waters, you might buy a copy of *Electric Current Abroad,* latest edition. Listing type and frequency, nominal voltage, types of plugs used, and other data, the book is published by the U.S. Department of Commerce and is for sale by the Superintendent of Documents, U.S. Government Printing Office, Washington, D. C. 20402. Price is 30¢.

A.C. Switches Aboard the Boat

To meet safety standards, switches wired into the boat's a.c. system must be the kind that simultaneously disconnect both current-carrying conductors: the black and the white. This eliminates the use of ordinary hardware switches of the type found in home and office. In shoreside domestic, 115 volt electrical work, single pole switches are used, wired in the black (hot) conductor only.

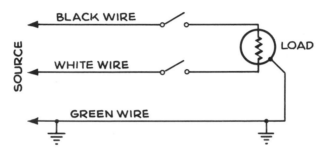

Fig. 4-7 Aboard the boat, switches are wired to interrupt both the hot and neutral conductors. The equipment ground is never switched.

Switch gear aboard the boat is different. Double pole switches are recommended, one pole breaking the black, the other breaking the white. There is a reason for breaking the connection in both wires when the switch is off: Even though the boat itself is correctly wired, the white neutral wire being grounded, there is a possibility of the system being plugged into dock power with white and black wires reversed. There is also the possibilty that incoming shore power may be wired with reversed polarity—the white wire hot, the black grounded. Electricians, particularly amateur ones, can make mistakes. In that case, aboard the boat if there were single pole switches, wired in the black conductor circuit only, you would open the ground circuit, leaving the white wire hot. That is not safe, and is why both wires should be switched on board.

Where single pole switches have been used in a.c. systems aboard older boats, they should be wired in the black conductor only. The white neutral wire must not be switched, nor must the green or bare equipment grounding wire. Naturally, when the single pole switch system is used, it is most important that the boat be plugged into dockside power with correct polarity: Black wire hot, and white wire grounded.

Testing Polarity

If you are ever in doubt as to correct polarity of incoming power, make a simple, quick check as follows: Using an inexpensive miniature neon light circuit tester, touch one test prod to the black conductor, the other prod to an earth ground such as the engine block or a below-waterline, metal, thru-hull fitting. The light should glow. Touch the test prod to the white conductor; the light should not glow. Polarity is correct. However, if the light remains dark when you touch the black, but glows when you touch the white, polarity is backward. Reverse the shore connection.

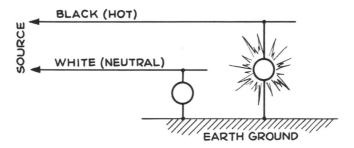

Fig. 4-8 A test light between black wire and ground should glow, but between white and ground it should not—if polarity is correct.

Suppose both shore plug and on-board receptacle are of the correct, polarized, 3-blade, non-reversible type, but you find that the marina receptacle is wired backward? If yours is a one-night tie-up, you will have to live with it, or alternately, make up a temporary cord that will restore correct polarity aboard. If the reversed situation exists at the marina where you "live," urge the operator to have the wiring corrected.

Receptacles Aboard the Boat

Power receptacles located on deck, in cockpits, or other areas exposed to the elements must be watertight and incorporate a self-closing, water tight, cap. Receptacles for attachment to the

FIBERGLASS

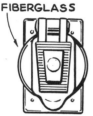

Fig. 4-9 Corrosion resistant receptacles with tight fitting protective covers are required in exposed locations.

shore cable must be the reverse service grounding type. All other a.c. receptacles on the boat must be grounding type with specific provision for the green equipment grounding wire.

We keep emphasizing that green grounding wire for a reason. Its purpose is not to conduct electricity when the situation is normal. But it *is* there to conduct current and protect humans against shock in the event the appliance it serves develops a fault. The green wire in an appliance cord connects to the third (centered) blade on a modern electrical plug. That blade mates with the third hole in the approved type receptacle, and in that hole is a connection to the grounding conductor.

Fig. 4-10 The black and white current-carrying conductors connect inside the appliance to its working windings. The green equipment grounding wire simply attaches to the frame.

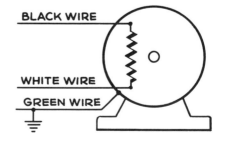

BLACK WIRE

WHITE WIRE

GREEN WIRE

In the unhappy event that a hot wire inside the appliance touches the device's frame or exposed metallic case, that case will become electrically "hot" unless tightly grounded. Purpose of the green equipment grounding wire is to ground the appliance and to conduct fault currents to earth, preventing them from passing through a human to ground.

Shock Hazard

Because of the inevitable dampness around a boat, shock hazard is naturally greater than in a home living room. That's why the protective grounding green wire is so important on floating equipment. But the green wire cannot do its job unless plugs are the three blade type, and receptacles have three holes to accept the plugs.

In the name of safety, boats fitted with the old fashioned two blade receptacles should be refurbished with the modern three blade type. And the third (green) connection should be securely grounded.

Fig. 4-11 The modern "pansy face" receptacle can accommodate the mating plug's grounding blade.

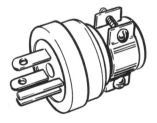

Fig. 4-12 The equipment grounding blade is prominent on an approved type of straight blade appliance plug.

The On-Board 115 Volt System

Shown in Figure 4-13, this system may be used on any non-metallic boat. It may also be used on a metal boat having

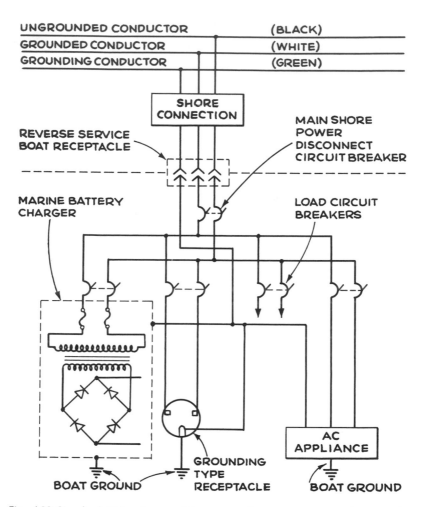

UNGROUNDED CONDUCTOR (BLACK)
GROUNDED CONDUCTOR (WHITE)
GROUNDING CONDUCTOR (GREEN)

SHORE CONNECTION

MAIN SHORE POWER DISCONNECT CIRCUIT BREAKER

REVERSE SERVICE BOAT RECEPTACLE

MARINE BATTERY CHARGER

LOAD CIRCUIT BREAKERS

AC APPLIANCE

GROUNDING TYPE RECEPTACLE

BOAT GROUND

BOAT GROUND

Fig. 4-13 Standard 115 volt a.c. wiring uses a three wire system and receptacle.

protection against galvanic corrosion. (More about corrosion protection is found in Chapter 13.)

The ground (white) and ungrounded (black) shore current wires are connected via the cable to the boat's a.c. circuit through a main disconnect circuit breaker. This main breaker, when tripped on overload or manually opened, breaks the circuit to both on-board current-carrying conductors, white and black. Neither current-carrying conductor is ever grounded to the boat at any point whatever.

The shore equipment grounding conductor, green or bare, is connected directly to all non-current carrying parts of the a.c. system. These are the power panel, junction boxes, and the like. The protective grounding wire is also connected to the boat's common ground point. Breakers, fuses, and switches are never placed in the grounding conductor. Its integrity must never be violated.

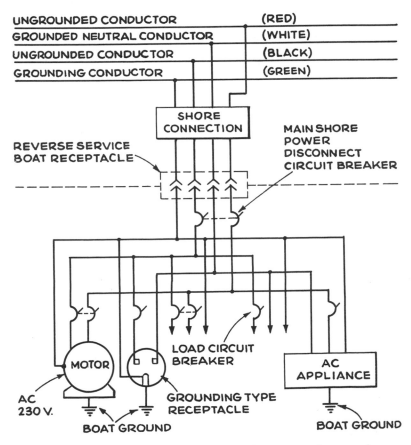

Fig. 4-14 Standard 115/230 volt a.c. wiring has four wires and receptacle.

The On-Board 115/230 Volt System

Similar to the 115 volt system, and shown in Figure 4-14, this system is used on larger boats, particularly those having high capacity air-conditioners and electric galleys. ABYC rates this system as ok on any non-metallic boat or on a metal boat having protection against galvanic corrosion.

In this arrangement, the shore grounded neutral conductor (white) is connected directly to the neutral white wires aboard the boat. No circuit breaker is required in the white. An acceptable alternate is to provide a breaker in the white neutral wire, *provided* it simultaneously opens all white, black, and red conductors when it trips.

In the standard system, red and black ungrounded shore conductors are each connected to the boat's system through a single pole circuit breaker. None of the three current-carrying wires is ever grounded on the boat.

On the 115/230 volt system, as with the plain 115 volt one, the green equipment grounding conductor is connected directly to all non-current-carrying parts of the a.c. system. It is also tied to the boat's common ground point. Because it is intended to protect the crew against electrocution, the green wire is never switched or overload protected in any manner.

The On-Board Isolation System

Recommended by ABYC as an excellent a.c. electrical system for most boats, the isolation transformer circuit reduces shock hazard. It also reduces the possibility that the floating a.c. system will cause galvanic corrosion. Because of the latter, it is recommended for use aboard steel and aluminum craft.

Heart of the isolation system is an on-board isolation transformer. Electrically, it offers complete separation of shore power from the boat's circuits. Shore generated electricity flows through the transformer's primary winding and back to shore. Its energy is transferred to the boat's system magnetically. But there is no direct electrical connection between shore juice and the boat's circuits.

An isolation transformer allows the boat's current-carrying conductors to float completely free of ground. They behave, in a sense, as though they were "dead" wires with respect to earth; but there is voltage *between* them. Because it circulates in its own closed circuit, electricity from the isolated system does not try to flow through people or other conductors to true earth ground. It

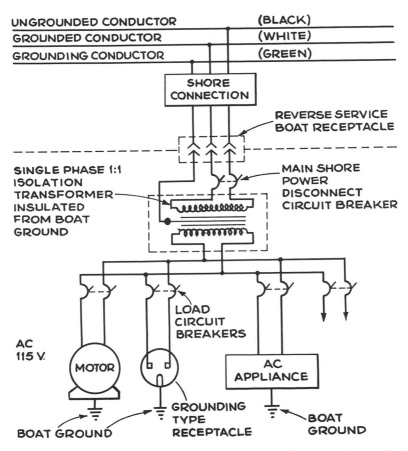

Fig. 4-15 In the isolation system, current-carrying conductors make no direct connection to the boat's distribution wiring. The equipment grounding conductor terminates at the transformer shell.

is, therefore, safer for sailors and gentler on boats from a corrosion standpoint.

Figure 4-15 shows an isolation transformer system for 115 volts a.c.; and a similar system is used where 115/230 volts is brought on board via an isolation transformer. In all cases, the transformer is insulated from the boat. Its primary winding is energized from shore power through circuit breakers; these breakers, when tripped, simultaneously open the black and white current-carrying conductors.

The isolation transformer frame is tied to shore "earth" via the green equipment grounding wire; but the frame is insulated from the boat. The green grounding wire need not be brought aboard any farther than the transformer, and is not run through the boat's a.c. distribution system.

A negative reason for not carrying the green equipment grounding wire through the boat's receptacles served by an isolation transformer is this: Since the black and white current-carrying conductors are both floating free, having essentially no potential to ground, neither will shock a person who touches one while simultaneously touching a ground, such as a water pipe. Should an appliance develop an internal fault, it will not shock the user who is grounded. Consequently, the green protective wire is not required.

There is also a positive reason for not tying the green shore grounding wire to the boat's central ground point. Because of circuit unbalances in the shore system, the green grounding wire may actually be a volt or two different in potential from the true ground potential of the water in which the boat floats. When this happens, current will flow from the boat's ground through the water in which it floats; and the current will cause electrolytic corrosion to underwater hardware.

Protection for On-Board A.C. Circuits

Your home is protected against fire caused by electric overload or short circuit. Fuses or circuit breakers are the protection; the same kind of devices protect your boat. As back-up, certain switches and disconnects are also needed.

Trip-free circuit breakers are a recommended protective component for on-board application. These are designed so that the reset handle cannot be manually held to override the current interrupting mechanism. "Cheating" on the breaker is impossible.

Two types of breaker are available for on-board use; Magnetic breakers convert current to a magnetic field; and when the field becomes too strong it operates a mechanism, opening the protective switch. Thermal breakers convert current to heat; and when temperature rises beyond predetermined setpoint, the heat operates a bi-metal or other switch mechanism. Many marine electricians, and men at marinas, prefer the magnetic type because it does not derate itself in the hot sun or when cabin temperatures get torrid. Advantage of the termal breaker is that it offers a time lag before tripping, thus allowing motors to overload the line momentarily while starting.

Correct size fuses offer safe on-board circuit protection. However, fuses have several disadvantages as compared to circuit breakers:

- When a fuse blows, it is more difficult to replace it than simply to re-set a circuit breaker.
- It is dangerously easy to replace a blown fuse with an improper one of excess current-carrying capacity.
- If a fuse blows and no replacement is handy, there is the temptation to shunt it with a length of wire, a practice which leads to fire.
- In damp corrosive atmospheres, fuse clips tend to corrode, offering a high resistance connection which results in voltage drop.

Where fuses are used aboard the boat, the skipper is urged to carry plenty of spares, and to store them close to the active fuse. It is certainly not unrealistic to carry a half dozen spares for each size fuse used on the boat.

Shore Power Disconnect

A safe on-board a.c. electric system must have a shore power disconnect switch which simultaneously shuts off all current-carrying conductors from shore to boat. Of course, it does not interrupt the safety equipment grounding conductor. The multi-pole disconnect switch should be located as close to the shore power inlet receptacle as possible. Naturally, to serve its purpose, it must be in a handy, readily accessible location.

Feeder Protection

Feeders from shore power to the boat should be protected as required by ABYC standards. The Council says: "Each current-carrying conductor from the shore power inlet receptacle to the boat's main a.c. switchboard or panel, except the grounded neutral of a three wire, 115/230 volt a.c. service, shall be protected by a circuit breaker or fuse having a rating equal to no more than 125 percent of the total normal load."

As mentioned earlier, all current-carrying conductors in branch circuits must have fuses or trip-free breakers. Also, each circuit serving an a.c. motor must be protected by a device rated not more than 125 percent of the motor's full load rated current.

Full Power with Safety

If the boat is to have full voltage through all circuits, and if wiring is to operate cool and safe, a.c. conductors must be of adequate size. This is a basic rule in wiring. For common wire types, with not more than three conductors cabled or bunched in a raceway, the National Electrical Code allows the following ampacities for insulated conductors. This table also indicates the approximate voltage drop per ampere per 100 feet:

From the table, it is apparent that the voltage drop at 15 amps through 100 feet of 14 gauge wire is approximately 7.2 volts; but the same current passing through 100 feet of 10 gauge wire suffers a voltage drop of only 3 volts. Heavy boat wiring pays, especially because it is possible that voltage from the marina and through the power cord may be low to start with.

Gauge Awg	Ampacity	Voltage Drop
14	15	.48
12	20	.31
10	30	.20
8	40	.13
6	55	.08

When inspecting old wiring or installing new, make sure that your boat's a.c. wiring is as heavy as or heavier than specified by the code. Lighter wire is not only risky but also makes appliances sluggish.

Where you're in doubt about the current a circuit handles, energize the circuit, placing on it all the loads it will be asked to carry; then measure the flow of current with a clip-on a.c. ammeter. If the current is greater than the ampacity rating of the wire, rework the circuit with heavier wire. Alternately, lighten the circuit's load; and run a new circuit for part of the equipment it served.

Regarding wire gauge, a good rule is: "Where there's doubt, use the next heavier gauge." This is particularly true in cabins and bilges baked by the sun where heat increases conductor resistance while decreasing insulation durability.

SYNOPSIS

The housepower a.c. system coming aboard the boat is the same kind of 4-wire circuitry found in households, but with modifications. Both current-carrying conductors are switched and fused, whereas in household electricity, only one current-carrying conductor is ever "opened." One current-carrying conductor is grounded ashore, but not on the boat. The protective green equipment grounding wire is grounded ashore, and may be grounded on the boat; but it is never switched or fused. Dockside receptacles must be 20 amp size, and the locking type. The a.c. system is particularly safe, and contributes to corrosion reduction. All onboard systems should be fitted with trip-free circuit breakers, and must have a shore power disconnect switch.

CHAPTER V

Boats, Like Bankers, Must Be Bonded

A HUSKY, low resistance bonding system is a *must* on inboard powered, non-metallic boats. It is, in fact, required by the American Boat and Yacht Council on boats meeting ABYC's high standards.

What is Bonding?

Bonding comprises a heavy electrical conducting system which electrically "ties together" the entire boat. It acts somewhat the same as the guard grounding conductor in household wiring, but its functions are even more important. In both cases, all exposed metallic enclosures for electrical equipment are held close to ground potential in the event wiring develops a fault.

ABYC cites four important reasons for requiring electrical bonding on non-metallic boats. These are:

1. Bonding provides a low resistance electrical path between otherwise isolated metallic objects, reducing the possibility of electrolytic corrosion due to stray currents between objects.

2. Bonding prevents the possibility of above-ground electrical potential on exposed electrical equipment if there is an electrical fault.

3. Bonding provides a low-resistance path to ground for voltages higher than system potential, as, for example, during a lightning strike.

4. Bonding minimizes radio interference.

Bonding is Independent

It is important to know that the bonding system is definitely *not* intended to function as the current-carrying conductor in the boat's a.c. or d.c. electrical system. For example, it must not be used as the ground return conductor in the d.c. system; and it must not be used *in place* of the equipment ground conductor in the a.c. system. In short, the bonding network is intended to act as a heavy electrical back-up, but is not to be intentionally used as a current-carry circuit. You don't intentionally hook circuits to the bonding network for it to conduct working currents.

Details

Where a bonding system is installed aboard a boat having a grounded electrical system, both the bonding system and the electrical system's grounded conductor must connect to a common ground point. Notice that the two systems come together only at this one point; they are not interconnected at several points throughout the boat.

Bonding conductors must be independent of the electrical system's grounded conductor except at the point of attachment to the one common ground terminal. This prevents the bonding from carrying operating current, which it must not be asked to do.

The bonding conductors must be permanent, continuous, and of sufficient size to conduct safely any currents likely to be imposed on them due to stray currents or short circuits.

Usually running from bow to stern, the common bonding conductor should be uninsulated copper or bronze strip, or copper tubing. The kind of tubing used for refrigeration and

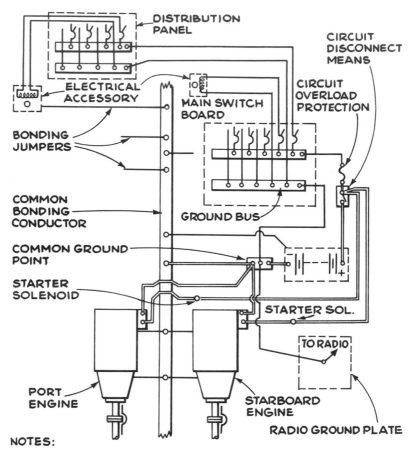

NOTES:
1. WIRES ADJACENT TO EACH OTHER THROUGHOUT SYSTEM.
2. ELECTRICAL EQUIPMENT MAY BE INTERNALLY GROUNDED.
3. SYSTEM SHOULD BE POLARIZED THROUGHOUT.
4. SWITCH BOARD AND DISTRIBUTION-PANEL CABINETS, IF
   CONSTRUCTED OF METAL, SHALL BE BONDED.

Fig. 5-1 Schematic shows a bonding system on a boat having a grounded direct current electrical system.

plumbing work is good for the purpose. Also acceptable is bare copper or tinned copper wire of heavy gauge. Wire, tubing, or strip must be of thick gauge, not only to provide heavy current-carrying capacity, but to offer ease of accepting low resistance connections. Copper braid, sometimes used to bond aircraft or electronic gear, is not recommended for use in bonding boats. It is difficult to connect to, and is subject to deterioration by corrosion.

Common bonding conductors made of copper or bronze strips must be no less than ⅟₃₂″ thick, and no less than ½″ wide. As a matter of fact, on well constructed yachts it is not uncommon to

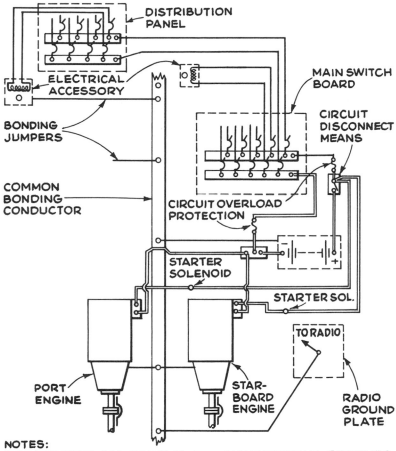

NOTES:
1. ALL ELECTRICAL EQUIPMENT WITHOUT INTERNAL GROUNDS.
2. SWITCH BOARD AND DISTRIBUTION-PANEL CABINETS, IF CONSTRUCTED OF METAL, SHALL BE BONDED.

Fig. 5-2 Schematic shows a bonding system on a boat having an ungrounded direct current electrical system.

see the main fore-and-aft bonding strip $\frac{1}{32}''$ thick and $2''$ to $5''$ wide, laid right down the centerline of the boat.

Where round wire is used as the common bonding conductor, it must be #8 AWG wire gauge or heavier. Where tubing is used, it must, of course, have conductivity equal to or greater than #8 wire. Standard $\frac{3}{4}''$ or $1''$ copper refrigeration or plumbing tubing serves well as a common bonding conductor. It is easy to handle, convenient to connect to, and has adequate conductivity.

The Master Conductor

Named the common bonding conductor, the main bond must be installed fore-and-aft, from bow to stern, preferably along the boat's centerline. It must have a short, heavy, direct connection to the boat's common ground point; and it must be positioned so bonding jumpers can be as short and direct as possible.

Preferably, there should be no splices in the common bonding conductor. Where they are necessary, connections must provide electrical continuity and mechanical strength equivalent to the original conductor. Joint laps must be at least $2''$ long, brazed or soldered, and secured against failure due to vibration or strain.

Watertight bulkheads present a special problem to the installation of the main fore-and-aft bonding conductor. An acceptable method of carrying the conductor through a bulkhead is to use a very heavy through-bolt of bronze or copper, the through-bolt or bolts, being heavier in electrcal cross-section than the bonding strip itself. When through-bolts are used, they should attach to the bonding conductor and pass through the bulkhead well above maximum bilge water level. Also, where possible, it is a good idea to sweat the connections after tightening the through-bolts firmly.

Fastenings used to secure the common bonding conductor to the hull or other surfaces must be of a metal equal to or more noble than the copper conductor. Thus, screws, nuts and bolts of copper silicon bronze, Inconel, or 18-8 type 304 passive stainless

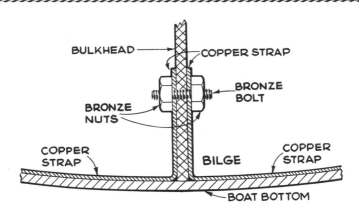

Fig. 5-3 One method of carrying a bonding strap through a bulkhead by heavy copper or bronze hardware above the bilge water level.

steel are fine, but "household" brass screws will corrode, and are no good for the purpose.

ABYC requires certain accessibility to the common bonding conductor: "The point of connection to the common ground point, points of connection to the bonding jumpers, and splices in the common bonding conductor shall be accessible for inspection and maintenance," says the safety standard book. This means that when a bonding system is installed, there should be some kind of removable floorboards or cover plates at the points cited above. Makes sense.

Naval architects say that the main bonding conductor should preferably be routed as close to the centerline of the boat as is practical. However, they say, "On small boats where the electrical components are predominantly on the side of the hull, the common conductor may be routed in a manner to minimize length of the bonding jumpers."

Bonding Jumpers

Shorter than the fore-and-aft main bonding conductor, the bonding jumpers form the ribs of the system. They connect the metal non-current-carrying parts of the boat to the common

93

bond. Naturally, they must be tightly connected at each end with corrosion and vibration resistant fastenings. Where the bonding jumpers attach to the common bonding conductor, strain relief must be provided so the connections remain secure.

The jumpers, like the common bond, need not be insulated. One exception might be where the jumper is close to current-carrying wires, and where chafing might possibly cause a short circuit. Size of wire must be more than great enough to handle maximum expected current, and in no case should be smaller than #8 AWG wire or the equivalent in copper strip or tubing.

Things You Should Bond

If you are installing a bonding system or inspecting an existing one, see to it that all large metal blobs are attached to the boat's system. Include such items as:

• The propulsion engine or engines on a motorboat, and the auxiliary motor on a sailboat are bonded. If the boat has an auxiliary electric generating plant, that, too, must be bonded. To make sure that the prop shaft is well bonded, install a brush or rubbing contact adjacent to it as described in Chapter 13, "Taming Electrolytic Corrosion."
• Electric motor and generator or alternator frames are included. However, where the motor or generator is attached firmly to a bonded engine, as the starter and alternator are, separate bonding is not needed; the engine's bond will serve very nicely.
• Larger cabinets and control boxes housing either d.c. or a.c. power components are connected to a jumper. However, it is not necessary to run a heavy bond to every small switch plate or receptacle. These are individually grounded on a.c. circuits by the equipment grounding conductor, the bare or green wire.
• The cabinets and enclosures of electronic gear must be included in the bonding arrangement. Good bonding protects the electronics against damage from lightning, meanwhile reducing their pick-up of static, spurious signals, and electrical noise. Bonding also acts as a backup in protecting the user against electrical shock

hazard from the gear which is energized from the 115 volt a.c. line.

• Where metallic sheath or conduit is used to carry conductors, it should be connected to the bonding.

• Heavy cables, tubes, pipes or rods comprising part of the rudder or clutch control arrangement should be bonded.

• It is most important that fuel tanks, fuel-fill deck fittings, fuel feed lines, electrically operated fuel tanks and valves be tied to the bonding system. Good bonding of the entire fuel system is a step toward preventing fires caused by static discharge or lightning side flashes.

• Bonding should include metal or lead lined battery trays, should also include water tanks and their connecting fill hardware on deck.

Metal Boats

Aluminum and steel boats need not be bonded, provided good electrical continuity is maintained between all the items which normally require bonding. A tight electrical connection to the hull will usually more than suffice.

There are two points to watch carefully when using the metal hull as a common conductor:

1. Underwater hardware which might create a galvanic couple with the hull should not be electrically attached to it. In this case, the hardware should be completely insulated from the hull. For example, a copper or silicon bronze underwater fitting should be insulated from the hull. Otherwise, the hull would try to "protect" the fitting, and the hull would corrode.

2. In order to avoid galvanic action between a through-hull fitting and the metal hull, the following should be done with electric pumps: The sea water connection must be insulated from the hull, and an insulating rubber hose placed between fitting and pump. The pump casing and motor frame may be grounded as long as there is no electrical connection between pump assembly and through-hull fitting.

95

SYNOPSIS

The bonding system is a heavy set of conductors used to electrically "tie the boat together." Bonding is normally non-current-carrying, and completely separate from either the boat's d.c. or a.c. system. It is never used as the ground return wire for electric circuits; and those circuits are attached to it at one point only: The boat's common ground point.

CHAPTER VI

The Charging Circuits

THIS CHAPTER applies to the generator and alternator charging circuits drvien by the propulsion engine, serving the engine and auxiliary batteries. "Plug-in" chargers, deriving their energy from the 115-volt a.c. line are discussed in Chapter 7.

The System

Heart of any charging circuit is the generator or alternator, with secondary components comprising the regulator, ammeter, and (in some circuits) a protective device such as a fuse or circuit breaker.

Conventional Generator

The "old fashioned" conventional generator is replaced by the modern alternator on the majority of newer marine engines. However, the older type is still very much alive, being found on some diesels, numerous imports, and on many older engines still in service. It has one advantage over the newer alternator in that it can stand more electrical abuse and still come back fighting.

How the Generator Works

Shown schematically in Figure 6-1, the conventional generator closely resembles a shunt-wound, direct-current motor. So close is it electrically, that if connected to a direct-current power source it will run as a motor.

The field or stationary windings, excited by feed-back of direct current, create a strong magnetic field in which the armature rotates. Driven by the engine via a V-belt, the generator's armature and its integral coils spin through the magnetic field; and

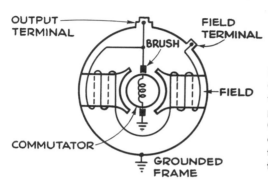

Fig. 6-1 Electrical schematic of two-brush generator shows that armature furnishes output current via the brushes. One end of the field wiring is connected to the hot brush, the other end to the external field terminal.

electricity is generated in the armature windings. At one end, the armature carries a commutator against which stationary brushes ride or slip, as in a direct-current motor (See Page 258). In the most popular circuits, one brush is grounded to the machine's frame; the other is insulated and connected to the generator hot output terminal.

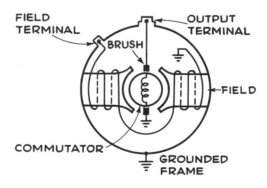

Fig. 6-2 Less frequently used than the circuit in Fig. 6-1, this circuit has the field grounded inside the generator frame. Field excitation is through external resistance connection to the output terminal.

Heavy Current Commutated

Since the current which is induced inside the generator orig-inates in the armature or rotor, it must all pass through the brushes and commutator to reach the output terminals. This means that in an ordinary size generator, the brush-commutator combo must handle as much as 25 or more amperes. Both the brushes and commutator must be heavy, clean, and well adjusted or unwanted arc will eat away both assemblies.

Start-Up

When the engine is first started, and the generator begins to spin, its field coils are deenergized, and it would seem that it could not start generating. However, it chain-reacts itself into operation because of residual magnetism in the field coil pole pieces. When the generator is at rest, there remains a trace of magnetism in the field iron. This residual magnetism generates a weak current which, fed to the armature, quickly builds up to many amperes, and the machine is in full swing within split seconds.

Output Control

The generator's output is conveniently controlled by varying the magnetic strength of the field. Since field strength depends upon the current in the windings, if we weaken that current we will reduce generator output. That's the way it is done in prac-tice. An external resistance is inserted in the field circuit. As the external resistance is increased, field current and resulting mag-netic strength decreases, and generator output falls.

On a few larger generators field modulation is via a simple hand-adjusted rheostat of perhaps 10 ohms overall resistance. But most propulsion engine driven generators have a variable resistor in a voltage control box, and this resistor is automatically positioned by electrical signals to maintain generator output

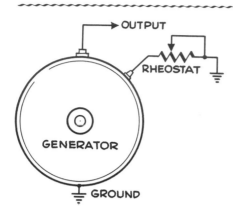

Fig. 6-3 A variable resistance between field terminal and ground
adjusts generator output.

within the desired range. This is described in more detail in later paragraphs.

"Shorting" the Field

Since inserting an external resistance in the generator's field winding decreases output, it would seem that removing all resistance should increase the output. And it does. One internal field winding connection is hot, being fed by the armature. The external connection is normally open. Therefore, if the external connection is grounded or shorted to the generator frame, the machine will put out its absolute maximum charge. This is one way to test a generator, isolating a trouble to either the generator or its external control. The field is shorted to frame by a jumper. If output soars, the generator is ok, and the trouble probably lies in the control circuit.

A word of warning: Don't operate the generator more than a short period with shorted field connection or it will overheat and may be destroyed.

"Flashing" the Field

On occasion, particularly after a generator has been laid up for the winter, its field poles will lose all residual magnetism, and the generator will not put out, no matter how fast it is spun.

100

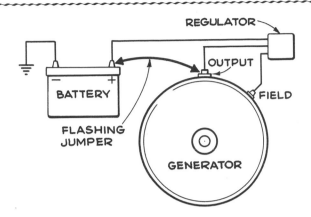

Fig. 6-4 A jumper from battery hot terminal to the generator's output connection flashes the field.

In this case, you can flash the field, restoring the lost residual magnetism.

Using a piece of heavy wire, make a jump circuit from the battery's hot, ungrounded, terminal direct to the output terminal on the generator. Energize this jumper for only a brief instant, and be careful. Don't get burned: a lot of current will flow. The high current will remagnetize the field poles, and the generator should then operate satisfactorily.

Reversed Polarity

If a generator has been wired into a circuit backward, and its field is magnetized in reverse, it will charge with reversed polarity, *discharging* the battery more and more severely as the engine is accelerated. To cure this rare trouble, simply flash the field with correct polarity, as described above.

Open Circuit is Harmful

Never operate a generator-equipped engine with the generator load circuit open. That is, don't run without a battery in the circuit, or with the wire between generator and battery disconnected. To do so may damage the generator, its regulator, or both.

The Generator Regulator

Three individual units, looking like wire wound relays, comprise the generator regulator. They control reverse current, voltage, and current limit. Operation of a typical regulator is shown schematically in Figures 6-5, 6-6, 6-7.

Reverse Current Cutout

If the generator's ouput terminal were wired directly to the battery, all would be well while the generator charged. But when the engine was shut down, current would flow back from the battery to the generator, discharging the battery. The reverse current cutout is simply a relay, preventing current from flowing back from the battery to the generator. So simple is its function that it is sometimes replaced by a single diode rectifier which allows current to flow from generator to battery, but not backward.

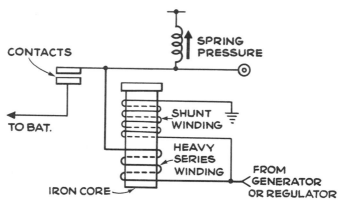

Fig. 6-5 Schematic of reverse current relay shows series and shunt windings around a common soft iron core.

Figure 6-5 shows a reverse current relay schematically. Around its magnetic core, two coils are wound: A shunt winding with many turns of fine wire, and a series winding comprising only a dozen turns of heavy wire. Close to the core pole, urged open by a spring, is the relay contact arm. When the core is magnetized by the windings, the contact arm is pulled down, making a connection from generator to battery.

The shunt winding is designed to pull down the relay arm, closing the contacts, when generator voltage slightly exceeds battery voltage. As the contacts close, current starts flowing through the heavy series winding, adding to the magnetism holding the contacts closed.

When the generator slows or stops, current commences flowing from battery to generator, reversing the direction of flow through the series winding, but not through the shunt. This makes the coils buck magnetically, all but destroying magnetic attraction. Immediately, the relay opens, disconnecting battery from generator.

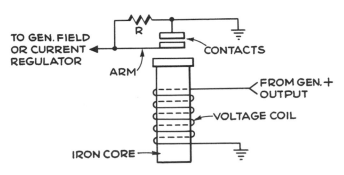

Fig. 6-6 When increased generator voltage is impressed on the coil, the contacts are magnetically pulled apart, inserting resistance R in the generator field circuit.

Voltage Regulator

Shown in Figure 6-6, the voltage regulator is essentially a heavy duty voltmeter which senses generator potential and increases the generator field resistance when output voltage exceeds setpoint.

Around the iron core is a voltage coil comprising many turns of fine wire. This coil is connected across the generator output; and the higher the generator voltage the stronger the pull of the electromagnet against the relay arm. When generator potential reaches regulator setpoint, the voltage coil urges the contacts apart against spring restraint.

The generator external field circuit is grounded, essentially without resistance when the contacts are closed, but when the contacts open, resistor R is added to field circuit resistance.

It was seen earlier that when field circuit resistance to ground is increased, generator output drops. In the present circuit, resistance is negligible when the contacts are closed. Therefore, when resistor R is thrown in the circuit, in series, generator output potential drops, voltage coil attraction decreases, and the contacts close. Instantly, voltage rises. The cycle is repeated many times a second, as the contacts vibrate to maintain setpoint voltage in the charging circuit.

More sophisticated regulators use two sets of contacts and two steps of resistance to give wide range control throughout the span of generator output. But in all electro-mechanical instruments, the general principle is as described for the regulator in Figure 6-6. And in most instruments, a current limiter is included in the circuit, working together with the voltage regulator, as described below.

Current Limiter

Located between the voltage regulator and reverse current cutout, the current limiter protects the generator from overheating or burning when the battery is badly discharged or the load very heavy. In that event, the voltage regulator keeps the field grounded, calling for absolute maximum charge rate, and at substantial generator speed, current must be limited.

A simple current limiter is shown in Figure 6-7. Wound on the pole piece, the current coil is a few turns of very heavy wire, transmitting full charging current from generator to reverse current cutout. The contact set is normally closed, urged shut by a spring; and current in the coil creates a magnetic field tending to pull the contacts open. The contacts are in the generator field

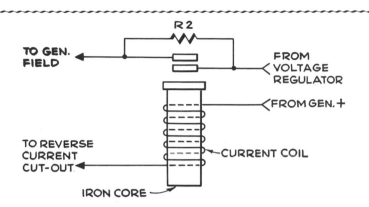

Fig. 6-7 As generator current reaches maximum allowable value, the current winding pulls the contacts apart, increasing generator field resistance, and lowering output.

circuit, between the voltage regulator and generator field terminal.

Assume that the voltage regulator has grounded the field, making the generator work hard. When current flowing through the limiter's current coil exceeds setpoint, say for example 35 amperes, the contacts are pulled apart by magnetic force. Then resistor R2 is inserted in the field circuit, and generator output falls. So does the current coil's pull; and the contacts close. Current rises; and the cycle is repeated many times a second, as the vibrating contacts limit current to a safe value.

Effect of Spring Tension

Spring tension opposes electro-magnetic attraction operating the contacts in each of the devices: reverse-current cutout, voltage regulator, and current limiter. It is apparent, then, that magnitude of spring force has considerable influence on regulation.

Spring tension is adjustable. In expensive regulator assemblies, it is adjusted by set screws, and in less costly units by bending the spring hanger. In regulators operating on the principles described earlier, effect of *increasing* spring tension is as follows:

a. Reverse current cutout: Cut-in voltage is raised, meaning that the generator must spin faster before being able to charge the battery. On a nominal 12-volt system, typical cut-in voltage is 12.8 volts.

b. Voltage regulator: Operating voltage is raised, meaning the generator will charge harder, other parameters being equal. On a nominal 12-volt system, the usual voltage setting is about 14.3 volts. On an infrequently used weekend auxiliary, it can be raised to almost 15 volts for faster charging.

c. Current limiter: Maximum current is raised, meaning that when heavily loaded, the generator will deliver more current. Adjustment is dictated entirely by generator maximum rating. For a generator rated 20 amperes, the regulator would be set to that value with the generator working into an extremely heavy load.

The Alternator

Doing the same job as the conventional generator, described in earlier pages of this chapter, the alternator looks and works quite differently. For a given output, it is generally more compact, and its regulation is simpler. Also, it can be spun at faster ratios to engine speed, offering superior charge rate at engine idling speeds. Generally, the alternator requires less maintenance than the older type generator.

Alternator Function

In some ways, the alternator is just the reverse of the generator: In the alternator, the armature is the stationary member, called the stator; while the field rotates, and is called the rotor. Such "backward" circuit arrangements allow the high charging current from the stator windings to be conducted directly to the battery circuit without being transmitted through commutator and brushes. The concept eliminates arc, spark, burning, and the maintenance which results.

Granted, the alternator has two brushes running on slip rings. But the brushes handle only two to four amps, and the rings are smooth, not segmented as in a conventional commutator; therefore, arc and wear are negligible.

Stator Windings

The alternator shown in Figure 6-8 incorporates a three-phase stator winding, star connected, with the common point of the windings at a neutral terminal which "floats" and is not grounded. Contrasted to a single set of windings, use of three-phase or individual windings increase the number of pulses

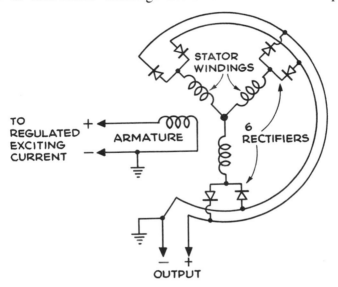

Fig. 6-8 The alternator has three individual stator windings, each terminating at a pair of rectifier diodes which convert a.c. to d.c.

generated by the alternator, resulting in an electrically smoother output. Three individual phases also reduce the required ampacity of the rectifier diodes, discussed later.

Rotor

The alternator's rotor is much different from the armature in a conventional generator. The rotor has but a single winding, wrapped around the center of the shaft, each end of the winding terminating at a copper slip ring. The winding is wrapped around the shaft, not formed in lengthwise hanks as in the ordinary generator. This gives the rotor winding terrific strength to resist centrifugal force, allowing alternator speeds of 10,000 rpm and more without danger that the rotating member will "throw a winding."

Fig. 6-9 Interleafing iron fingers encompass the rotor coil which gives alternate magnetic polarity to the rotating "spokes."

Iron pole pieces radiate from the center of the rotor, six at each end. They curve and parallel the shaft at their outer ends, interlacing like bent fingers, presenting twelve surfaces to the stator. When the center rotor coil is energized or excited by direct current, the pole pieces become powerful electro-magnets, spinning about inside the stator, inducing three-phase alternating current in the stator windings.

Rings and Brushes

The rotor coil must be energized with a few amperes of feed-back exciting current from the battery. Since the rotor spins, the coil cannot be energized by direct conductors; therefore, it is fitted with two smooth copper slip rings at which the winding terminates. The slip rings pick up their exciting current from two small graphite conducting brushes, one brush being grounded, the other being connected to the voltage regulator which modulates rotor excitation current. Since the rings and brushes carry only a few amps of exciting current, they are subject to little wear or pitting, usually lasting the life of the alternator.

Rectifiers

Each of the three phases in the stator terminates its hot end in a pair of diode rectifiers. These are solid state components which pass electricity in one direction only, rectifying alternating current to pulsating direct current. Without moving, they perform the function of the conventional generator's commutator, brushes, and reverse current cutout. As indicated in Figure 6-10, three diodes are connected to the positive alternator terminal; and three are connected to ground, which is the alternator's negative termination.

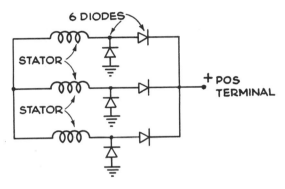

Fig. 6-10 In most popular alternators, six diodes rectify three phase alternating current to direct current suitable for battery charging.

Reverse Polarity

A little study of Figure 6-10 will show why alternator manufacturers put on red tags with big letters saying, "Don't connect to wrong polarity!" If a battery is connected backward, positive post to alternator ground, negative post to alternator output terminal, there will be fireworks. The diodes, rated for perhaps 40 amps, will try to conduct battery short circuit current, hundreds of amps, and will blow like so many fuses. A diode's weakness is that a short circuit will blow it faster than any ordinary fuse.

The moral is: "Don't ever, but ever, connect an alternator with reverse battery polarity."

Rotation

Most alternators are symmetrical both mechanically and electrically, and can be rotated in either direction.

Effect of Dead Battery

The alternator has a weakness. It will not charge an absolutely dead battery. We have seen that modest feed-back of current from battery to rotor is required to excite the alternator. If the battery is completely dead, unable to deliver so little as an ampere (a rarity), the generator is unable to charge, since excitation is unavailable.

There is an emergency procedure that you can use to get things going again when the battery is absolutely flat. A lantern battery, or even a half dozen flashlight batteries, in series, can be used to tickle the rotor. The emergency exciting source is connected between ground and the "field" terminal which is the hot brush. Then, when the alternator starts putting out, the regular battery can take over.

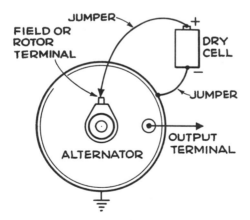

Fig. 6-11 When the boat's storage battery is dead, the alternator can be tickled into operation by exciting the rotor with a dry battery, as shown. A lantern battery or several flashlight cells in series will do it.

Regulation

The conventional generator control box has a reverse current cutout, voltage regulator, and current limiter. But most alternators use only a voltage regulator.

110

Reverse Current

No electro-mechanical reverse current cutout is required in the charging circuit since the diode rectifiers inside the alternator prevent the backward flow of current from battery to alternator stator. However, excitation current must be prevented from flowing to the rotor when the engine is shut down. This is done by connecting the exciter circuit to the ignition key, or by providing a simple relay for the function.

Current Limiting

Most alternators require no current limiter since their inherent impedence restricts current output to a safe value. Therefore, no external limiting device is used.

Voltage Regulation

A good voltage regulator is a definite necessity since, if unregulated, the alternator will go wild, grossly over-charging the battery. The voltage regulator senses battery system voltage, and controls flow of exciter current to the rotor so as to maintain system voltage within tolerance.

Figure 6-12 is a schematic drawing of an electro-mechanical

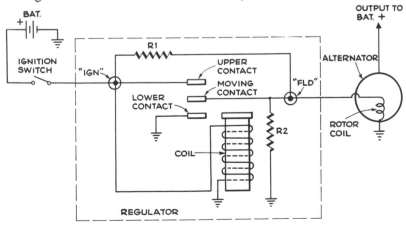

Fig. 6-12 Schematic drawing shows principal of alternator voltage regulator.

voltage regulator used on many popular engines. Mounted on or near the engine, the regulator is connected in the rotor circuit between alternator and the battery's hot terminal. One regulator terminal is marked IGN, the other FLD. The IGN terminal is connected to the ignition switch, allowing the rotor circuit to be energized only when the ignition switch is turned on. A third connection to the regulator is made from its frame to ground: the engine block.

Inside the Regulator

Heart of the regulator is a relay having two fixed contacts, and one movable double-faced contact. The arrangement is shown in the schematic. The upper fixed contact is connected to the IGN terminal; the lower one is grounded. The center contacts are connected to the FLD terminal, and are urged upward; away from the coil by spring tension.

Resistor R1 is connected directly between the IGN and FLD terminals, shunted across the upper set of contacts. Resistor R2 is connected from FLD to ground; and its function is to reduce arc at the contacts.

Consisting of many turns of fine wire, a voltage coil is connected between the ignition switch terminal and ground. When the ignition switch is closed, battery voltage forces current through the coil; and the resulting magnetic pull from the coil's core attracts the moving contact.

Low Voltage Mode

When battery voltage is low, current flowing through the voltage coil is proportionately low; and magnetic attraction of the coil's pole piece is insufficient to overcome spring tension holding the moving contact against the upper stationary contact. In this mode, battery voltage pushes current through the upper contacts, through the rotor coil to ground. Since the rotor circuit resistance is now low, maximum current flows through the rotor coil. On a 35 or 40 ampere alternator, full rotor current is on the order of 2.5 amps. Rotor magnetic field strength is now high, and alternator output is maximum for given rotor rpm.

Higher Voltage Mode

When battery voltage rises, magnetic attraction of the voltage coil assembly overcomes moving point spring tension, opening the upper contacts. Now, the moving contact floats, touching neither the upper or lower stationary contact. Battery current now flows through resistor R1 to the rotor, thence to ground.

Resistor R1, in series with the rotor coil, reduces rotor magnetic strength, correspondingly lowering the alternator's output for a given rotational speed. Because potential falls, the voltage coil's magnetic pull is weakened: Spring tension then overcomes the weaker magnetic pull, reclosing the upper contacts. The sequence is repeated many times a second.

Heavy Load

When the electrical load is relatively high, the moving contact oscillates, making and breaking with the upper contact. This alternately modulates rotor circuit resistance, limiting alternator output voltage.

Light Load

When engine speed is high and electrical load low, alternator output voltage tries to increase. Battery voltage, now higher, induces the voltage coil magnetic force to pull the moving contact against the lower stationary contact which is grounded. Current now completely ceases flowing through the rotor since both ends of its coil are grounded.

Bypassing the rotor coil causes alternator output to cease momentarily: The coil loses magnetic pull, and the moving point returns to the neutral or no-contact position, floating between the upper and lower stationary contacts. Now, current flows through resister R1 to the rotor; and alternator output rises. Consequently, at high rpm and low electrical load, the moving contact oscillates between floating position and the lower contact, thus limiting charging voltage.

Charging Rate

In discussing generator and alternator controls, we have described voltage modulation and current limiting. The reader may wonder, "What determines the charging rate indicated on the ammeter?"

The voltage control determines charging rate, increasing rate when the battery is low or heavily loaded, decreasing rate when the battery is fully charged. By maintaining (or trying to maintain) generator output voltage at exactly one level, the voltage regulator creates a "constant potential" charging system. As explained in Chapter 7, if a given voltage, above nominal, is applied to a dead battery, that voltage will force a high charge rate; if the voltage is maintained unchanged as the battery comes up to charge, the identical potential will charge the battery at a much slower rate.

Voltage regulators are usually set so that, when the battery is fully charged, the residual charging rate will be but 3 or 4 amps. On a nominal 12-volt system, this dictates that the regulator be set at approximately 14 volts.

Ammeter

The ammeter is wired into the battery circuit as shown in Figure 6-13 and indicates the net current flowing into or out of the battery, excluding the current furnished for engine starting. The starter circuit is not wired through the ammeter because starting current is a hundred amperes or more, whereas most dashboard ammeters are rated for only 30 to 40 amps.

As shown in the diagram, generator current flowing to the battery passes through the ammeter, deflecting its pointer in one direction. On the other hand, battery current flowing to the accessory load flows through the ammeter oppositely, deflecting its pointer in the reverse direction. However, if generator output exactly matches accessory demand, no current flows through the ammeter, even though the generator may be delivering heavy current to the load.

On a few larger installations a separate uni-directional ammeter is wired in the circuit right at the generator output terminal. This extra meter helps the boatkeeper monitor generator performance, separating it from the "net effect" reading of the conventional ammeter.

Voltmeter

Shown in Figure 6-13, a direct-current voltmeter, wired from the hot load terminal to ground, is a fine system-monitoring and trouble-shooting instrument. It is not standard, but is found as an extra on better d.c. systems.

For a nominal 12-volt system, the best kind of voltmeter is one with suppressed zero and expanded scale. The face of this

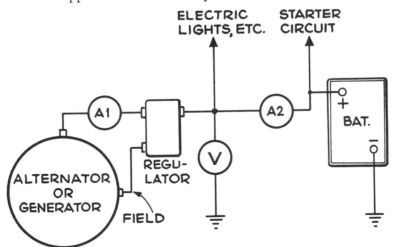

Fig. 6-13 The customary ammeter A2 responds to new current flowing to and from the battery. Meter A1 indicates generator current only; while the voltmeter monitors system voltage.

type instrument indicates from about nine to 16 volts, yielding attractive resolution for the important part of the voltage scale. On this meter, a change of less than half a volt is readily apparent, and movement as little as a tenth of a volt is readable.

The experienced boatman learns to interpret the readout from his voltmeter particularly after he has lived with it for a few weeks and become accustomed to its behavior. Low voltage after the system has been idle indicates loss of charge due to leakage or aged battery cells. Abnormally high voltage indicates that the generator voltage regulator is set too high. Low voltage while the generator operates signifies that the regulator is adjusted too low, or that system load is beyond the generator's capacity.

Wiring

The conductor from generator or alternator output terminal to its feed point must be of heavy gauge because considerable current flows when the generator is working hard. Resistance in this circuit cuts generator charging ability, adds load to the generator and creates dangerous heat. A 30 ampere machine should be wired with #10 gauge wire or heavier; and #8 gauge should be used for currents of 40 to 45 amperes.

Since the generator or alternator's frame is commonly the ground conductor, it must be well connected to the engine. On occasion, the pivot point, used for V-belt tightening, has been known to offer a high resistance connection, electrically noisy. For this reason, it is a good boatkeeping procedure to ground the generator or alternator frame to the engine via a flexible cable or wire braid.

Protection

Generator and alternator output circuits are usually unprotected by fuses or circuit breakers because if this circuit is opened, source voltage will rise to a magnitude damaging to the machine. However, it is perfectly good practice to protect the cir-

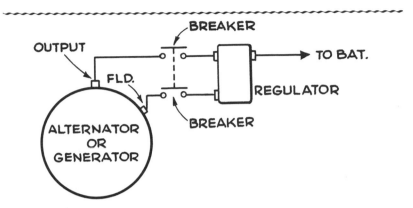

·Fig. 6-14 If the alternator or generator output circuit is protected by a circuit breaker, another pole of that same breaker should be wired in the field circuit.

cuitry, *provided* a two-pole circuit breaker is installed. The breaker senses charging current, one of its poles being in the generator or alternator output conductor, the other pole wired in the field or rotor circuit. With this arrangement, as shown in Figure 6-14, when the breaker trips on overload, it not only opens the charging circuit, but also opens the control circuit. Because both circuits are open, the generator or alternator can spin without harm.

Master Switch

If there is a master switch in the battery system, as dictated by safest practice, it should have an auxiliary switch for the generator or alternator control circuit. Much smaller than the master, the auxiliary switch opens the field or rotor circuit when the master is open circuited. Ganged double switching, as shown in Figure 6-15, prevents generator voltage from surging wildly should the master switch be open circuited while the engine is running.

Boatkeeper Maintenance

Inspect and adjust the V-belt driving the alternator or generator. Do this frequently because the belt works hard, and slight

117

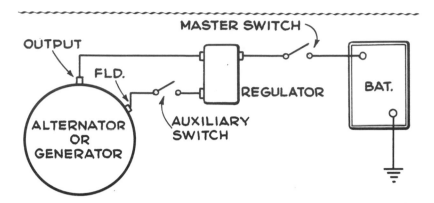

Fig. 6-15 Ganged with the master switch, an auxiliary switch must open the field circuit when the charging circuit is opened.

looseness will allow it to slip. When it slips wear increases quickly, and soon the machine is running slowly, with decreased output. This leads to complete belt failure in short order.

Replace the driving belt when it looks the slightest bit worn; and always carry a spare. After you install a new belt and tighten it properly, operate the engine for 10 to 20 minutes, then re-tighten the belt. It will stretch and "seat" in the first few minutes. Good idea, also, to double check belt tension after a day of operation.

Generators and alternators have ball bearings at the drive pulley end, and require no lubrication there. But a few have an oil cup at the other end, where a sleeve bearing is used. Put a few drops of oil in this cup about twice a season.

Once a month or so, give the wiring a quick once over, making sure that all connections to the generator and regulator are secure. Also inspect the wiring to the battery. Loose connections or faulty wiring in the charging circuit cannot only result in a run down battery, but can also damage the regulator and generate radio frequency interference.

After several seasons of hard use, a conventional generator may need commutator or brush service. Remove the cover from the brush section and, using a flashlight, inspect the brushes and commutator. If the copper commutator segments appear burned, worn or pitted, the unit is due for a trip to the overhaul shop. If the brushes are worn down to short nibs, they need replacing, because when they wear too short they cause arc, and will ruin the commutator. They'll also cause radio noise.

Shooting Alternator Trouble

The following are alternator troubles and possible causes:

- Alternator will not charge, even into a low battery:
  1. Drive belt very loose or broken.
  2. Badly worn brushes or slip rings on rotor.
  3. One or both brushes stuck out of contact with slip ring.
  4. Open rotor circuit inside or outside alternator.
  5. Open stator (charging) circuit inside or outside alternator.
  6. Blown rectifiers.
- Low, Unsteady Charge:
  1. Loose drive V-belt.
  2. High resistance in the charging circuit wiring or connections.
  3. High resistance in the alternator-to-engine winding.
  4. Open or poor connection in the stator winding.
- Low Charge and Low Battery:
  1. High resistance in the charging circuit.
  2. Low voltage regulator adjustment.
  3. Shorted rectifier or open rectifier.
  4. Grounded stator winding.
- Excessive Charge to a Charged Battery:
  1. Voltage regulator adjusted too high.
  2. Regulator contacts stuck shut.
  3. Voltage regulator coil open circuited.
  4. Regulator not properly grounded.
- Noisy Alternator:
  1. Alternator loose in its mount.
  2. Worn, frayed, "lumpy" drive V-belt.
  3. Worn ball bearings.
  4. Bent drive pulley or cooling fan.
  5. Open or shorted rectifier (causes singing).
  6. Open or shorted stator winding.

- Excessive Ammeter Fluctuation:
  1. High resistance in the rotor circuit.
  2. Defective regulator.
  3. Loose wiring in charging or control circuit.

Shooting Generator Trouble

- Generator will not charge, even into a low battery.
  1. Drive belt very loose or broken.
  2. Badly burned brushes or commutator.
  3. Weak brush springs, or brushes out of contact with commutator.
  4. Open circuit to the field winding.
  5. Spring tension on reverse current cutout too tight.
  6. Voltage regulator adjusted for lower than battery voltage.
  7. Open wiring or connections in the charging circuit.
- Low, Unsteady Charge:
  1. Loose drive V-belt.
  2. High resistance in the charging circuit.
  3. High resistance in the generator-to-engine mount.
  4. Poor connection or high resistance in the field circuit.
  5. Worn brushes, dirty commutator.
  6. Spring too loose on the current limiter.
  7. Dirty, pitted contact in the reverse current cutout.
- Low Charge and Low Battery:
  1. High resistance in charging circuit.
  2. Voltage regulator spring too tight.
  3. Worn brushes, dirty commutator.
  4. Open circuit or very high resistance in field circuit.
- Excessive Charge to a Charged Battery:
  1. Spring too tight on voltage regulator.
  2. Voltage regulator contacts stuck shut.
  3. Open circuited voltage regulator coil.
  4. Grounded field circuit between generator and regulator.
  5. Grounded field coil inside generator.
- Noisy Generator:
  1. Generator loose in its mount.
  2. Worn, frayed, "lumpy" drive V-belt.
  3. Worn ball bearings.
  4. Bent drive pulley or cooling impeller on generator.

- Excessive Ammeter Fluctuation:
  1. High resistance in the field circuit.
  2. Defective regulator.
  3. Loose wiring in charging or control circuit.
- Generator Discharges Battery with Dead Engine:
  1. Contacts stuck shut in reverse current cutout.
- Generator Discharges Battery when Running Fast:
  1. Polarity is reversed. Field must be flashed for correct polarity.

SYNOPSIS

The conventional generator delivers direct current to the load via its armature, commutator and brushes; while the alternator does the job from its fixed stator coils via diode rectifiers. The generator commonly has a three-element regulator, controlling field current, but the alternator usually has a voltage regulator alone, to control rotor current. Advantage of the generator is that it can stand more abuse than the alternator. But the alternator offers the advantages of higher capacity, better low speed performance, and reduced routine maintenance.

Charging rate is controlled by maintaining voltage nearly constant, and is indicated on an ammeter between generator and battery. A voltmeter is a good indicator, supplementing the ammeter. When a master disconnect switch is wired in the battery charging circuit, it should have an auxiliary switch which opens the control circuit simultaneously with the charging circuit.

CHAPTER VII

The Boat's Battery Charger

THE BATTERY CHARGER, sometimes referred to as a rectifier unit, is the crossover or connecting link between the boat's a.c. and d.c. systems. Energized from 115 volt alternating current, from dockside or onboard a.c. generator, the charger keeps the boat's batteries charged when the engine-driven alternator is not operating.

Function

The charger's function is first to transform 115 volt house-power to lower battery voltage, then to *rectify* the reduced voltage from alternating (a.c.) to direct (d.c.) current. Additional functions in some chargers include voltage and current regulation, automatic line compensation, automatic turn-on and turn-

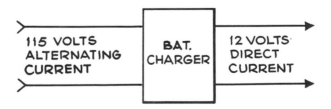

Fig. 7-1 The charger is a connecting link between the boat's 115 volt housepower system and the battery. However, the a.c. is isolated from the battery, there being no direct connection between the two.

off, and remote control. Better types of charges also include fuses, circuit breakers, and output instrumentation.

Automatic Control

Modern charging units having solid state or magnetic control are particularly suited to boats with many battery-powered accessories. This kind of unit maintains constant voltage on the d.c. system which the batteries serve. Note that controlled unit does not constantly trickle charge: On the contrary, upon detecting falling d.c. voltage, the unit charges the system bringing voltage back to normal. The rectifier will automatically charge whether falling potential results from slow "shelf life" discharge or from the current drained by an active load such as an automatic direct-current operated refrigerator.

Hum and Ripple

Low level of hum or ripple in a charger's d.c. output is a desirable characteristic in a unit used aboard a boat fitted with extensive electronic equipment. Electrical hum ensues when a high percentage of alternating current leaks through the charging circuit and is superimposed on the direct current. Then the direct-current circuits are said to have high a.c. ripple. A reasonable percentage of ripple is tolerable for most purposes; but when too much is imposed on the d.c. lines, it causes unpleasant hum in radios and can adversely effect other d.c. gear.

Better chargers use full-wave rectification to minimize ripple, rectifying both sides of the a.c. cycle, rather than just one. Some more expensive units incorporate filters to still further reduce the hum component. As a matter of fact, the battery itself acts as something of a filter. The reader will notice less alternating current hum on the boat's line when the battery is connected than when the system is energized by charger alone, the battery being removed.

Direct Operation

It is feasible with some chargers to operate direct-current

motors or lights directly from the rectifier without a battery in the system. However, this is not advisable unless the charging unit is rated for this specific service. In some circumstances, it is hard on the charger; and unless the rectifier is filtered, ripple and hum level will be objectionably high, with voltage regulation poor. Instructions accompanying each individual unit will tell whether or not it is rated as a power pack for direct operation without a battery in the circuit.

Chargers rated to be used as a direct source of energy, without a battery floated in the circuit, are often called battery eliminators. One such piece of equipment is the Heathkit Model IP-12. Typical of the breed, it furnishes well filtered, regulated six and 12-volt current at five amperes (more for short periods). Of course, it may also be used simply as a battery charger.

A Simple Charger

The basic battery charger is not complex; and a simple one is shown in Figure 7-2. Incoming 115 volts (or 230 volt) a.c. power is dropped in transformer T1 to battery charging voltage and fed to the rectifier. Then, rectifier diode D1, either a vacuum tube or solid state device, passes half wave pulses of current to the battery, 60 times a second. This circuit, found on inexpensive chargers, was typically used on the old Tungar chargers; and its output is rich in hum and ripple.

An Improvement

A better charger is that in Figure 7-3. In it, the transformer's low voltage winding is center-tapped for negative return, and the two sides of the winding feed two rectifiers D2 and D3 to give full-wave rectification. Output is 120 pulses a second, ripple being lower than from the charger in Figure 7-2.

More Versatile

Multiple battery voltages or several charge rates or both may

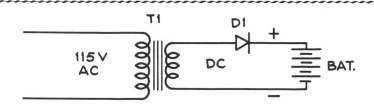

Fig. 7-2 Simple battery charger is a transformer and single rectifier.

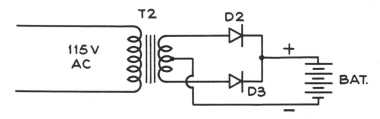

Fig. 7-3 A center-tapped secondary winding and two diodes feed direct current to the battery in this full-wave charger.

be selected manually in the charger shown schematically in Figure 7-4. The low voltage secondary transformer winding in T3 is tapped for selected voltages. Switch SW1 selects the desired voltage, feeding the full-wave bridge rectifier having four rectifiers D4, D5, D6, D7.

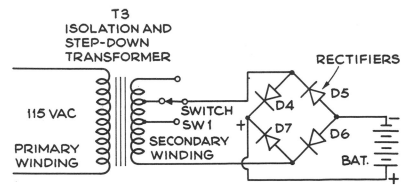

Fig. 7-4 The selector switch in this charger allows several rates of charge to be chosen manually.

Infinitely Variable

The charger shown in Figure 7-5 accommodates a wide variety of battery voltages and charging rates. Intelligently used and monitored, it can be used to energize d.c. equipment directly, because its output voltage can be adjusted to match the load, provided, of course, that the load is not beyond its capability.

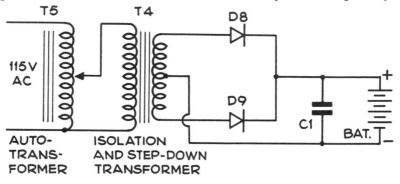

Fig. 7-5 A manually adjustable auto transformer gives this charger eliminator wide charging rates.

A manual, almost infinitely variable auto-transformer such as a Powerstat or Variac, selectably reduces line voltage fed to the isolating and voltage dropping transformer T4. Through the rectifiers D8 and D9, low voltage from the transformer is changed to d.c. and then applied to the battery.

Capacitor C1, of several thousand microfarads, is connected across the output circuits, and acts as a ripple filter, reducing hum and allowing the unit to be used as an eliminator. Note that in this circuit an auto-transformer is used to vary output voltage. However, the second transformer is a true isolating transformer, effectively separating the shore power circuit from the battery circuit. It would be unthinkable to use the auto-transformer alone as the voltage reducing means, because with its single winding it offers no isolation between the circuits. For more on the theory of the isolation transformer, see Chapters 4 and 13.

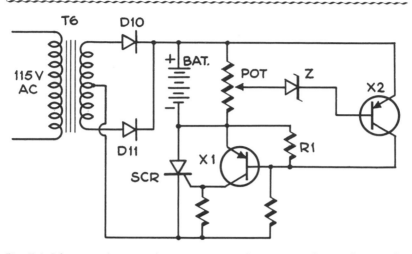

Fig. 7-6 Schematic diagram shows one type of automatic charger having the ability to turn itself off when charging is complete.

Fully Automatic

The charger circuit shown schematically in Figure 7-6 is used in one of those sophisticated types capable of charging the battery to the equivalent of full voltage and then shutting itself off. When circuit voltage drops, due to sagging battery voltage or appliance demand, the charger turns itself on.

Transformer T6 and full-wave rectifiers D10 and D11, deliver charging current to the battery through silicon controlled rectifier SCR in the negative or ground return line. The SCR is a solid state electrical trigger or gate, very much like a relay. Transistor X2 compares battery voltage with zener diode Z voltage. A zener diode provides reference voltage much as a laboratory standard cell does. When battery voltage falls, transistor X2 is cut off. Immediately a positive voltage is developed across resistor R1 and between the emitter and base of transistor X1. Promptly, X1 conducts, firing or triggering the SCR just as though it were a relay being closed; and, of course, the SCR conducts like a closed switch, applying charging current to the battery.

Charging current slowly forces battery voltage to rise; then

127

when battery voltage reaches nominal, X2 again commences to conduct, cutting off X1, and killing the gate signal to the SCR. Charging now ceases completely. The manually variable resistor POT allows the operator to adjust the voltage at which charging starts and stops.

Trickle Charging

Because many pleasure boats are used on weekends only, it would seem a simple, workable arrangement to leave the batteries on a slow trickle charge of perhaps a quarter ampere all week long. In theory, this should keep the cells fully charged. However, as explained in Chapter 2, the idea is not too good. Battery experts don't like the constant trickle because of its adverse effect on the cells.

Timed Charging

For the boat "plugged in" at dockside, a 24-hour timer can provide a good means of keeping the batteries charged during the week. The charger, in series with the timer's switch, charges the battery at from 3 to 6 amperes per 75 ampere-hour battery. Typically, the timer is adjusted to turn on the charger from 15 to 45 minutes per day, or as required to keep the electrolyte specific gravity at peak reading. General purpose timers may be used for this purpose, and are available in many hardware stores

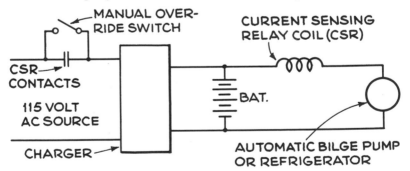

Fig. 7-7 With this simple rig, the bilge pump or refrigerator automatically energizes the charger when current is demanded.

and electrical supply houses carrying lamps, intrusion alarms and the like. A good timer for the job is Tork Model 8001, which can be set in increments of from 15 minutes to 24 hours.

Demand Charging

A circuit the author has used successfully on a boat with automatic bilge pumps incorporates a current-sensing relay. Wired in series with the battery conductor serving the bilge pumps, the sensing relay "feels" when the pumps draw power from the battery, and immediately turns on the charger which forces more d.c. into the battery than the pumps draw.

The demand charging circuit is shown in Figure 7-7 in which CSR is the coil of the current-sensing relay in series with the bilge pump's automatic float switch. The reader with ingenuity, who is also a reasonable electrician, can construct a rig similar to the one shown. It takes a little experimenting to adjust the current-sensing relay to close at the desired value, and open smartly when the load is removed. A reverse-current relay from a conventional generator may be modified for the job, or an ordinary general-purpose relay may be stripped and rewound with a dozen turns of heavy wire, converting it to a current-sensing relay.

Another approach to automatic charger activation is shown in Figure 7-8. An ordinary general-purpose, direct-current relay is

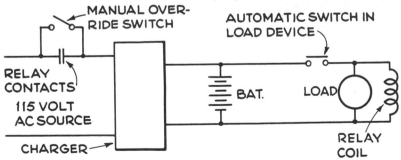

Fig. 7-8 An ordinary across-the-line relay energizes the charger when the load is turned on.

wired across the line on the appliance side of the automatic switch, such as the float switch handling a bilge pump. The practical difficulty is that in most bilge pump or refrigerator switches it is difficult to get at the cold connection between switch and motor.

For safety and neatness, the relay and switch are fastened inside a small metal enclosure, and the wires lead out through neatly fitting grommets. Purpose of the manual override switch is to permit normal operation of the charger regardless of commands from the current-sensing relay.

Isolation Required

Code making bodies insist that a marine charger have electrical isolation between the 115 volt a.c. service and battery circuit. There must be no direct electrical connection, all power being transferred magnetically through a two-winding transformer.

The isolation requirement rules out the auto-transformer because it has but a single winding, more like a single winding reactor than true transformer. Note that where the auto-transformer is used in Figure 7-5, it is followed electrically by an isolation transformer, so that through-leakage is blocked.

Isolation Test

Should the reader want to check his charger for isolation between a.c. input and d.c. output, he may do as follows:

1. Locate the charger near a water pipe or other good earth ground and plug it into a 115 volt receptacle. Turn it on.

2. Connect a small dashboard size six or 12 volt test light to the charger's positive output lead. Touch the other test lead to the grounded pipe. The bulb should not glow.

3. Using the charger's negative lead, perform the same test; and the bulb should not glow.

4. Reverse the 115 volt a.c. plug in its receptacle, and repeat the tests with positive and negative. The bulb must remain dark.

If the bulb glows in the tests, there is electrical leakage between the a.c. lines and d.c. circuits, and the charger should not be used aboard the boat.

Charge While Starting?

When you hit the starter switch to crank the engine, battery voltage may be momentarily dragged down to seven or eight volts on a 12-volt system. Will low voltage, resulting in high charge demand, damage the charger? That depends. Some chargers will blow a fuse or open a breaker, others are designed to cope with the load. The reader must check the owner's manual on his particular unit.

Technical Requirements

The American Boat and Yacht Council has a standard for marine chargers or rectifiers. The following suggestions, useful to the owner in judging a charger, are based upon the ABYC standards:

1. Automatic chargers should have a type of control which will properly charge at rates generally acceptable to battery manufacturers. As a guide, automatic units should be designed to maintain voltage of between 2.15 and 2.35 volts per cell. This applies under no-load conditions with the batteries fully charged, and the electrolyte at 77°F.

2. If the automatic unit has output capability of 20 amperes or more, it should incorporate automatic or manual control to compensate for variations in alternating current input.

3. Input voltage or voltage range should be clearly marked on the unit's nameplate. This sounds like a minor matter, but it is important because a few chargers operate on 230 volts, and some also have taps or adjustments which must be manipulated to match the rectifier to its input.

131

4. Rectifier circuits should be full wave, or filtered, or both, to minimize objectionable ripple and hum in the output.

5. Cabinets, supporting brackets, and other structural parts, if made from corrodable metals, must be well galvanized, coated, or otherwise well protected against rust and corrosion.

6. Transformers must be the isolating type, well doped, treated, or coated for use in damp, salty environments.

7. All marine chargers should have an ammeter to indicate output current. More sophisticated units should also have a voltmeter; this is particularly true of chargers having adjustable input or output.

Installation

ABYC specifies that chargers be installed in a dry accessible location, well removed from engine exhaust piping or other heat radiating surfaces. Specifically, chargers should not be located where the ambient temperature exceeds 122°F, or where they are exposed to direct radiant heat.

Chargers should never be located directly above batteries where they will be bathed in rising electrolyte vapor, nor should they be exposed to drips or from cowl openings, ports, or ventilators. Best location is a least two feet above normal bilge water, and protected against splash. Many good installations are made with the charger mounted well up on a machinery compartment fire wall or bulkhead. The unit should not be buried under other machinery because controls and meters must be readily available and visible.

Electrical Protection

The rectifier's circuits must be protected, of course, and there must also be means of disconnecting the 115 volt a.c. power as well as the d.c. output power. Specifically, standards making bodies require the following:

1. An easily accessible manual disconnect switch should be provided in the a.c. power leads to the charger; and this switch

must open both conductors simultaneously. Also, fuse or circuit breaker protection must include both feed wires.

2. Direct-current output wiring between charger and battery must have fuse or circuit breaker overload protection.

Shore Power Connections

A good charger has three internal terminals to receive shore power. Two terminals are for the black and white hot and neutral wires, the third is for the equipment grounding conductor. Terminations are clearly marked, with input and output connection points well separated.

Parallel Connections

The Constavolt marine charger is one of the better known makes; and its manufacturer, LaMarche Manufacturing Co., makes the following suggestions regarding parallel installation. The instructions are typical, applying in most instances to other makes of chargers:

"A Constavolt charger can be used across sets of batteries connected in parallel. For each additional parallel battery across the charger output, an additional 5 amperes of charge must be used for charging current."

Twin-Engine Connections

Twin-engine cruiser installations require a special switching arrangement. LaMarche advises as follows for this kind of circuitry:

"When a charger is used with double-battery systems in a twin-engine cruiser, the two-battery systems are connected across the output of the charger in parallel so that both sets of batteries are maintained at full charge. However, when both engines are running, the batteries should be disconnected from each other or an unbalance between the separate alternator systems might develop.

"In order to electrically separate the batteries when both

engines are running, a 200 ampere vapor-proof switch must be installed between the two battery sets in the ungrounded conductors. One set of batteries remains connected to the charger; the other set is disconnected. However, the switch can be closed for starting one engine on both sets of batteries, or for charging both sets of batteries from one engine, the other engine being shut down."

SYNOPSIS

The charger converts a.c. dock power to d.c. battery power, charging the boat's batteries under fixed, automatic, or manual rate control. Battery chargers use full-wave rectification or incorporate some kind of filtering to reduce ripple and hum. Some chargers may be used to operate d.c. appliances directly; but this is not true of all. True marine chargers must incorporate isolating transformers rather than auto-transformers. Constant trickle charging is undesirable, and to eliminate it, fully automatic, timed, or demand charging is suggested. Rectifiers should be installed high above the bilge water, must have overload protection, and should have switches in both a.c. and d.c. connections.

CHAPTER VIII

~~~~~~

Alternating Current
Generating Plants

An on-board alternating current power generator, gasoline or diesel driven, offers several advantages to the cruiser of roughly 32 feet and larger.

1. The generator frees the boat from dependence on a shore power cord.

2. It allows the boat to be cruised anywhere, and to moor or anchor where its skipper pleases, without regard to shore power availability.

3. Self-provided power allows the use of electric cooking, baking, heating, and air conditioning, all of which draw more current than can be easily provided by the marina.

4. A generating plant can be selected which provides 230 volts as well as 115, the higher voltage being demanded by larger appliances, particularly man-sized galley stoves.

5. Battery charging is always available on the boat having a generating plant. Should the propulsion engine starting batteries become discharged, they can be recharged by the self-powered on-board power station.

Size and Weight

The following table is averaged from several kinds of power plant, and is intended to show the magnitude of size and weight to be expected for a given wattage output.

Output Watts	Weight Lbs.	Width	Length
2,500	200	17"	26"
5,000	475	17"	38"
10,000	800	20"	47"
15,000	1,200	21"	48"

First Cost

Purchase price varies considerably depending upon the accessories such as fresh water cooling, type of starting, silencing arrangement, and whether the engine is gasoline or diesel. However, a ballpark idea of cost can be gleaned from the following list prices averaged from quotes made in late 1972 on basic models:

Output Watts	List Price
2,500	$ 850.
5,000	$1,600.
10,000	$2,600.
15,000	$2,900.

The above approximate prices are for true marine, water-cooled units of high quality. Complete radio shielding adds about $75 to the cost, and top quality silencing adds about the same amount. Automatic "demand starting" costs something like $75 to $100.

What Capacity Required

How large a generating plant do you need on your cruiser? That depends upon how many accessories and appliances you have on board, and upon how many are likely to be operated at any one time. The size of the largest electric motor has a bearing on the matter, too, since alternating current induction motors draw 4 to 5 times more current when starting than when running.

The following tabulation gives an idea of the wattage demand by various 115 volt appliances. It is not specific, but is intended to give the magnitude of demand for planning and estimating:

Item	Approximate Watts
¾ HP air conditioner	800 Watts
Electric blanket	100 Watts
Coffee percolator	600 Watts
Electric stove	1,000 Watts per element
Fan	50 Watts
Electric fry pan	1,200 Watts
Space heater	1,400 Watts
Pressing iron	1,000 Watts
Toaster	1,100 Watts
Vacuum cleaner	800 Watts
Water heater	1,200 Watts
Waffle iron	1,200 Watts
Can opener	100 Watts

Estimate the Demand

Should you turn on all those appliances at once, the load on the generator would exceed 10,000 watts. Fortunately, you will probably never have more than 40% to 60% of the stuff on the generator at any one instant; and therefore an electric plant of 4,000 to 6,000 watts capacity will handle the job. It's up to you to appraise the situation and make an intelligent selection depending upon your and your crew's habits.

In the table we see that the electric stove demands 1,000 watts per element. If the stove has four "burners" all energized at once, it will load a 4,000 watt generator to the gunwales with nothing else turned on. Keep the cooking habits in mind when choosing a power plant.

Watch those Induction Motors

Remember that it is skating on thin ice to talk about the wattage demand of alternating-current induction motors, the kind used on refrigerators and air-conditioners. Although we may estimate that a ¾ HP motor draws 800 watts from the system, its *current* demand may be closer to that drawn by a 1,500 watt heater. The difference is due to the low power factor of the induction motor. (See Page 270). The point is, when estimating the capacity of generator required, you can about double the wattage for induction motors to arrive at required current.

Volt-Amperes are Better than Watts

A still better approach is to think in terms of volt-amperes. Add up the total of amperes required, then specify the size of power plant you need in this term. Alternator manufacturers tend to think more in volt-amperes than in watts. For the current demand of various size induction motors, see Page 277. For the current demand of light bulbs, heaters, stoves, toasters, and other resistive loads on 115 volts, obtain current by dividing wattage by 115. Thus, a resistive device rated 1,000 watts demands 8.7 amps approximately. Fluorescent lights have a poor power factor; and before you compute their current demand, double the published wattage. Your answer will be in the ballpark.

Fuel Cost

Since most generating plants are operated but a few hours a day, and at partial load, fuel consumption represents a small fraction of that burned by the propulsion engines. The following published figures give an indication of fuel consumption in gallons per hour for several sizes of power generators at partial and full load:

138

Output & Type	50% Load	Full Load
2,500 Watt gasoline	.49 Gal/Hr.	.60 Gal/Hr.
4,000 Watt gasoline	.60	.82
10,000 Watt gasoline	1.3	1.7
15,000 Watt diesel	1.1	1.8

The above figures indicate that the 10,000 watt plant, when delivering 5,000 watts, burns 0.6 gallons an hour. Using gasoline at 38¢ per gallon, this results in a cost per thousand watts hours (KWH) of about $0.046. Assuming that the 15 KW diesel uses fuel costing 28¢ per gallon, it delivers a KWH of power for about $0.034 at full load.

On-Board Location

The best place for a generating plant is in the engine compartment. That enclosure has ventilation for the propulsion engines, is often sound insulated, and has stringers capable of carrying the generator plant's weight.

Regarding position, the manufacturer of Kohler electric plants has the following recommendations:

"We recommend that if the plant is mounted parallel to the keel, the engine be located forward of the generator or in such a manner as to facilitate minor servicing. Remember that oil changing, filter element changing, and carburetor adjustments occur more frequently than do changing the generator brushes.

"Maintain as much space as possible around the engine portion of the electric plant. If possible, a removable hatch should be placed above the electric plant engine. Sufficient space should be allowed for regular maintenance needs; and be sure that easy access is allowed to the seacock on the water intake."

Mounting

The plant should be mounted on stringers which distribute its weight over many frames, or on a platform which distributes

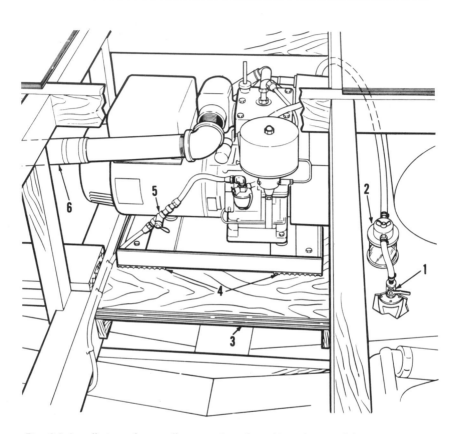

Fig. 8-1 Installation of a small generating plant. Note the good features:
1. Seacock in water line
2. Water filter
3. Heavy mounting base that distributes weight evenly.
4. Vibration isolation pads
5. Fuel shut-off valve at engine
6. Flexible axhaust section

its weight evenly over a fiberglass boat. It should be mounted high enough to be out of bilge splash and low lying vapors, and high enough so the exhaust line can pitch downward from its engine. Where the assembly is located close to or below the waterline, the exhaust must be arranged as shown in Figures 8-5 and 8-6.

Vibration Elimination

To prevent vibration transmission through the hull, the electric plant should be mounted on first class vibration eliminators, resilient pads, or springs. When mounted in this way, the assembly has no rigid connection to the hull or superstructure and is free to vibrate and shake independently. No part of the plant must touch deck supports, bulkheads or hull. All connecting lines, such as water, fuel, exhaust, and electric must be flexible. Should any one of these be rigid, not only will it telegraph noise to the boat, but will soon fracture due to fatigue.

Cooling

Whether cooled by direct circulation of raw water, or by a heat exchange system, the motor should be connected as prescribed by its manufacturer. A seacock must be fitted at intake on the hull, and this seacock should be turned off when the boat is left unattended. A water filter or strainer is desirable, and it is a good idea to have some kind of automatic alarm or shut-down which operates if the engine should overheat. Where the generator installation is below the flotation waterline, it is extremely important that all connections have the highest integrity, that flexible hoses be of top quality, and all hose connections be double clamped. If the cooling system should spring a leak while the boat is unattended, the boat may go to the bottom.

Water pick-up scoops or scuppers in the hull bottom should not be in line with those for the propulsion engine or immediately aft of any projection which might make the water turbulent. Also, the scupper should have some kind of strainer grill to keep twigs and other debris from entering.

Fuel Supply

The electric plant should use the same fuel as the boat's propulsion engines, and can draw from the same tanks, if that is desired.

Safety is the key word in fuel system installation and inspection; and every inch of the way, the fuel system should conform to the requirements of American Boat and Yacht Council and National Fire Prevention Association. If the reader plans to install an electric plant himself, or to have one installed (which he will inspect), he is urged to first get the following publications which are safety guides: *NFPA #302.* or *Safety Standards For Small Craft.* Addresses for NFPA and ABYC are found on Page 340.

Highlights of a safe fuel system are these:
- The fuel tank must be secured against shifting by means which are beyond possible reproach.
- Tank must be vented overboard so spill and vapors never enter the boat.
- Tank, fill plate, and fuel lines must be electrically connected to the boat's bonding system.
- Fuel must be drawn from the top of the tank via a dip tube. No outlet must ever be made in the side or bottom of a tank.
- An anti-siphon orifice inside the tank in the dip tube must prevent siphoning of fuel after the engine stops. Also, there must be a shut-off valve in the fuel line close to the tank. Preferably the shut-off should be an approved solenoid actuated valve which will block the fuel flow when the engine is shut down.

FUEL LINE TO PROPULSION ENGINE   **FUEL LINE TO ELECTRIC PLANT**

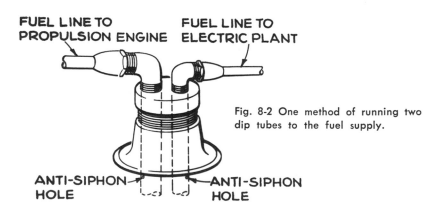

Fig. 8-2 One method of running two dip tubes to the fuel supply.

ANTI-SIPHON HOLE   **ANTI-SIPHON HOLE**

• The carburetor float must *never* be depended upon to shut off fuel flow when the engine stops. On an installation where the carburetor is below the fuel tank, it is suicidal to do so.

• In addition to the mandatory fuel shut-off at the tank, an additional valve may be installed near the carburetor, allowing engine work to be done without the contents of the fuel line being drained, and also acting as an added safety.

• The use of a T fitting in the propulsion engine fuel line is discouraged. If the generator's engine feeds on the same line as the big engine, the smaller one may be starved when the boat is underway.

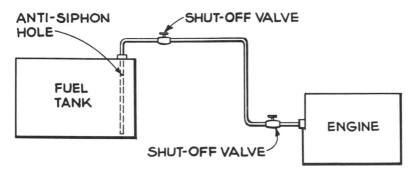

Fig. 8-3 Generating plant engine must have a fuel shut-off valve close to the fuel tank, and should have one near the carburetor.

Exhaust System

A quiet exhaust arrangement is more important on a generating plant than on the main propulsion machinery because the generator often operates at night when the crew (and neighbors) are trying to relax. The exhaust must do its job without allowing water to flow back into the engine. It must form a flexible, not rigid, connection between generating plants and the hull; and it must be adequately water cooled. As shown in Figures 8-4 and 8-5, the exhaust line must pitch down about 1″ per foot from the point of cooling water injection to its termination. Naturally, special arrangements are made for installations below the waterline, as shown in Figure 8-5.

Exhaust lines must be of adequate size to keep back pressure moderate. 1½ ″ pipe is recommended for plants up to about 3 KW; 2″ pipe for plants up to 7.5 KW; and 2½ ″ pipe for plants up to 15 KW. Runs should be as straight as possible, with long radius bends where turns must be made.

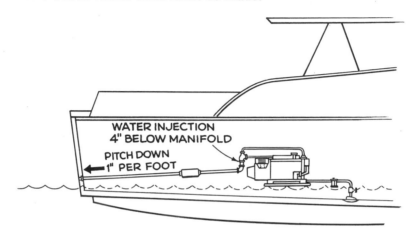

Fig. 8-4 Getting enough downward pitch for the exhaust is relatively easy on a power boat installation.

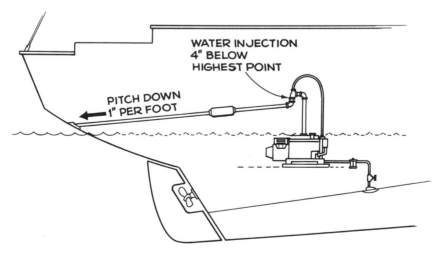

Fig. 8-5 One method of handling exhaust on a sailboat installation where the generating plant is below the waterline.

Silencing

A good muffler is appreciated on the generator, not only by your crew, but by yachtsmen on boats moored or tied nearby. Several especially effective muffling systems are offered by marine electric power plant manufacturers; and these are designed specifically for the application.

Onan's Aqualift is a tank-like muffling system into which both engine exhaust and spent cooling water are discharged. Using exhaust energy, the device then lifts the water and gases up to as much as four feet, and spews the matter overboard. Aqualift not only quiets the exhaust; it also solves the cooling water disposal problem for below-waterline generator installations.

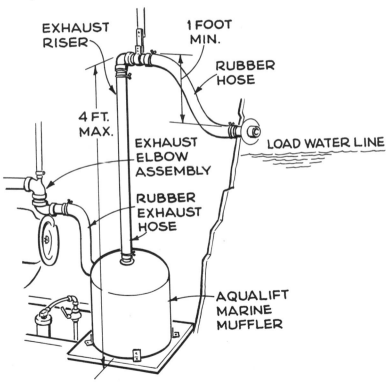

Fig. 8-6 Onan's Aqualift muffler silences engine and lifts cooling water above the waterline.

The makers of Kohler electric plants offer a Super Silencer which, fitted in the exhaust line, also cools exhaust gases, mixes exhaust with water, and expels the water-gas mixture out of the boat. It can lift spent water up to four feet, eliminating the inverted U often found in below-waterline installations. Super Silencers cost about $60.

Sound Absorption

Acoustically absorbent conforming covers are offered by several electric plant manufacturers under such names as Hush Cover and Sound Shield Enclosure. Provided with convenient snap or clip openings for maintenance, these covers soak up a great deal of airborne sound, and contribute substantially to a mute generator complex. One of these muffling covers is well worth installing on a plant which is operated late into the night. Cost of a cover is in the $300 area for most sizes of unit.

Wiring

Battery wiring follows the same principles as discussed in Chapters 2 and 9. Heavy cables are required to handle starting currents; and battery polarity must match that of the generating plant where battery current is used not only for starting but for alternator excitation.

Alternating current wiring for the "housepower" is made as described in Chapter 4, and, in most cases, is the same wiring as used for the shore power.

Ship to Shore Transfer Switch

An absolute *must* where shore power is also connected to the boat's a.c. system, the shore transfer switch is double throw. As shown in Figure 8-7, in one position the switch connects the boat's conductors to the generating plant, in the other, it connects shore power. Simultaneously, it disconnects the unused system. This is vital, because if both systems are on the line together, there will surely be fireworks as one system bucks the other.

Notice that the transfer switch opens the current-carrying conductors, but does not open the equipment grounding conductor. The latter is the green "safety" wire discussed in Chapter 1.

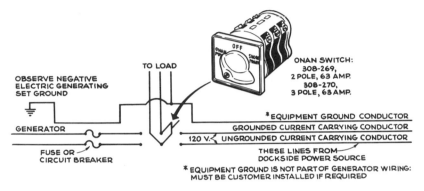

Fig. 8-7 The load transfer switch is wired to prevent simultaneous connection of generator and shore power to the boat's housepower circuits.

Starting

Several starting systems are found on generating plants:

1. Conventional starter motor with manual control.
2. Starter windings in the generator with manual control.
3. Starter windings in generator with automatic demand control.

Conventional Starting

Found most often on larger generating plants, particularly on diesels, the conventional starter is identical to that used on propulsion engines. This kind of starter is discussed at some length in Chapter 9.

Manual Generator Starting

By adding starting windings to the alternating current generator, the machine is converted to a powerful direct-current motor, operating from battery power fed through a commutator and set of brushes. This type of starting is simple, quiet, and fast spinning, eliminating the mechanical drive found in the conventional starter. With this system, the operator throws a switch located anywhere in the boat, and the engine starts. Several switches may be installed so that the generator can be started from, say, the galley, head, and main cabin. When power is no longer needed, the switch is simply opened, and the driving engine stops.

Demand Starting

An electric control box replaces the simple manual switch in such systems as the Onan Control-O-Matic and others. On the control console is a switch offering Run, Automatic, and Off. In the Run position, the switch eliminates the automatic start feature and simply locks the generator on. In Automatic selection, the controls function as follows:

1. Direct-current battery voltage is conducted on the 115-volt a.c. power lines. Little or no current flows since there is no load on the line.

2. Someone turns on a light or appliance, causing a little direct current to flow. A control relay senses the current, flips, and starts a chain reaction. First, it turns on the bilge blower, if the system includes the blower feature. Then, after a time delay, the controller energizes a contactor, cranking the engine and getting it up to speed.

3. When a.c. voltage rises close to normal, a main contactor applies a.c. voltage to the lines and locks the generator on.

4. When the load is removed, as by the light being turned off, a current transformer senses the open circuit, and "pulls the switch" opening the contactor, and shutting down the generator. Battery voltage is reapplied to the lines, awaiting another load signal.

Safety devices are included in automatic starting. If the engine fails to start in 45 seconds, the starting power is shut off, and the system must then be manually reset. Should oil pressure fail to rise, the engine is shut down; and if the engine overheats, it is also shut down.

Frequency Control

Line frequency is directly related to speed; and the faster an alternator rotates, the higher the frequency. 60 Hertz generating plants commonly spin either 1,200, 1,800, or, in a few cases, 3,600 rpm. To keep revolutions at design speed, the driving engine is fitted with a mechanical governor; and this is adjustable.

A simple way to check on your generator's speed and frequency is with an ordinary synchronous electric clock having a sweep second hand. Use the clock and a watch or stopwatch. Plug in the clock, run the power plant, and compare the electric clock with the watch. If the electric clock runs fast, slow the generator as required to make the clock "keep time." If the clock lags, speed up the engine via governor adjustment. Without much difficulty, you should be able to make the clock keep time within a second per minute.

A.C. from the Propulsion Engine

Because the boat's propulsion engine runs at speeds varying over a range of 4 to 1 or more, in the past it was almost impossible to use it to drive a 60 Hertz alternator. Obviously, as the skipper maneuvered, the frequency would vary all over the lot. However, several new approaches have made it possible to use the propulsion engine to run a 60 Hertz power plant. One method is mechanical, the other hydraulic, and both incorporate constant speed drives.

Mechanical Drive

Named Auto-Gen, an engine mounted and driven alternator is made by Mercantile Manufacturing Co. It delivers 115 volts at 4,250 watts intermittent, 3,750 constant load, at 60 Hertz, plus or minus about three cycles per minute. Heart of the assembly is a V-belt constant speed drive. Through a governor, the mechanism senses engine speed, then varies the diameter ratio between two V-pulleys to maintain alternator speed synchronous. One end of the constant speed drive is propulsion engine driven, the other end connects to the alternator.

Auto-Gen can be mounted directly on the propulsion engine, or placed near it where it can be belt driven. The drive includes a magnetic clutch, similar to those on air-conditioner compressors, allowing the unit to be shut down when not needed. Weight is just under 100 pounds; and the alternator uses battery power for excitation.

Hydraulic Drive

Onan manufactures a constant frequency marine power alternator which they call Hydra-Gen, and it is rated at 6,000 watts. The system is easy to understand. The propulsion engine drives a hydraulic pump; the pump, via connecting tubing energizes a constant speed hydraulic motor, and that motor drives the alternator at snychronous speed for 60 Hertz.

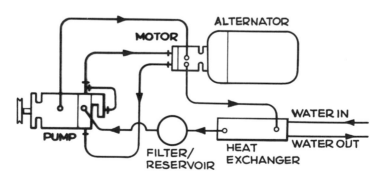

Fig. 8-8 Plumbing schematic shows how engine-driven pump transmits high pressure fluid to hydraulic motor. In turn, the constant speed hydraulic motor spins the 60 Herz alternator.

150

The hydraulic pump is belt driven, and may be mounted on the engine or near it. The alternator can be tucked anywhere that offers a dry location and enough ventilation, making the unit ideal for auxiliary sailboats. Frequency regulation is plus or minus about three Hertz with the hydraulic pump varying between 1,300 to 4,000 rpm.

Off Season Layup

If the electric plant is to be decommissioned for any length of time, proper storage is essential. The following is based on recommendations made by Kohler Company for gasoline powered equipment:

1. Drain crankcase oil while engine is hot. Flush with clean oil, then refill.

2. Shut off the fuel valve and run the engine until it starves.

3. Remove the spark plugs; then pour a teaspoon of oil into each cylinder. Rotate the engine by hand several times, then install the plugs.

4. Drain the cooling system, including engine block and seawater pump. On closed-cooling systems, fill completely with clean water and anti-freeze.

5. Clean the exterior and wipe it down with light oil.

6. Disconnect and remove the batteries to where they can be stored in a dry, cool place and kept charged.

7. Cover the entire unit with a dust cover. But do not cover it with a polyethylene or other non-breathing plastic sheet which might make it sweat and rust.

SYNOPSIS

Freeing the boat from the dockside power cord, an on-board housepower generator can energize almost unlimited electrical accessories. Cost of a 5,000 watt plant is roughly $1,600; and cost of a KWH of power is something under five cents. The power plant should be vibration and sound proofed, and special attention given its exhaust installation. A ship to shore transfer switch is essential. Several varieties of propulsion engine driven alternator are now available.

~~~~~~

CHAPTER IX

Engine Starting Circuits

ONE CHARACTERISTIC of engine cranking circuits is that most of the components are electrically and mechanically rugged. The circuits are basically simple, but their husky construction springs from the work they perform, involving up to several hundred amperes of current, and more than a horsepower in work. Another characteristic is that the heavy components are, in the main, designed for short duty cycles: They work very hard for brief intervals, but tire easily:

Components

Principal components in the standard engine starting system are:

1. Starter motor
2. Mechanical drive
3. Solenoid relay
4. Neutral safety switch
5. Starter switch
6. Heavy cables and control wiring
7. Battery

The Motor

Energized by battery current, most engine starting motors are shunt wound, 4-pole, 4-brush, high-current machines using very heavy windings in both field and armature. Because of the high currents flowing, the windings appear more as bus bar than ordinary magnet wire. Figure 9-1 shows the internal connections and circuit arrangement in a starter.

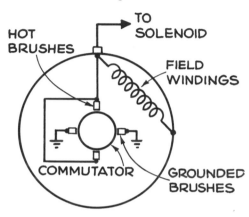

Fig. 9-1 Starter wiring schematic shows field windings, with two brushes grounded, and two hot. All windings are very heavy wire.

Both mechanically and electrically, the starter resembles the conventional d.c. charging generator, except that its windings are much heavier, its brushes and commutator conduct more current, and it ordinarily has plain shaft bearings. Because of its extraordinary power, coupled with limited efficiency, the motor heats up quickly when working at capacity. After 10 or 15 seconds of full load output, the motor windings are usually up to fully allowable temperature, and the motor must be given a short rest before being worked again. A representative duty cycle might be 5 seconds on, 15 seconds off, or thereabouts.

The Mechanical Drive

Several different kinds of mechanical drive are used to transmit starter motor high speed rotation to the slower turning engine; and all incorporate reduction gearing of some kind. In addition to reducing armature-to-engine speed by a ratio as high as 50 to 1, the mechanical drive also provides means to engage and disengage the starter from the engine. Three types of drive are common: helical shaft, shifter fork and double reduction.

Helical Shaft Drives

Often called a "Bendix Drive," the helical variety of drive is found on older engines, and on some modern auxiliary motors. This drive automatically engages the starter's small pinion gear with a large diameter ring gear on the flywheel. It does so by inertia.

The small starter gear is carried on a spirally threaded shaft, the shaft comprising an extension of the armature. Free to rotate several revolutions, the pinion can screw itself along the helical shaft for about an inch. When electric power hits the starter, the armature shaft suddenly accelerates, but the weighted pinion gear, because of inertia, stands still for a brief instant. Since the shaft is spinning and the gear is not, the gear screws itself forward and into mesh with the engine flywheel ring gear. There, its fore-and-aft motion ceases against a stop, and the pinion rotates the engine flywheel.

The engine starts. Now, the flywheel spins faster than the pinion, kicking it back out of engagement, where it remains as the engine continues operating. Because the pinion gear assembly is counterweighted out-of-balance, it cannot idly drift back into engagement with the flywheel ring gear.

To absorb the crashing shock when the little pinion hits the flywheel gear, and to help it recoil from that gear when it has finished its job, the pinion assembly incorporates a heavy, tough helical spring. The spring is between the sprial drive and small gear, carrying full starter motor torque. If the spring breaks, as it may on occasion, the drive is rendered useless.

Advantage of the helical shaft drive is is simplicity and lack of external mechanical parts. Disadvantage is the heavy mechanical shock it delivers when it slams its pinion into the engine's flywheel. Compared to other drives, it is also slightly more susceptible to troubles created by rust.

Shifter Fork Drive

Used extensively on modern engines, the shifter drive positively engages the starter pinion with the flywheel ring gear before the starter motor starts to spin. In this device, the pinion is carried by the armature shaft extension, and the extension is splined, allowing the pinion to slide freely fore-and-aft while transmitting torque. A shift fork or yoke slides the pinion along the shaft; and an overrunning clutch integral with the pinion allows the starter motor to crank the engine, but prevents the engine from spinning the starter.

As a refinement, between the shifter fork and pinion, there is a spring connection offering "snap" to the pinion's sliding motion. If the pinion should fail to mesh with the flywheel ring gear at first, but should engage tooth-on-tooth, the spring will

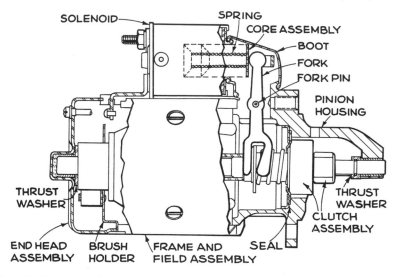

Fig. 9-2 Cutaway side view shows how shifter fork slides the pinion fore and aft to engage flywheel ring gear. The flywheel is not shown.

snap it home the first split second that the starter motor rotates. Unlike the heavy spring in the helical shaft drive, the pinion "snap" spring carries no starter torque, is less subject to breakage.

When the engine is to be cranked, the shifter mechanism first slides the pinion into mesh with the flywheel gear; then immediately power is applied to the starter motor, spinning the assembly. When the engine fires and runs, the operator releases the shifter, disengaging the pinion from flywheel. Simultaneously, the starter motor is deenergized.

Should the operator hesitate and not immediately release the pinion from the engine ring gear, the overrunning clutch will prevent the engine from accelerating the starter to explosive revolutions. Since the engine may quickly climb to 4,000 rpm, and since gearing of 20 to 1 between starter and engine is common, without the overrunning clutch the engine might try to spin the starter 80,000 rpm. Naturally, at this absurd speed, the starter would explode centrifugally, spraying its parts over an acre. But the one-way clutch prevents this catastrophe.

The most common method of synchronizing shifter actuation with starter motor electric switching is via a solenoid relay. This device is discussed below.

Double Reduction Drive

A modification of the shifter fork drive, the reduction variety is found on larger gasoline engines and diesels. The flywheel engaging mechanism is as described for the shifter fork drive; but between the starter motor's armature shaft and the pinion shaft, there is a reduction gear. The design allows reduction ratios as high as 50 to 1 between starter armature and engine, obviously giving the starter terrific torque at the engine crankshaft.

Solenoid Relays

Electromagnetic relays or solenoid starting switches perform one or more of three functions: 1. Close the heavy current circuit

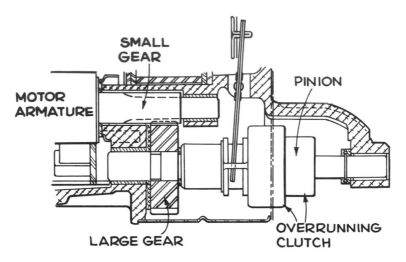

Fig. 9-3 Reduction gear drive gives this starter almost twice the cranking torque of the direct drive starter.

between battery and starter; 2. Shift the starter drive; 3. Apply extra voltage to the ignition circuit. Being heavy duty, special purpose relays, starter solenoids comprise a magnet winding, plunger, heavy current contacts, and special accessories tailored to the application. Battery voltage to actuate the solenoid comes via a control circuit in which we find the manual starter switch or button, and possibly a safety device to prevent starting "in gear."

Solenoid Switching Function

When control current from the manual starter switch flows through the solenoid winding, it generates a strong magnetic field, pulling a soft iron plunger against spring pressure. Near the end of its travel, the plunger closes a heavy-current switch, usually a copper disc and two rugged contacts. When the disc is pressed against the contacts, it conducts battery current from one heavy terminal to the other. Externally, one terminal is connected to the hot battery cable, the other to the starter.

Solenoid Shifting Function

When serving starters which have a shifter fork drive, the solenoid plunger invariably does the work of sliding the pinion into mesh with the flywheel gear. Linkage connects the solenoid plunger to a shift lever arranged that when the solenoid is energized, plunger travel throws the pinion into mesh during the first part of its travel. After engaging the gears, the plunger closes the starter switch, the sequence preventing the starter from spinning and stripping its gears before engagement.

Because it requires substantial force to move the shifter smartly, the solenoid coil is of heavy wire and draws appreciable current. On some larger solenoid packages, current is reduced through use of two windings: A heavy, high-current winding and auxiliary winding are both energized momentarily to throw the plunger home with force. But at the end of its travel, at the point where it energizes the starter motor switch, the plunger opens the circuit to the high-current winding, leaving the lighter auxiliary winding to hold the switch closed. The dual circuit reduces battery drain during the interval when the starter is cranking the engine.

An unusual pseudo solenoid is used on one make of starter. One of the starter motor's field poles is hinged to move farther

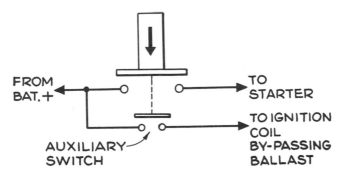

Fig. 9-4 Small auxiliary switch in starter solenoid assembly furnishes battery voltage to ignition coil while starter is energized.

and closer to the armature. When the starter is energized, the pole piece is drawn down magnetically, and a linkage from the pole piece engages the starter device.

Solenoid Ignition Function

Numerous starter solenoid switches feature an auxiliary switch, wired into the ignition circuit. Movement of the solenoid plunger actuates this switch; consequently, it is closed during the interval the starter motor is drawing battery current. The auxiliary switch shunts the ballast resistor out of the ignition coil's primary circuit, thereby increasing primary voltage and intensifying spark while the engine cranks. The idea is to make the engine start easier.

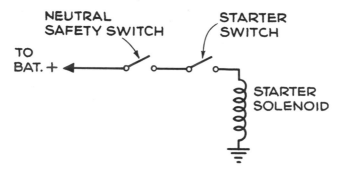

Fig. 9-5 Neutral safety switch in starter control circuit is closed only while marine transmission is in neutral. It is wired in series with the manual switch.

The Neutral Safety Switch

On many engine installations there is a switch on the marine transmission, actuated by the shift lever. When the lever is in other than the neutral position, the switch is open circuited preventing the engine from cranking by opening the control circuit between manual starter switch and solenoid. Purpose of the safety is, of course, to prevent the boat from starting "in gear" and charging ahead or astern, out of control.

If yours is an older boat, not equipped with a neutral safety, you might want to make a morning's project of installing one.

Kits are available for many models of transmissions. However, if you cannot locate a kit, you might apply a little ingenuity and rig a Microswitch on the transmission or manual control, wiring it into the solenoid control circuit to prevent starting in forward or reverse.

The Manual Starter Switch

Often combined with the ignition switch, the manual starter switch handles only the moderate current demanded by the starter solenoid relay control circuit, not the heavy current demanded by the starter. Some starter switches are also wired to furnish battery voltage directly to the ignition coil, by-passing the ballast resistor during the short interval when the engine is being cranked.

Cables and Wiring

Those heavy cables connected from battery to ground, battery to solenoid, and solenoid to starter, are an important part of the starting complex. Even the slightest excess resistance in these cables will deteriorate starting performance unbelievably.

Consider a cranking circuit with 100 amperes flowing from battery to starter. Unwanted additional resistance as tiny as 1/100th ohm will decrease starting voltage by a volt. If the original condition was 100 amperes at 10 volts, adding the mere 1/100th ohm will reduce voltage to nine and current to 90. This means that instead of being able to draw 1,000 watts, the starter motor can only demand 810 watts. Surprisingly enough, that added 1/100th ohm reduced started capacity by almost 20%.

The example points up the attractive feature of 24-volt starting for diesels, which are tough to crank. In a 24-volt system, cable resistance has only half the effect that it has on a 12-volt system, because for a given power, current is half. (Voltage drop equals current times resistance.)

The surface where the starter assembly mounts to the engine

is just as much a part of the heavy current system as the battery cables. Battery juice flows to the starter through the cables but returns to the battery via the starter frame, engine block, and ground strap. For this reason, it is important that the starter flange and engine housing to which it attaches both be shiny-clean when a starter is mounted. Rust, dirt, or loose fastenings offer high resistance, preventing the starter from performing well.

The above paragraph shows why it is a good idea to connect a substantial ground strap directly to the starter's mounting bolts or cap screws. Ground circuit resistance is minimized. Furthermore, heavy starter currents, a potential cause of corrosion, need not be conducted by the engine's cast iron block.

Control wiring is of much smaller gauge than that of the battery cables, since it carries but a few amps, compared to a possible several hundred in the cables. Nevertheless, control wiring must be heavy enough to carry solenoid current, on the order of 15 amps, and must be free of shaky connections which will cause chatter in the solenoid and difficult starting.

The Battery

The battery's role in the starter circuit is vital, obviously; and the all-important storage battery is treated in some depth in Chapter 2.

Starter Trouble Diagnosis

Troubles relating to a hard starting engine are discussed in Chapter 12. Additional and specific troubles found in the starter itself are pinpointed in the analysis that follows here, where common malfunctions are cited.

Starter Motor will not Operate

Where the starter motor acts completely dead, not struggling or attempting to operate, look into the following:

1. Dead battery
2. Loose, broken, or disconnected battery cable
3. Starter very loose on its mount
4. Open circuit in manual starter switch or wiring
5. Burned contacts in solenoid relay
6. Open coil in solenoid relay

Starter Struggles, Won't Crank

If the starter draws current, hums, growls and seems to be drawing appreciable amps, investigate the following:

1. Weak battery
2. Loose connection or corrosion on cables
3. Starter loose in mount
4. Internal ground in starter motor windings
5. Armature rubbing on field poles inside motor
6. Damaged, jammed, or rusty drive
7. Water in engine cylinders causing hydrostatic lock

Starter Spins Smartly; Engine Does Not

1. Broken overrunning clutch
2. Pinion and shaft rusted, dirty, sticky
3. Broken Bendix spring on helical shaft drive
4. Broken linkage or spring in solenoid shifter mechanism
5. Broken teeth on engine ring gear

Solenoid Plunger Clicks and Chatters

1. Discharged battery: Weak battery will pull in the solenoid plunger; but when solenoid connects starter to battery, added load drops voltage, dropping out the plunger. This sequence continues, causing chatter.
2. Corroded solenoid contacts
3. High resistance in battery cables or connections

YOUR BOAT'S ELECTRICAL SYSTEM

Starter will not Disengage

1. Broken solenoid plunger spring
2. Faulty manual starter switch; won't open
3. Rust or dirt on drive mechanism

SYNOPSIS

The starter, a short duty cycle motor, draws high currents from the system, necessitating the use of heavy components and wiring throughout. Mechanical drives are either the helical shaft or shifter fork type, and sometimes incorporate a reduction gear. A heavy solenoid relay switches starter current on, and in the shifter fork drive it also meshes the starter pinion with flywheel ring gear. In some designs an auxiliary switch shunts the ballast resistor during the starting cycle. The manual starter switch, often ganged with the ignition switch handles the moderate current required by the solenoid.

CHAPTER X

Ignition—How It Works

A BOOK on marine electricity would be incomplete without good coverage of power plant ignition. Certainly the marine engine's ignition system is the most vital and hard working electrical system on board a gasoline powered boat; and it's also the system which causes the most acute embarrassment when it fails.

Because of ignition's importance, and its vulnerability to attack by the marine environment, two chapters are devoted to the subject. This chapter describes ignition systems, telling how the components work together to generate spark; the following chapter covers ignition trouble-shooting and tune-up.

Starting with the ignition switch, let us look into the system's components one by one as an aid to understanding the entire complex:

The Switch

Usually provided with a key lock, the ignition switch is connected in the circuit between the battery hot terminal and the ignition coil hot primary winding terminal. Terminals on both switch and coil are usually identified by the marks "bat" or "ign." Many ignition switches incorporate secondary contacts and extra terminals energizing the starter circuit when the key is turned to its extreme position against a stop. Because of the dual function, you must remember, when servicing the ignition switch, to observe correct connections when attaching wires. It's a good plan to tag all wires before unhooking them from the switch; then you will know what's what when making new connections.

Switch Troubles

Mechanics seem to ignore the ignition switch when trouble-shooting, yet you should keep in mind that it can be a trouble-maker. Because of the damp marine environment, this is true to a greater extent aboard a boat than in a car or truck. A switch making poor or intermittent contact can cause the engine to start hard, miss, and quit completely just when it is needed the most. Many a diagnosis of "bad coil" or "wet plug wires" has in reality been a faulty ignition switch.

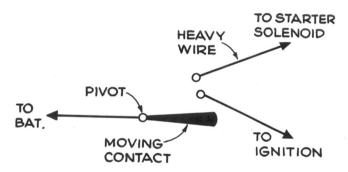

Fig. 10-1 Schematic of ignition switch shows that when the moving blade touches both starter and ignition contacts, starter is energized. Partial motion of blade energizes ignition only.

The Wire from Switch-to-Coil

The low voltage wire running from the ignition switch to coil, carries from two to five amperes, and the conductor may be ordinary copper, or in a few instances it may be alloy resistance wire. Resistance wire is occasionally used as a substitute for a ballast resistor, the function of which is described in subsequent paragraphs.

If the wire from switch-to-coil is resistance conductor, it must never be used to furnish juice for another accessory. Voltage drop through the resistance is computed on the basis of ignition coil load only. If you add an additional load at the coil end of the wire, you will reduce the coil's primary winding voltage; this, in turn, will lower spark voltage. Even if the switch-to-coil wire is copper, it is best not to hang any new accessory on it since that will load the switch circuit, possibly reducing spark intensity.

The Ballast

Roughly half an ohm in resistance, the ballast resistor is connected in the circuit between the ignition key switch and the coil's primary winding. Ballast function is to drop battery voltage

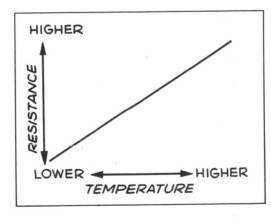

Fig. 10-2 Ballast resistor drops voltage to coil's primary winding, reducing voltage more when the ballast element heats.

to a lower potential allowing favorable ignition coil design without excessively high current in the primary winding. The ballast increases resistance as it warms, automatically furnishing higher voltage for cold engine starts, then reducing voltage and resulting current demand as the engine warms to its job and the ballast follows suit. On most marine engines the ballast resistor is a wire-wound component, coiled in a ceramic case. However, in a few installations, it may be a simple length of alloy wire connecting the ignition switch to the coil. This arrangement was described in the preceeding paragraph.

In some circuits, the voltage reducing ballast is by-passed and switched out of the system while the engine is being cranked by the starter. Here, a shunt is actuated by the starter circuit, usually by the starter solenoid, shorting out the ballast while the engine cranks. Purpose of the shunt is to maximize primary voltage and generate hot spark during the starting period, when battery voltage is severely decreased by the starter motor's enormous current demand. Several by-pass systems are found: One uses an auxiliary contact in the starter solenoid; another employs an extra contact in the starter key switch; yet a third consists of a relay which is closed by energy from the starter switch.

Ballast Problems

Like all electrical components, ballast resistors are subject to trouble. Corrosion is a menace which sometimes eats away at the windings, increasing resistance and lowering primary circuit voltage. Sometimes a ballast will burn out, opening the circuit completely, and stopping the engine. At other times its terminals corrode making intermittent contact, and causing the engine to misbehave horribly.

The Coil

A rose is not always a rose, and a coil is sometimes not a coil, particularly when it is really a transformer. In reality, an ignition "coil" is what electronic people call a "loosely coupled transformer." It has two separate windings, and is a step-up transformer. But since it has been called a "coil" these many years, we will follow suit in our nomenclature, knowing down deep that the thing is a transformer.

Inside the Coil

The coil's primary winding of several score turns of heavy wire is wrapped around a magnetically soft iron core. Energized by the battery, several amperes flow through the primary, which has only a few ohms resistance. Much different is the secondary winding which is also wound around the same soft iron core. The secondary is the high voltage spark winding, comprising several thousand turns of fine gauge insulated wire, and offering a resistance of perhaps 10,000 ohms. How different the windings are, even in terminations: The primary winding terminates at two ordinary screw-type low voltage terminals, but the high voltage secondary terminates in a high voltage, highly insulated tower into which the distributor wire fits. The cold end of the

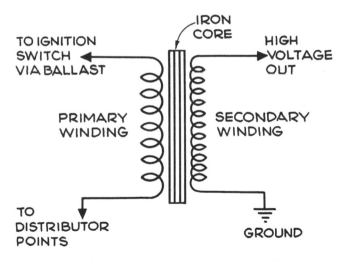

Fig. 10-3 The ignition coil is actually a step-up transformer of high ratio. Primary winding is a few turns of heavy wire; secondary wiring is comprised of thousands of turns of hair-like wire.

high voltage secondary simply fastens to ground or to the primary winding terminal.

Magnetic Activity

Current flows through the primary winding, generating a healthy magnetic field around the iron core. Then, when primary current flow is suddenly interrupted by opening of the breaker points, the magnetic field rapidly collapses. The contracting magnetic lines of force now slice across the multi-thousand turn secondary winding, inducing potential of 10,000 volts or more. Intense spark voltage is then conducted to the special high voltage termination on the coil's tower.

Causes of Trouble

High voltage leaks, invited by moisture, dirt, salt, and small cracks in the coil's high voltage insulation cause most secondary circuit troubles. On the other hand, corrosion and poor connections generate most primary circuit grief. Seldom does a coil's voltage slowly weaken with age. More often, the unit will quit stone cold all of a sudden because a connection has broken, because of a drenching, or because one of the windings has open circuited, and the component has failed outright.

RFI Suppressor

To suppress radio frequency interference, many ignition coils are fitted with a suppression capacitor, wired between the hot primary coil terminal to ground. Do not confuse this capacitor with the similar appearing ignition condenser. The suppressor unit must always be connected to the coil's battery or ignition key terminal, *never* to the coil terminal which is connected to the distributor. If you connect the RFI suppressing capacitor to the coil terminal which is connected to the distributor, it will fail in its job. Worse, it may degrade ignition performance.

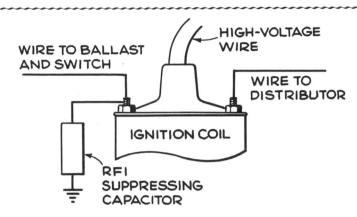

Fig. 10-4 Radio interference suppressing capacitor is connected between battery terminal and ground.

High Voltage Wires

The main high voltage ignition wire transmits spark voltage from the ignition coil to the center terminal in the distributor cap, thence to the rotor. Radiating from the distributor are similar heavily insulated wires carrying high voltage to the spark plugs. This set of wires, the ignition *harness* may have stranded copper conductor or a resistance conductor made of carbon impregnated string or resistance alloy. Where used, resistance conductors are intended to suppress radio frequency interference.

Possible Trouble

High voltage wire problems usually originate with cracked insulation, broken wire, or a widely separated connection at coil, distributor or plug. If the circuit between coil and distributor is broken, the engine dies. If, however, continuity to just one plug is interrupted, the engine (if multi-cylinder) will continue to run; but it will miss with an even cadence.

High voltage plug wires, particularly on high compression engines, must never be closely harnessed, bunched or paralleled in a tube or raceway. As far as practicable, high voltage wires should be separately dressed, spaced from one another, and also kept away from ground. Tight bunching of ignition wires can induce misfiring and cross-firing.

Cross-firing of spark plugs is where two plugs are fired at the same time, or where the intended plug misfires, and another does fire. Tight bunching of adjacent plug wires causes a pair to respond as a capacitor. When the surging pulse of voltage appears in one wire, it is capacitively coupled to the next wire, both wires then carrying spark, when only one is intended to do so. The moral is to keep the wires neatly separated.

Distributor

The distributor and all its inner workings "times" the spark and sequentially directs high voltage to each spark plug in a predetermined firing order. It is the engine's nervous system, subject to no end of ills in the marine environment. Comprising the complete conventional unit are the points, condenser, cap, rotor, and advance mechanism. These will be described individually.

Breaker Points

Inside the distributor housing, the breaker points determine the exact time at which each spark discharge is generated as the engine rotates. The points are a high-speed switch. When closed, they complete a circuit from the battery, through the coil's primary winding to ground. "Ground" in this case is the distributor housing.

The magic moment is when the points separate, breaking the primary circuit, and inducing spark. Ignition timing is dependent on the exact split second that the points "break" and they must open crisply, at exactly the right time in the engine's cycle.

Clearance and Dwell

Driven by the engine camshaft, the distributor shaft rotates, and its lobes or cams, one for each cylinder, push the points open against spring pressure. The distance which the points are forced

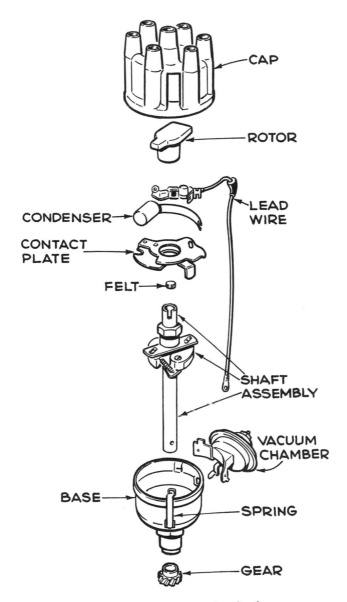

CAP

ROTOR

CONDENSER

LEAD WIRE

CONTACT PLATE

FELT

SHAFT ASSEMBLY

VACUUM CHAMBER

BASE

SPRING

GEAR

Fig. 10-5 Exploded view of a distributor.

173

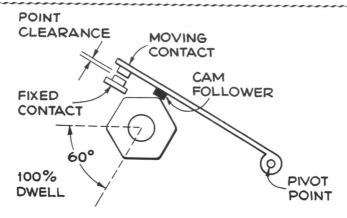

Fig. 10-6 Point clearance is measured with cam follower at top of a cam lobe. On the six-cylinder distributor shown, dwell must be less than 60°, since that angle represents 100% dwell.

apart is called "point clearance," and the angular degrees of shaft rotation during which they remain closed is termed "dwell." The dwell can be defined in angular degrees or percent; and dwell increases as point clearance decreases. If clearance were decreased until the points no longer opened at all, dwell would be infinitely great, defined 100% or 360° dwell.

Correct dwell is seen to be a function of point clearance, and determines the length of time, at a given engine speed, that the ignition coil's primary winding can magnetically energize the iron core. It takes a finite time to magnetically "saturate" the core. If points are adjusted with excessive clearance, dwell time is too short to saturate the iron, and, at high speed, spark will be weak.

On the other hand, long dwell, caused by insufficient point clearance, results in the points being "scraped" open rather than being snapped open smartly. Spark becomes weak, indeterminate, and sour; the engine tends to stall, and starting becomes sluggish.

Breaker Point Springs

So much attention is ordinarily lavished on the points that the

174

springs are sometimes overlooked as a source of good or bad ignition. Since the breaker points are urged toward the closed position by a spring, it is apparent that the spring must be very much alive to actuate the points at high speed. Because of its mass, though small, the moving point resists following the cam at high speed. If the spring is weak, the points will bounce (racing men call it "float") at high speed. Performance then deteriorates as the engine develops a surging high speed miss.

There is however, a practical limit to how much force the point spring can exert. Heavy spring pressure can act as a drag on the advance mechanism, and may distort or even break the point arm. Distributor makers publish specifications for correct spring tension; and tune-up mechanics often consult these data, adjusting tension accordingly. In most distributors, adjustment is made by careful bending of the spring, which is a flat leaf, or, on some cases, by selection of appropriate shims or washers.

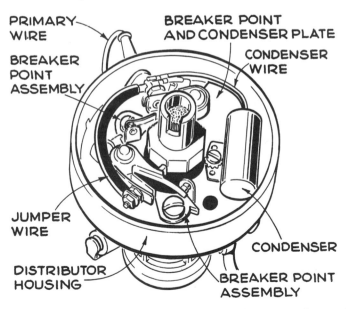

Fig. 10-7 Shown is a distributor with two sets of breaker points. One set breaks the primary circuit; the other makes it.

Double-Point System

On opening the distributor on some eight-cylinder marine engines you will see two sets of breaker points. Dual sets are used to give maximum possible dwell while retaining reasonable clearance and reducing the possibility of point bounce. The points are angularly arranged that one set breaks the circuit; then the other set closes it almost immediately.

In single point-set distributors, the greatest dwell practical in an eight-cylinder machine is on the order of 28° to perhaps 32°. But in a distributor having two point-sets, dwell can be raised to 35° or even 38°. The maximum theoretical dwell is something less than 45°, since that is the total angle between adjacent cam peaks in the distributor shaft.

Double Points, Two Coils

Usually offered as a custom option for high speed, high performance marine engines, the dual-point coil system is excellent ignition. In effect, it is two almost completely separate systems, each system firing 4 cylinders of an eight-cylinder power plant.

A four lobe, rather than eight lobe, cam is used in the 8-cylinder dual rig. The point-sets are disposed so that one set handles four cylinders, the other set handles the other 4 in alternate firing order. One big advantage is that dwell (and coil saturation) can be as high as 60°, whereas in the conventional distributor it is seldom higher than 30°, as explained in earlier paragraphs. The system functions beautifully at the highest speeds. Another advantage is that point life is extended because each point-set shares the work with the other, each assuming half the total load.

Point Troubles

Points spawn just about every kind of ignition trouble imaginable: Corroded points cause missing; wide point clearance can cause knock; insufficient clearance generates back-firing through the carburetor air horn; excess dwell makes the engine hard to start; weak spring "breaks up" the engine at high speed; pitted points stall the machine; and a broken point kills it entirely. Obviously, points must be serviced and adjusted frequently.

The Rotor

Perched on top of the distributor shaft, the rotor is a high speed rotating switch. It picks up spark voltage pulses from the ignition coil, sequentially distributing the spark to the plugs in correct firing order. It is made of insulating material and has a metal conductor carrying ignition voltage from its center pivot point to its tip.

Rotor Troubles

Since the rotor handles very high voltage, its insulation must be excellent. If resistance breaks down, or if the rotor develops small cracks, becoming electrically leaky, spark hotness suffers. An electrically leaky rotor can cause hard-to-trace loss of spark, even when all other ignition components check out correctly.

Condenser Function

A condenser and capacitor are the same thing, and the word "capacitor" is more often used in electronic work. However, since "condenser" has been popular in distributor work for years, we will use it here.

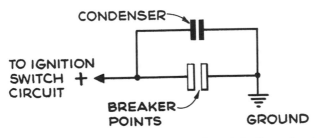

Fig. 10-8 This electrical schematic shows relationship of distributor breaker points to condensor.

Physically, the condenser is most often located inside the distributor, close to the points, although sometimes it is fastened to the ignition coil. Electrically, it is connected across the points as a shunt, from the hot point to ground. Its function is to provide a high frequency path from the coil primary winding to ground. At the instant the points open, collapsing the magnetic field in the coil, the condenser, in series with the primary winding, resonantly "rings" the coil. This jacks up spark voltage. Lacking a condenser, the circuit will generate only the most anemic spark, with voltage too puny to fire the spark plugs, even under favorable conditions.

Condenser Ills

It does not wear out, and, unlike the points, the condenser is a relatively trouble-free component. On occasion, because of the damp marine environment, a condenser will become electrically defective and inefficient. However, as a rule, if a condenser gives trouble at all, it fails completely due to an internal short circuit or an external open lead.

Distributor Cap

More than just a top closure for the distributor, the cap performs an important function, and on better distributors it is made of a superior quality plastic. Imbeded in the plastic are conductors carrying high voltage from the coil's secondary winding to the distributor rotor, and from rotor to the plug wires. Continuity and insulation for the high voltage are essential in the cap, or ignition will be interrupted.

Cap Defects

More marine ignition trouble is generated by defective distributor caps than is sometimes suspected. As the plastic ages, it sometimes develops hairline cracks. These fill with invisible traces of a salt which attracts moisture and spawns a spark grounding network, killing spark during damp weather. Unhappy mechanics have traced hot spark all the way through to the distributor, but have then found no spark at the plug wires. Later, after considerable trouble-shooting, they determine that the spark is leaking away to ground via a defective distributor cap.

Centrifugal Advance

In the lower distributor housing, underneath the breaker points, is a set of centrifugal governor weights. These are attached to the rotating distributor shaft and spin with it, flying out farther and farther as the engine accelerates. Moving centrifugally against restraining springs, the weights, through cam action, advance the distributor lobes ahead in phase relationship to the engine crankshaft. At speed, the points break earlier in the cycle, advancing spark timing as required for optimum performance. Pulling the weights in, the restraining springs retard the spark for easy starting and smooth idling.

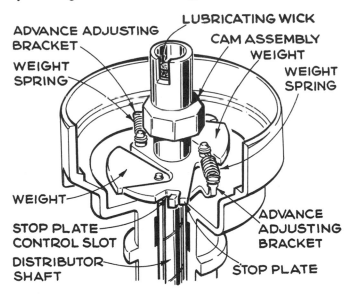

Fig. 10-9 Centrifugal advance mechanism, showing weights and springs.

Centrifugal Defects

In the marine distributor, the centrifugal advance mechanism and its springs sometimes rust, sticking in one position, or responding in a limited range to speed changes. Such trouble is occasionally overlooked by the mechanic accustomed to working on auto and truck engines where, because of kinder environment, the advance seldom malfunctions. Most frequently, the advance rusts into the retarded position, giving the engine a smooth idle, but forcing it to lose power, overheat, and sometimes pop back through the carburetor at high speed. The cure is to disassemble the distributor and clean the mechanism.

Vacuum Advance

Supplementing centrifugal advance in some distributors is a vacuum actuated timing control which modifies ignition advance in response to the magnitude of mainfold intake vacuum. Intake vacuum is largely a function of engine loading. Therefore, the vacuum advance modifies ignition timing largely in accordance with load and throttle setting.

High vacuum in the intake manifold signifies light load. Sensing this, the device advances spark farther than the mechanical weights have already done. Low or weak vacuum indicates acceleration and heavy load on the engine. On detecting low vacuum, the device retards timing relative to that which would be given mechanically.

Many vacuum advance mechanisms detect intake vacuum at an accurately positioned, small-diameter, rifle drilled hole in the carburetor. The little hole is located so that it is exposed to vacuum beneath the throttle butterfly valve when that valve is open more than for idle. But the little hole is blocked off and cannot feel vacuum when the throttle is closed for idling. This design directs virtually no vacuum to the advance actuator during idle. Response is retarded spark, a parameter contributing to smooth idling. But as the throttle is advanced to a position faster

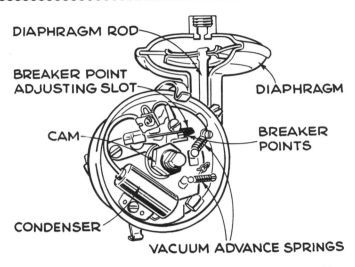

DIAPHRAGM ROD

BREAKER POINT
ADJUSTING SLOT

DIAPHRAGM

CAM

BREAKER
POINTS

CONDENSER

VACUUM ADVANCE SPRINGS

Fig. 10-10 Cutaway shows how vacuum acts on diaphragm to modify ignition timing.

than idle, it exposes the hole to vacuum on the manifold side of the butterfly valve, and the vacuum mechanism responds by advancing spark timing.

Vacuum Control Defects

A diaphragm is ordinarily the device used to measure vacuum and to position the timing mechanism: From the diaphragm come most of the troubles associated with vacuum advance. After cracking or perforating with age, the diaphragm leaks. Slowly, it ceases functioning, and to compound the trouble, it bleeds air back into the manifold, where unwanted air upsets idle performance and reduces acceleration. Best cure, of course, is to renew the diaphragm assembly.

Spark Plugs

In this book, our interest in the spark plug is as an electrical component, not so much as a member of the engine's thermodynamic team. Electrically, the spark plug is simplicity itself: It comprises a center electrode separated from the side electrode by a ceramic insulator. Inside the cylinder high voltage spark leaps from the center electrode to the one on the screw shell, and that is that. For good ignition, the plug must be of the correct heat range, must have proper threads, and a tight gasket.

Plug Troubles

Spark plugs are subject to many ills as anyone knows who has tinkered with engines. If the plug operates too cool, or is subjected to rich mixtures, it will gather black soot and misfire. If the ceramic cracks, the plug may short, particularly during damp weather or when the engine is heavily loaded. Undersized electrode gap causes uncertain ignition, accompanied by sluggish high speed performance. An oversized gap may cause high speed miss, and contributes to hard starting. Too wide a gap forces ignition voltage to rise above normal, and may damage the coil.

Surface Gap Plugs

Inside the combustion chamber, the tip of a surface gap spark plug appears as two concentric rings in the same plane, separated by a ceramic ring between them. When the plug fires, high voltage travels from the small center ring, across the ceramic surface to the outer ring. Advantage of the plug is that it operates cool, having no projections to gather incandescent points of carbon. This feature makes the surface gap particularly suitable for use in outboard motors where fouling is a persistent problem.

Particularly suited for use in motors having capacitor discharge ignition, surface gap spark plugs usually don't do too well with conventional spark. Consequently, if your engine has the conventional system, you will do well to stick with the type plug recommended by the manufacturer.

However, if your engine has capacitor discharge ignition, the story is different. In fact, the surface gap plug was developed in response to the spark characteristics of CD ignition. It takes full advantage of CD's lightning-like, ultra fast spark discharge. But when married to ordinary ignition, the surface gap plug tends to slowly bleed away the charge before an arc can flash across the electrodes, and this is particularly true after the plug becomes a little sooty.

Capacitor Discharge Ignition

Electronic capacitor discharge ignition is quite different from the conventional variety, and in some respects it is an opposite. The following highlights indicate basic differences:

1. In the CD system, energy is stored in a capacitor and released at the crucial moment. In standard ignition, energy storage is magnetic.

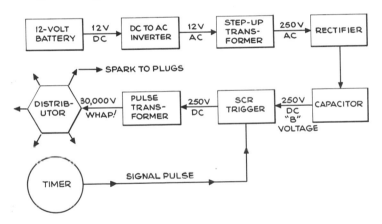

Fig. 10-11 Block diagram shows functions in a capacitive discharge ignition system.

2. Spark can be triggered in the CD system when the points make, or when they break; or points can be eliminated completely. The point-break system is almost universal with standard systems.

3. The "coil" in a CD system is a pulse transformer of low primary impedance, sometimes using a ferrite core. It generates

183

spark on current inrush. The conventional coil, iron cored, throws its spark on current outrush.

4. CD spark is hotter, lasts for a shorter interval than conventional spark. CD voltage hits the spark plugs with more of an electrical hammer blow, giving it the ability to fire dirty plugs.

Figure 10-11 is a block diagram of a typical capacitor discharge ignition system. It shows the workings as follows:

The Inverter

Energized by the boat's battery, the inverter changes direct current to alternating current at hundreds of cycles a second. The inverter is a transistorized power oscillator, similar to an audio signal generator, and it furnishes all the power required by the CD ignition system.

Step-Up Transformer

Usually part of the power pack incorporating the inverter, the step-up transformer has its primary winding energized by high frequency alternating current from the d.c. to a.c. inverter. Output from the secondary winding is on the order of 150 to 300 volts; and, of course, that output is a.c.

Rectifier

Solid state rectifiers, usually the silicon variety, convert medium voltage high frequency current from the step-up transformer to direct "B" current of approximately the same voltage. In effect, all of the components thus far described could be replaced by a single "B" battery of, say, 250 volts. Function of the inverter, transformer, and rectifier are simply to convert 12-volt battery current to direct current some 20 times higher in voltage.

Capacitor

As the system name implies, the energy storage capacitor is the heart of the CD ignition. It soaks up "B" power from the rectifier power supply and stores it at the 150 to 300 volt level, ready to be shot forward to the next component on demand. Usually, the capacitor is a bank of two capacitors, one having 5 to 10 times the capacity of the other. The large one is kept highly charged all the time, acting as a reservoir of power. The smaller one discharges its energy on demand, is then immediately recharged by the big one.

SCR Trigger

The silicon controlled rectifier is a gate or electronic switch which, when closed, blocks flow of "B" current from the storage capacitor to the pulse transformer. The SCR switch is easily opened and closed, its operation requiring very little signal energy. When closed, it presents an almost completely open circuit. When triggered, it flips the other way, presenting a low resistance path through which power can flow. It can be thought of as a relay, operable with little signal power, and able to open and close incredibly fast. As a matter of fact, in modern circuits of other kinds, SCRs often replace relays.

Pulse Transformer

Replacing the ordinary ignition coil (and usually called a "coil" itself) the pulse transformer converts "B" voltage to extremely high ignition potential. When the SCR, acting as a trigger, snaps shut the circuit between capacitor and pulse transformer, there is a surge of current. Hitting the pulse transformer's primary winding like an electric hammer, the rush of current from the capacitor induces a blast of hot spark from the secondary winding. Compared to ordinary spark, the whap of voltage from the pulse transformer builds up much faster, and decays quicker. The sudden intensity of spark gives the system its ability to fire fouled up spark plugs. Because the standard system's voltage builds up more slowly, it can leak across the fouling before it has time to jump. The CD system's quick rise time, however, forces the spark to jump before there is time for leak-off of voltage.

The Timer

Breaker points comprise the timer in the stardard system. In the CD circuitry, the timer may be a point-set, a rotating magnet, a light beam and photo-cell, or a proximity switch.

In the capacitor discharge system, the points, or whatever timing device is selected, handle only a weak current, it being in the milliampere range as contrasted with the several amperes which the conventional point-set interrupts. Result of low current in the CD's timer is extended life and reduction in required maintenance.

The small timing signal generated by the timer, breaker points, magnetics, or whatever, is transmitted to the "grid" or trigger in the SCR, and the SCR fires allowing the capacitor charge to surge into the coil's primary as described. The timer is advanced and retarded by mechanical or vacuum means, the same as in the conventional ignition system.

A popular "pointless" timing system uses a magnet, slotted disc, and a pick-up coil. The disc, with a slot for each engine cylinder, rotates at half crankshaft speed, in a 4-cycle engine, and is interposed between the magnet and coil. As one of the slots rotates into position between the magnet and winding, the latter senses the lines of force and generates a blip of current. The blip is transmitted to the silicon controlled rectifier, the SCR triggers, and a rush of "B" voltage is thrust into the pulse transformer. Spark flashes immediately.

In the capacitor discharge ignition system, the distributor proper, rotor and cap, are relatively conventional. Often they are manufactured of a higher grade plastic than is customary in standard units because they must withstand the electrical stress generated by fierce voltage spikes.

An Interesting Experiment

The reader, having a little shop and an interest in electrical puttering, can simulate a capacitor discharge ignition system from his junque box. Figure 10-12 shows the principle of the thing.

Use any conventional ignition coil for the demonstration, a capacitor rated to match or exceed the "B" voltage, and some kind of "B" voltage supply, preferably between 100 and 250 volts. The resistor between the power supply and capacitor simply protects the supply against surges, and might be something like 500 ohms. Value of capacitor can be experimented with. You can try anything from .5 to 25 microfarads.

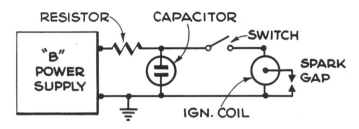

Fig. 10-12 Mock-up of CD ignition will throw a spark when switch is closed. The switch simulates timing points.

With the rig set up as shown, energize the "B" supply; then close the switch which simulates the SCR in a real system. You will get a whap of spark across the gap. For fun, experiment with various size capacitors. But a word of caution: Don't get bitten by the spark. And always give the spark a gap through which to jump to ground. Should you open-circuit the high voltage termination, the hot spark may arc-over inside the coil, and ruin the coil in doing so.

SYNOPSIS

Starting with the switch, and continuing through the ballast and coil's primary winding to the points, the ignition primary circuit is energized by battery voltage. When the points "break," interrupting primary current flow, high spark voltage is induced in the coil's secondary winding. The "coil" is actually a transformer.

High voltage from the secondary winding is conducted to the center of the distributor cap. From there it flows to the rotor which distributes timed high voltage spurts of spark to the plugs in correct sequence.

Point clearance determines dwell, which increases as clearance decreases. Dwell, in turn, controls coil saturation time at any given engine speed. In systems having dual-point arrangements, dwell interval can be desirably extended.

Shunted across the points, the condenser provides a low impedance path to ground, making the coil "ring" or resonate when the points suddenly open. Without a condenser in the system, spark will be very feeble.

As the engine speeds up, spark is automatically advanced to fire earlier in the cycle. Advance may be effected centrifugally, or by vacuum, or both.

Capacitor discharge ignition converts battery voltage to "B" voltage and stores this in a capacitor. Acting as a gate or trigger, a silicon controlled rectifier, on signal from the points or other kind of timer, dumps a charge of capacitor energy into the "coil" or pulse transformer which generates high voltage. The high voltage is then distributed to the plugs in correct firing order.

CHAPTER XI

Tuning the Ignition

WHEN A MARINE ENGINE looses power, accelerates grudgingly, starts with difficulty, and generally acts tired, chances are its ignition needs tuning. With a grasp of ignition fundamentals, the specifications, a few parts and tools, you can do a very respectable tuning job yourself. Rounding up and enticing a really good ignition mechanic aboard your boat is often a tougher job than doing the tune-up yourself. So why not try your hand at this most frequently needed electrical job?

Fundamentals

Ignition fundamentals were discussed at some length in the previous chapter. Review them, if you like, keeping in mind the function of each component: switch, ballast, coil, points, condenser, rotor, distributor cap, and spark plugs. These are the parts you will be manicuring.

Specifications

Before tackling the ignition, try very hard to get the specs on spark plug tightening torque, initial timing, point clearance, plug electrode gap clearance, and point dwell. If you find it impossible to get these data on your marine engine, attempt to find out on what automobile or truck engine the marine unit is based. Then see if you can get the specs on that machine. Lacking the specs, it is possible to do a reasonably good tune, provided you use some ingenuity and employ your "engine-ear." But on the whole it is most rewarding to work according to the good book.

Parts

Get everything on hand before tackling the ignition's innards. To do a really complete tune, purchase new points, condenser, distributor cap, rotor, and high-voltage wiring harness. There's a possibility you may need a new ballast resistor, too, if the old one is corroded and seedy looking.

Tools

The right tools make otherwise difficult jobs easy. For ignition tune-up, you should have the following implements:

- Set of miniature "ignition" wrenches.
- Pair of long-nosed pliers.
- Several small screwdrivers.
- Set of feeler thickness gauges.
- Spark plug adjusting tool with gauges.
- Point file.
- Torque wrench.
- Dwell meter.
- Timing light.

The reader may throw up his hands and say, "I can't afford to buy a dwell meter and timing light for the few tune-ups I do per year; that's extravagant!"

But it is not extravagant. Consider that you pay from $20 to $40 for the labor on a thorough ignition tune-up for each occurrence. You can buy a good dwell meter under $30, and a timing light under $20. After your second tune-up, you are ahead of the

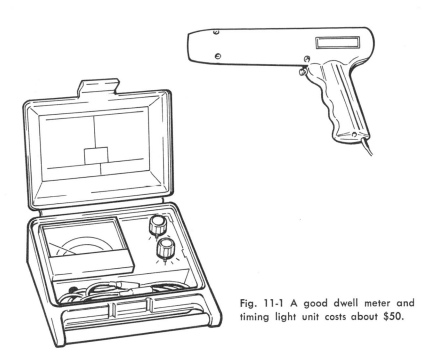

Fig. 11-1 A good dwell meter and timing light unit costs about $50.

game. What's more, having the tuning tools on hand, you are undoubtedly going to check on the ignition more frequently, and will tune more often. You will find that your dwell meter and timing light will be among your most frequently borrowed tools, proving, sir, that most boatmen should own these important instruments. (A side issue is that you'll probably end up tuning your automobile, as well—saving more money.)

Incidentally, the Heathkit Company, Benton Harbor, Michigan, sells engine tuning instruments in kit form, and they are excellent tools at a modest price.

Inspect the Switch

While you are puttering around the switch, trace the wires, making sure they are secure, well insulated, and free of fraying.

Replace conductors which appear ratty; and trace through to the ballast.

Look at the Ballast Resistor

Wired between the ignition switch and coil in the primary circuit, the ballast must be fresh looking and free of corrosion. Its terminals must be clean and tight. If it fails to meet these criteria, best plan is to replace it. It is not a costly item.

After checking through the wiring, switch, and ballast, run the engine a short time to be sure all's well. As a matter of procedure, it is smart to run the engine after each adjustment or replacement. Then, should the machine refuse to start or if it runs poorly, you will know what particular part or adjustment causes the trouble; and you will not have to go trouble-shooting the entire system to find the root of the malfunction.

Change the Plugs

You have been working through the primary system toward the distributor. Now, before you attack the distributor's innards, turn to the spark plugs a few minutes.

Brush, blow, or vacuum all the dust and dirt out of the spark plug recesses. Remove the old plugs. Using a feeler gauge, gap

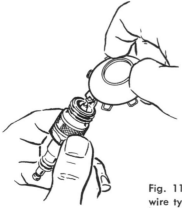

Fig. 11-2 Measuring spark plug gap is done with a wire type feeler gauge.

the new spark plugs to specification; don't simply install them fresh from the carton without adjustment. If you do not have the specification, adjust the gaps to 0.030''. Put a little oil or grease on the new threads, and install the plugs, being careful not to cross thread the bosses. Use your torque wrench and tighten the plugs to specified tightness. If you don't know the spec, tighten to 25 pound feet.

Start and run the engine.

Install New Points and Condenser

Carefully open up the distributor by removing the cap. Many caps are held in place with spring clips; some are fastened with two screws.

Take out the rotor. Some simply push on to the distributor shaft, others, shaped more like a wheel, are retained by two screws. In either case, removal is easy; but be careful not to drop the screws down in the bottom of the distributor where you will have a devil of a time retreiving them.

Note exactly how the point-set is installed, and how it is wired. Then remove both the points and condenser. Install the fresh components exactly as the old ones came out. Work carefully,

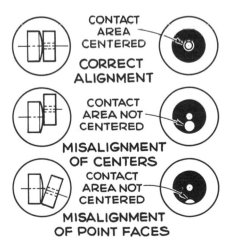

Fig. 11-3 Correctly installed, the breaker points "kiss" at centers.

being alert not to bend or distort the moving point arm. After installing the points, examine the way they seat together. The two contact surfaces should be concentric and square with each other. If there is a misalignment, very carefully bend the pivoted point, as required, to bring the points into true relationship. You want the centers of the contacts to kiss straight-on.

Adjust Point Clearance

With the new points correctly in place, you will set the clearance. This is the spacing between the point contact surfaces when the points are wide open; and this spacing directly effects dwell and timing.

Slowly rotate the engine by hand or by bumping with the starter until the point's cam follower is on top of a cam lobe. The points are now open to their widest possible position. You will see that the fixed contact is adjustable in some manner, allowing it to be shifted as to increase or decrease the point clearance. Using a feeler gauge, carefully adjust the points until the clearance is as specified in engine specs. Then tighten the set screw, if one is provided.

Calculating Point Clearance

By far, it is best to adjust to the clearance specified by the engine manufacturer. However, if, despite your best efforts, you can't find the specification, you can hit it fairly closely by the following procedure:

1. Nudge the engine over until the breaker point cam follower is centered on a flat between two cam lobes. The points are now closed.
2. Without moving the cam, adjust the points to exactly zero clearance. Now, the points are just kissing, and the cam follower is also touching a flat on the cam. The most minute rotation of the shaft will start to open the points.

3. Slowly rotate the engine until the points are wide open, the cam follower being on top of a lobe. You have now opened the points to absolute maximum possible clearance.

4. Using a feeler gauge, measure the maximum clearance. On a typical eight-cylinder distributor it might be, say, 0.028″.

5. Select *half,* or a little more than half, of absolute maximum as your operating clearance. For the eight-cylinder distributor cited in (4.) above, this would be from 0.014″ to 0.017″.

Set the Dwell

Button up the distributor, not forgetting to install the new rotor. Run the engine. Hook up your dwell meter in accordance with its instructions. Idle the engine and watch the dwell.

- If dwell is too great, increase point clearance.
- If dwell is too small, decrease point clearance.

Dwell by Rule of Thumb

Naturally, you will set the dwell to that recommended by the engine maker. However, if it is impossible to find the specification, you can proceed by a general rule; chances are you will be fairly close to home base. For conventional four-stroke cycle engines, use the following dwells:

Four-cylinders: 54°
Six-cylinders: 36°
Eight-cylinders: 27°

The suggested dwell angles are based upon the points remaining closed for saturation 60% of the time, and open for 40%. If the distributor has a dual-point, single-coil, system, the eight-cylinder dwell may be increased to 34°. At any rate, there is nothing sacred about these exact dwells because different cam shapes demand modified dwells. But the given angles should make the engine well and happy.

	4-Cyl	6-Cyl	8-Cyl
100%	90°	60°	45°
90%	81°	54°	40.5°
80%	72°	48°	36°
70%	63°	42°	31.5°
60%	54°	36°	27°
50%	45°	30°	22.5°
40%	36°	24°	18°
30%	27°	18°	13.5°
20%	18°	12°	9°
10%	9°	6°	4.5°
Closed Time	Dwell expressed in degrees		

Fig. 11-4 Table shows relationship of percentage dwell time to dwell, in degrees.

In custom distributors having two point sets and two ignition coils, each set firing four cylinders, the dwell is adjusted as for a 4-cylinder engine. Each point set is given dwell of 50° to 60°.

Re-Time the Engine

After the points are replaced and adjusted, the engine must be re-timed. This is so because any change in point clearance and dwell alters the timing.

The initial (idling speed) timing on modern engines is usually somewhere between top-center and 10° before top-center; and this adjustment is one of the most critical that you will make in your tuning program. Set the timing by the book," avoiding the temptation to wander too far from the specifications. Should you advance the spark excessively, cylinder pressures will be overly high, the engine may knock, will run rough, and may well be damaged. If you adjust the spark in retard, on the other hand, the engine will loose pep, may overheat, and may burn its exhaust valves.

Run the engine at idle, pointing the timing light at the appropriate marks on the rotating member and stationary pointer.

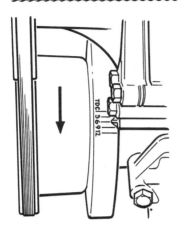

Fig. 11-5 These are typical timing marks on belt drive of engine. Timing is shown five degrees before top center.

Considering the direction of rotation, if the rotating mark appears "early," retard the spark by rotating the distributor in the direction of its shaft rotation. Do the opposite if the spark is "late." Once you're hooked up and ready, re-timing of the engine is the work of but a few minutes. However, avoid using the timing light in bright sunlight. Doing so obscures the strobe effect, making it difficult to see the spinning timing marks. Work in a subdued light, and scribe a thin white chalk line on the timing marks before starting the engine.

Check the Advance

After you are satisfied with the adjustment of the initial timing, determined at idle speed, test the advance. With the strobe light directed at the timing marks, speed up the engine. The light should show ignition timing advancing with speed. Usually, the advance will start at about 1,000 rpm, and continue until the engine has accelerated, reaching some 2,000 to 2,500 rpm, at which speed full advance will be achieved.

Finding Top-Center

On a few marine engines, particularly older ones, you will search in vain for any indication of timing marks either on the flywheel, vibration damper, or generator drive pulley where they are customarily found. If this happens, create your own top-center mark as follows:

1. Remove the spark plugs.

2. Carefully insert some kind of straight feeler such as a pencil, screwdriver, or piece of rod into the plug hole of number 1 cylinder.

3. Crank the engine slowly clockwise until the piston is felt to be at its highest rise in the cylinder.

4. Now, rotate the engine, continuing clockwise, until the piston descends about one half inch. Mark the feeler carefully at a point exactly flush with the spark plug hole boss.

5. Mark the flywheel or crankshaft-mounted V-belt pulley at some point in alignment with a fixed pointer on the engine block.

6. Rotate the engine counterclockwise to where the piston is at highest rise, and *continue* going counterclockwise slowly until the piston descends to where the feeler mark is exactly flush with the spark plug boss, (at one half inch descent).

7. Mark the flywheel at the fixed pointer on the engine block.

8. You now have two marks. Halfway between those marks is top-dead center of number 1 piston. Mark that point carefully; then repeat the routine several times for increased accuracy.

Install New Cap and High Voltage Wires

Before removing the old distributor cap and spark plug wires, note carefully which distributor wire goes to what plug. Make a simple sketch to help you reassemble the wires correctly. Now, remove the old distributor cap and all the plug wires. Before installing the new cap, spray a mist of ignition moisture repellent, such as CRC in the cap. Install the cap and wires; spray the exterior with moisture repellent; spray the high voltage wires, the plugs, and the ignition coil. A thin coat of moisture inhibitor coating the entire high voltage system will help a great deal toward easy starts on damp mornings when moisture tends to condense on the cool engine.

Run the engine.

General Suggestions

- After completing the tune-up, recheck every nut, bolt, screw, and adjustment, making sure that all is secure.
- Following the tune job, and after the engine has operated something like 15 hours, give the dwell and timing a follow-up test. Sometimes, in the first few hours of use, while the point's cam follower is seating itself, the clearance will decrease, dwell will increase, and, as a result, ignition timing will become retarded. If you readjust dwell and timing after the first 15 hours, the adjustments should remain in spec for the following one or two hundred hours.
- When working on a powerful engine, one difficult to crank, remove the spark plugs, relieving compression and making the engine easier to rotate while you are working on the points.
- Adjust new spark plug gaps on the small side of specification tolerance. As the plugs are used, the gap will grow.
- If, after the engine is re-timed, it knocks or pings at advanced throttle, retard the spark just enough to eliminate the trouble. Do so while using the kind and brand of gasoline you customarily buy.
- Should the engine idle rough, hard, and fast, after it is re-timed, try retarding the spark a little. However, do not retard the spark too much or the engine will be lazy at high speed, and may suffer from overheated exhaust valves.

For Your Log Book

Cruisers maintained Bristol fashion sometimes have an engine room log, having entries kept up-to-date by the boatkeeper. If you are one of those keeping a technical log, you might want to enter all or part of the following data in the book. It will be most useful for future tuning jobs or for trouble-shooting, should that unpleasant chore ever become necessary.

1. Date, engine-hours, and jobs done during tune-up.
2. Dwell and point clearance.
3. Plug gap and tightening torque.
4. Initial timing at idle.
5. Engine rpm required to give full advance.
6. Primary current flow, key on, points closed, engine stopped.
7. Primary current flow at fast idle.
8. Resistance of the ballast when cold.
9. Resistance of coil primary, and coil secondary when cold.

SYNOPSIS

Having the correct specifications, parts, and tools is important; and a timing light and dwell meter are a great help. Engine electrical tune up includes inspection and adjustment of ignition switch, ballast, plugs, points, condenser, and wiring, as well as the distributor cap and rotor. Work includes installation of new parts, adjustment of timing, dwell and advance.

CHAPTER XII

Electrical Trouble-Shooting on the Engine

ALAS, despite the best maintenance and most loving tune-up, the inboard marine engine is known sometimes to quit, run rough, or refuse to start at all. Electrical troubles are more common in the marine power plant than in the auto engine because the yacht's machinery is beset by nature's tougher opposition.

The most obvious enemy is the wet environment in which the marine engine lives, and we all know that electrons and dampness simply don't cotton to each other. The second adversary is lack of use. Most pleasure boat motors are used only on week ends, except during the owner's vacation, and are laid up when the season is over, decommissioned for months on end. Infrequent use, supplemented by periods of idleness, invites rust, corrosion, and dampness penetration, all three of which attack the electrical system.

When a marine engine fails to perk, simply refusing to start, chances are nine to one that the trouble is electrical, and not in the fuel or compression system. Once running, but performing badly, the chances are still 7 to 1 that electrical malfunction is at the seat of the trouble. Consequently, if you flush out the electrical gremlins, odds are that you will cure the malady.

In this chapter are found a variety of electrical engine troubles. In some cases, there is a simple listing of possible causes, the cures being obvious. In other instances, commentary is intended to be helpful in pointing up the cure for a specific trouble.

Starter will not Try

If the starter refuses to struggle, hum, or show any sign of trying to rotate when you close the starter switch, do these things, stopping when you locate the trouble:

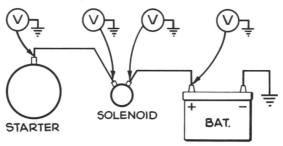

Fig. 12-1 With start switch closed, voltmeter or test light should indicate adequate voltage at the points shown.

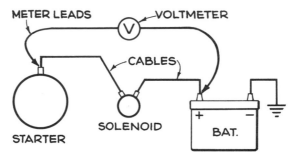

Fig. 12-2 When the starter operates, voltage drop from battery hot terminal to starter terminal should be but a fraction of a volt.

1. With starter switch closed, test for battery voltage on the battery terminals with test light or voltmeter.

2. Clean the battery posts and cable clamps. Test for voltage at the solenoid switch. Make sure the ground strap is ok.

3. Test for voltage on the starter side of the solenoid.

4. Test for voltage at the starter terminal.

5. If there is voltage all the way to the starter terminal,

between terminal and engine block, make sure the starter is tightly mounted to the engine. Its ground-return connection is through its hold-down bolts and flange.

6. If starter still fails to respond, remove it for bench repair.

Starter Struggles; Won't Rotate

1. If the starter won't crank the engine, or does so very slowly and with protest, test battery voltage with meter or test light while the starter struggles. Dim test light probably means battery needs attention. On a 12-volt system, potential below seven volts spells trouble.

2. If battery seems ok, check all cable connections: clean posts and clamps.

3. If voltage at starter terminals is almost equal to that at battery terminals, and if this voltage is seven to eight volts or more on a 12-volt system, while the starter struggles, the starter is probably defective. But before taking action, be sure there is no mechanical problem. Try this: Remove the spark plugs and see if the engine will then crank. If it has a cylinder locked with water, this procedure will clear it.

Engine Starts; Immediately Quits

If the engine fires, runs a few seconds, but stops as soon as you release the starter switch, look to the ballast resistor. If the ballast is open circuited, the ignition may be energized by an auxiliary starting shunt during the start period, but will be killed as soon as the start switch is opened.

Engine Cranks but Won't Fire

This is the most common of all troubles. When the engine fails to start after a few seconds of cranking, stop and find the trouble before wearing down the battery with fruitless grinding of the starter.

1. Find if the coil is throwing spark. Hold the high voltage

wire from the coil about a quarter of an inch from the engine block. Crank the engine. There should be spark.

2. Assuming there is no spark. Do as follows: Unbutton the distributor and make sure the points are opening and closing with shaft rotation. Close the points. Open and close the points with your finger. Each time they open, there should

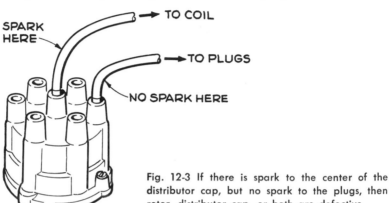

SPARK HERE

→ TO COIL

→ TO PLUGS

NO SPARK HERE

Fig. 12-3 If there is spark to the center of the distributor cap, but no spark to the plugs, then rotor, distributor cap, or both are defective.

be a spark from the coil's high voltage wire to ground. If there is no spark, check:

a. The moving point for being short circuited to ground, or corroded.

b. The condenser, by substitution.

c. All primary circuit wiring, by inspection and trouble light.

d. The ignition coil by substitution.

[Now, let's backtrack. Suppose that in Step 1 you found hot spark coming from the coil. Then proceed as follows to assure that this spark from the coil is conducted to the spark plugs:]

3. After rehooking the main high voltage wire to the distributor's hot connection, remove a wire from one spark plug, holding the end a quarter of an inch from the ground. With the ignition switch on, crank the engine. Spark should jump from wire to ground.

a. If spark *does* jump, remove and service the spark plugs; the trouble may be there.

b. If spark *does not* jump, you have determined that there is high voltage from the coil to distributor, but no voltage from distributor to plugs. Therefore, the spark is being grounded in either the distributor cap or rotor.

4. Open the distributor; remove the rotor and cap. Inspect both for cracks, breaks or chips. Wipe them dry, or, if possible, bake them in an oven at about 200°F for a quarter of an hour. Make sure they are bone dry. Spray them both with moisture repellent such as CRC, misting the cap both inside and out.

5. Try the spark test at the plugs again. If there is still no spark, and if the plug wires are bone dry, you are due to install a new cap and rotor.

Starter Spins; Won't Crank Engine

Some starter drives require sudden acceleration to force the small starter pinion into mesh with the flywheel ring gear. This kind of starter will sometimes wind up to speed, but fail to engage for any one of the following reasons:

1. Low battery voltage.

2. Dirty, corroded connections to battery cables at one or both ends.

3. Poor contact in starter solenoid.

4. Poor contact between starter mounting flanges and engine block.

5. Rusted, dirty pinion gear drive mechanism, preventing pinion from advancing on its shaft.

Stalling at Idle

This kind of stall has nothing to do with carburetion. As the ignition system "ages," and the point clearance decreases, there comes a state where at idle the points no longer completely open. The engine quits when the throttle is closed. The remedy is to tune the ignition, adjusting points to correct dwell.

Popping-Back

Backfiring through the carburetor, especially when the engine is cool and is being accelerated, is caused by retarded ignition timing. Remedy is to advance the spark.

Spark-Knock

Detonation, or pinging, sometimes called "knock," is invited by overly advanced ignition timing. Cure is to retard the spark. The assumption is made that the engine is not overheated, overloaded, or being operated on poor gasoline.

High-Speed Miss

Look into the following:

1. Improper dwell.
2. Fouled or improperly adjusted spark plugs.
3. Cracked ceramic insulator on one or more plugs.
4. Weak spring in the ignition point-set.
5. Cross-firing due to high voltage ignition wires being tightly bunched or having poor insulation.
6. Loose wiring, poor connections in the primary or secondary circuits, or an intermittent ignition switch.

No Generator Output

If generator or alternator output is weak or non-existent, look into the following:

1. Broken or very loose V-belt.
2. Disconnected field or battery wires.
3. Defective regulator.

4. Defective diodes in the alternator.

5. Burned brushes in the conventional generator.

One way to isolate generator output trouble to the voltage regulator or generator is as follows:

a. On a conventional generator, disconnect the wire from regulator to generator field terminal. Run the engine at fast idle; then short circuit the generator's field terminal to the grounded frame. If the generator is good, it will immediately put out, indicating that the regulator is defective. Don't run the generator for long with grounded field, however, or it will overheat.

b. On an alternator, disconnect the voltage regulator from the alternator. Use a jumper, and hook this in series between the battery hot (not ground) terminal and the rotor terminal frequently marked *F*, for field. This is the terminal which excites the alternator's rotor. If the alternator is good, it should put out when the rotor is excited, and the alternator is spinning at a good speed.

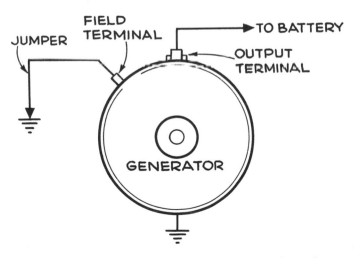

Fig. 12-4 Temporary jumper from field terminal to ground tests for output.

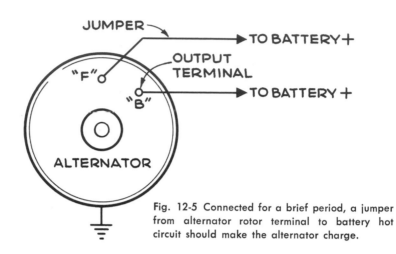

Fig. 12-5 Connected for a brief period, a jumper from alternator rotor terminal to battery hot circuit should make the alternator charge.

Reduced Alternator Output

If alternator output is somewhat low even when there are demands on the electrical system, one or more diode rectifiers may be open. If output is only half what it should be, there may be a short circuited diode. An alternator with a shorted diode usually whines; and the singing is more noticeable at idle speed.

If trouble-shooting tests indicate that either the generator or alternator is defective, remove the offender from the boat and have it overhauled in a well equipped shop. Voltage regulators, however, are usually replaced as a complete unit.

Trouble-Shooting of Components

Here is where a mite of foresight helps immeasurably. As a dedicated boatkeeper, spend a pleasant hour with your ohmmeter, making measurements on known good components. The information you gather may turn out to be a godsend next time the chips are down, and you are trouble-shooting in earnest.

Typical resistances are given here to indicate the magnitude of resistance expected, and may be a help when you are in a real pinch. But to make your ohmmeter a more useful trouble-shooting tool, measure and record your boat's critical resistances before you are in the heat of battle.

Always make your resistance measurements with the component disconnected from its circuits, and at room temperature.

Ignition Coil

Measure resistance between the two primary terminals: one to two ohms. Resistance between either primary terminal to the metal case should be infinite. Resistance of high voltage winding, measured from "hot" terminal to either primary terminal will be between 5,000 and 10,000 ohms. Resistance from hot terminal to case should be infinite.

Spark Plugs

Resistance from hot terminal to shell: infinite. If there is any appreciable conductance, the plug is fouled.

Condenser

Set the ohmmeter on a high range such as X1,000 or X10,000. Touch one ohmmeter prod to the condenser's metal case, the other to the pigtail lead. As the test leads touch, the needle should kick, then fall back to infinite. Reverse the leads. The needle should do the same, with an even greater kick. If the meter fails

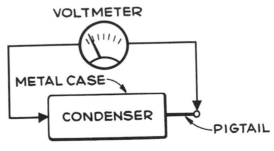

Fig. 12-6 A good distributor condenser will kick the voltmeter needle up-scale several minutes after the condenser has been charged to 100 volts.

to kick, the condenser is open. If the meter shows a finite steady resistance, the condenser is leaky. Replace it.

If you have a source of 100 to 150 volts direct current, you can give the condenser a real acid test: Charge the condenser to that voltage by touching the case to one power source terminal, the pigtail to the other. Careful! Don't get bit. Set your volt ohmmeter to a voltage scale equal to, or higher than the charging voltage. Wait half a minute; then touch the meter test leads to the condenser's case and pigtail. The needle should kick up scale almost to the charged voltage. In fact, a good, dry, clean condenser will show a snappy voltage even after sitting idle for half an hour after charging.

Ballast Resistor

Be particularly careful to measure the ballast when it is at room ambient temperature; its resistance increases with heat. Use the X1 scale, and the resistance should be barely readable, being on the order of 0.5 to two ohms for a 12-volt component.

Points

Resistance across the closed points should be zero, and across the open points should be infinite. Values from the grounded point to engine block must be zero, and from the hot, pivoted point to engine block, infinite. Wiggle the pivoted point with your finger when making that last test, and be sure all wiring is disconnected from the distributor.

Starter Relay

Solenoid coil in the starter relay, usually connected between the starter switch and ground, has immeasurably small resistance. Tested with an ohmmeter, a good solenoid coil will show a fraction of an ohm resistance.

Alternator

Beware the validity of resistance readings made on an alternator unless you have made the same measurements on the unit when in good condition. Various alternator designs have different internal hook-ups, making resistance quite different. So, make those measurements on a good unit while you can.

Typical resistance taken on a good Leece-Neville, 40 amp, 14-volt alternator, look something like this on the X1 scale of a common ohmmeter:

Battery (plus) terminal to ground is 40 ohms with meter test leads in one polarity, infinite resistance with test leads reversed. This shows the effect of the rectifier diodes. Field (rotor) terminal to ground is six ohms, showing the rotor winding and slip ring assembly is intact and terminate in the rectifiers.

However, when measurements are made in diode circuits, readings will change greatly from scale to scale on the ohmmeter. This is because a diode changes its conductivity with applied effective voltage. So, remember to use the same scale for all measurements, using the results only for a rough guide.

A 12-volt active test light, as described in Chapter 19, is useful for quick trouble-shooting of an alternator. Connected in one polarity between output (battery) terminal and ground, the light should glow. Connected in reversed polarity, it should extinguish. The same applies to the connections between output terminal and neutral. Connected in either polarity between ground and rotor (field) the light should glow.

SYNOPSIS

Because of the corrosive environment in which it lives, the marine engine is subject to more ills than the auto engine. Many of those troubles are, of course, electrical.

Starter troubles can originate in the battery, cables, or switch. Hard starting is frequently traceable to ignition; and troubles at all speeds often originate with trouble in the points. Knock is eliminated by retarding the spark; high-speed miss frequently starts with bad plugs or crossfiring. Generator and alternator troubles can be separated from those spawned in the regulator by isolating the two systems. Each component can be tested with an ohmmeter as an aid to trouble-shooting.

CHAPTER XIII

Taming Electrolytic
Corrosion

BOATMEN often refer to galvanic corrosion as "electrolysis corrosion" or more often simply as "electrolysis." This old terminology is technically incorrect and is being phased out by such bodies as the American Boat and Yacht Council. There are two reasons for improving the terminology:

1. Electrolysis refers to chemical or electro-chemical changes in a liquid solution or electrolyte due to the passage of electricity. By inference alone does the word describe the effect of electrolysis on a metal submerged in the electrolyte.
2. Incorrectly used, the loose word "electrolysis" gets applied to matters related to stray current corrosion; but the meaning is not specific. It is desirable, therefore, to adhere to the terminology adopted by standards making bodies.

Galvanic Corrosion

Most boatmen are familiar with galvanic corrosion: It occurs when dissimilar metals are immersed in an electrolyte and are touching each other or are electrically connected by a conductor. Boating waters, both fresh and salt, are electrolytes, salt being the stronger of the two. Simply tie a strip of aluminum and a strip of copper together by wire, dunk the pair in your local waters, and two things will happen: Electricity will flow through the wire; and the aluminum will corrode. By your experiment, you have created both a weak electric cell and have generated corrosion.

In the above demonstration, the two metal plates are called electrodes, and the boating water is the electrolyte. Of the two metals, the least noble (aluminum) corrodes, while the more noble (copper) resists corrosion; and in the process, water is subjected to electrolysis.

Those Noble Metals

The least noble metals are active ones; and they corrode easily. Magnesium, aluminum, zinc are typical examples. These are called anodic and are electrically positive in polarity. The most noble metals are passive; they are electrically negative, said to be *cathodic* and having high corrosion resistance. Nickel, In-

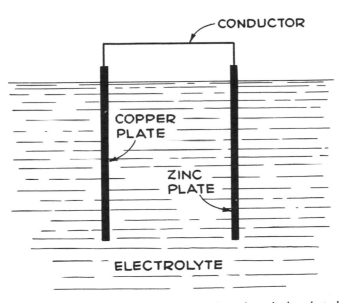

Fig. 13-1 Electric current flows from plate to plate through the electrolyte, returning via the conductor. In the electrolytic process, the zinc plate is corroded.

conel, and 18-8 stainless steel are popular examples of noble metals. The table in Figure 13-2 lists a series of maritime metals, giving their relative order in the galvanic series in sea water. Least noble metals are at the top, most noble at the bottom in this tabulation made by the American Boat and Yacht Council.

Fig. 13-2 Prepared by the American Boat and Yacht Council, this table gives the galvanic series of metals in seawater.

ANODIC OR LEAST NOBLE—ACTIVE

Magnesium and magnesium alloys
CB75 aluminum anode alloy
Zinc
B605 aluminum anode alloy
Galvanized steel or galvanized wrought iron
Aluminum 7072 (cladding alloy)
Aluminum 5456
Aluminum 5086
Aluminum 5052
Aluminum 3003, 1100, 6061, 356
Cadmium
2117 aluminum rivet alloy
Mild steel
Wrought iron
Cast Iron
Ni-Resist
13% chromium stainless steel, type 410 (active)
50-50 lead tin solder
18-8 stainless steel, type 304 (active)
18-83% NO stainless steel, type 316 (active)
Lead
Tin
Muntz metal
Manganese bronze
Naval brass (60% copper—39% zinc)
Nickel (active)
78% Ni.-13.5% Cr.-6% Fe. (Inconel) (Active)
Yellow brass (65% copper—35% zinc)
Admiralty brass
Aluminum bronze
Red brass (85% copper—15% zinc)
Copper
Silicon bronze

5% Zn.—20% Ni—75% Cu.
90% Cu.—10% Ni.
70% Cu.—30% Ni.
88% Cu.— 2% Zn.—10% Sn. (Composition G-bronze)
88% Cu.—3% Zn.—6.5% Sn.—1.5% Pb (composition M-bronze)
Nickel (passive)
78% Ni.—13.5% Cr.—6% Fe. (Inconel) (Passive)
70% Ni.—30% Cu.
18-8 stainless steel type 304 (passive)
18-8 3% Mo. stainless steel, type 316 (passive)
Hastelloy C
Titanium
Platinum

CATHODIC OR MOST NOBLE—PASSIVE

Self-Corrosion

In some instances, galvanic corrosion occurs in a single piece of hardware immersed in sea water and not in contact with a more noble item. Common red brass household screws offer an example. Non-marine brass is an alloy of zinc and copper, and the two are combined metallurgically in flake or crystal forma-

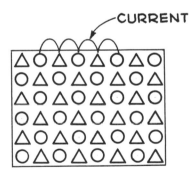

CURRENT

O = ZINC BIT

△ = COPPER BIT

Fig. 13-3 Corrosion can occur when current flows between bits of copper and zinc in common yellow brass immersed in an electrolyte.

tion. When put in sea water, such brass corrodes rapidly: Electric current flows internally, near the surface, between the tiny bits of zinc and copper. Because it is less noble, the zinc is eaten away, and the remaining object is reduced to spongy copper.

The above explains why you must not use ordinary land-lubber brass bolts and screws as marine fastenings. Monel, stainless steel, or copper are much better. Even good, hot, galvanized iron fittings will inevitably outlast kitchenware brass ones.

Environmental Effects

Increase in either water temperature or salinity increases the rate and severity of galvanic corrosion. Deterioration also increases as water pollution gets worse and as the adjacent metals are more dissimilar on the galvanic scale. Not surprisingly, corrosion abates when water temperature, salinity, and pollution decrease. It is also reduced when the metals are galvanically similar, when they are insulated from each other, and when they are physically separated to the maximum possible distance.

Prevention

There are four important ways the boatkeeper can prevent or reduce galvanic corrosion:

1. Fasten underwater hardware with screws, nuts and bolts of the most noble metal practicable. Join underwater parts with fastenings equal to or more noble than the basic part. Should electrolysis now occur, the fastening will be protected at the possible expense of the heavier hardware; but the boat will not suffer because of hardware failure. A fraction of an ounce of metal eaten away from the heavy hardware probably won't hurt anything. But that same weight of metal corroded from the smaller, more highly stressed fastening, may spell major trouble.

2. Paint underwater hardware with vinyl or other plastic, non-metallic paint. Acting as an insulator, paint will suppress current flow and reduce galvanic action. Avoid brushing metallic-base, anti-foul paints on underwater hardware such as propellers, rudders, and struts. Usually, the metal in the

paint will react with the base metal, and the paint will not adhere well, nor will it act as an anti-foul.

3. Insulate dissimilar underwater metals where possible so no current can flow from one to the other except through the water. This is usually difficult because of conductivity inside the wet hull. In that event, take the opposite tack and bond all underwater fittings with heavy wire (#8 gauge or heavier) and protect the entire system cathodically as later described.

4. Offer cathodic protection to all underwater fittings, both individually and collectively. This suggestion is made last because it is important and warrants considerable expansion.

Cathodic Protection

Galvanic anodes, usually zinc, or battery operated impressed current systems should be installed on any boat having underwater hardware. A possible exception is the trailered boat, used but a few hours a week, and stored dry. But on moored boats, good cathodic protection, intelligently installed, will reduce galvanic corrosion to the vanishing point. It will not, however, eliminate *stray current corrosion*; but we will discuss that in later paragraphs.

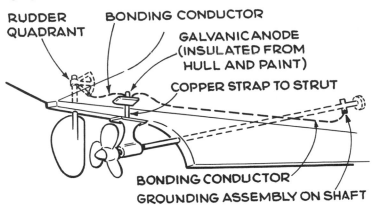

Fig. 13-4 ABYC suggests this anode arrangement on a non-metallic hull. Note that the anode is unpainted.

When you fasten a mass of zinc to a plate of copper or bronze and immerse the assembly in boating water, electric current flows from one metal to the other through the water, returning to the first metal through the metal. In this example, because zinc is the less noble, it will assume positive polarity and become the circuit's anode. The copper plate will become negative, forming a cathode to which the current flows through the water. Here we have an electric cell in which the zinc will corrode and deteriorate while the copper will be protected.

The practical effect of attaching zinc to a copper or bronze plate is that we sacrifice the zinc and protect the plate. This is a typical way of protecting a metal rudder.

But note carefully: If the zinc is to protect the plate, it must make good electric contact with it, and must be dunked in the same body of water.

For example, to protect a propeller strut, the zinc can be firmly attached to the hardware making secure electrical contact. Alternately, but not as desirable, the zinc anode can be attached to the fiberglass or wood hull, a wire or strap electrically connecting it to the strut. The electrical circuit between the zinc anode and the hardware it is supposed to protect must be complete or the zinc will do nothing. You can attach as many anodes as you like to the bottom of your boat, but they will protect nothing unless connected to the hardware electrically.

Probably the easiest way to protect underwater gear, is to tie it all together electrically: Bond such items as rudders, struts, propeller, prop shaft, through-hull fittings, and the hull's ground plate. Thus bonded, the entire network is then protected with adequate zinc masses.

Anodes

The American Boat and Yacht Council suggests that you purchase zinc galvanic anodes that conform to Military Specification MIL-A-18001. The spec defines a balanced alloy that

218

corrodes at a relatively uniform rate without forming a crust which would reduce efficiency in later life.

Attaching Anodes

The best anode is of limited efficiency if not correctly attached to the metal it is supposed to protect. Herein lies the weak point of many commercial anodes: These simply have holes through which the mechanic passes screws and attaches the anode to the hardware. This is satisfactory when the anode is new; but after some weeks of corroding, the drilled holes are eaten away. They expand, and, as a result, the fastening becomes loose and sloppy. Obviously, electrical resistance is increased between anode and hardware, with resulting reduction in protection. Better zincs are made with a cast-in galvanized iron or steel insert. Making intimate contact with the anode, this insert is tightened to the hardware, assuring longer useful anode life.

Anode Area

What area of anode is required to protect specific hardware? That depends upon composition of the underwater metal, water temperature, salinity, and paint condition. However, a good general rule is given in Military Specification MIL-A-18001:

One square inch of quality zinc anode will protect 800 square inches of freshly painted steel, or 250 square inches of bare steel or bare aluminum alloy. A square inch of good anode will protect about 100 square inches of copper or copper marine alloy. However, when the boat is underway, the protection ratio is reduced; more anode area is required to maintain the same degree of protection. For this reason, it is wise, where feasible, to use a somewhat greater area than indicated by the general rule. Anodes are not that expensive.

Don't Paint

"Protect the zinc and ruin the hardware," might be a way to

state it: Never paint the boat's anodes, because paint will act as an insulator, substantially reducing the zinc's efficiency. Each time you paint your boat's bottom, install fresh anodes. If you have the work done by a yard, specify what anodes you want installed; and inspect the job before the hull goes overboard. Make particularly sure about how the anodes are fastened, and, naturally, see that they are bright and unpainted.

Extra Dockside Protection

Most boats spend a great percentage of their time tied to the pier or resting at a mooring; consequently, most corrosion takes place while the boat is idle. Fortunately, it is easy and cheap to increase dockside protection against corrosion; and several marine suppliers sell portable anodes for the purpose. One of these, called "Guppy," is fashioned of zinc, in the shape of a fish: Fastened to a heavy wire, the anode is dangled over the boat's side and into the water while the boat lies idle. At the other end of the conducting cable there is a clamp, and this is gripped onto the boat's power plant or other component of the bonded system. The portable anode then does yoeman's duty protecting the boat's underwater hardware, propeller, rudder, and the like. Not only does the extra anode protect the underpinnings, but it also greatly extends the useful life of the permanently installed zincs.

Protecting the Prop

By all means, protect the propeller against corrosion; but avoid fastening shaft collar anodes around the propeller shaft close ahead of the wheel itself. Zinc shaft collars disturb the water's laminar flow, may decrease prop efficiency or even create cavitation. If you do use a collar type anode, fasten it on the prop shaft, as far forward as possible, close to where the shaft emerges from the hull.

In arrangements where you protect the propeller and shaft by a remote anode, you must provide special bonding between anode and shaft. It is not safe to depend on the electrical conductivity between the power plant, flange couplings, and prop shaft. Conductivity between engine and shaft is unreliable. The way to overcome this is to install a brush, wiper, or sliding contact to bear on the rotating shaft. Then, using adequate size wire, electrically connect the sliding contact to the boat's bonding system. The propeller and its shaft will now be at the same electrical potential as the remainder of the bonded system.

Bottom Paints

Many bottom anti-foul paints contain copper or mercury and are electrically conductive. Regarding the interaction between such paints and anti-corrosion anodes, ABYC states:

"Where galvanic anodes are mounted on bottom paints that may have conductive elements, or where there is a possibility of paint damage in the anode area due to high current density, the anodes should be insulated from direct contact with the paint by a suitable nonconductive coating or gasket. Insulation of the anode from the paint should not interrupt the electrical continuinity of the anode with the metals being protected."

Steel Boats

Boats with steel hulls may be protected by zinc, aluminum or magnesium anodes attached tightly against the steel bottom. ABYC points out that steel hulls should usually have anode protection both forward and aft. Non-metallic hulls, with most of the exposed hardware aft, usually require protection aft only.

Aluminum Boats

Corrosion protection of aluminum boats presents a special case where the protection must be more carefully controlled than on boats of other materials. Aluminum is unusual, being amphoteric,—having both acid and basic properties. It must be neither

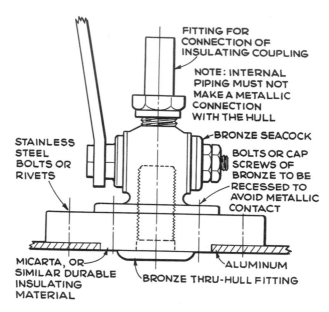

FITTING FOR
CONNECTION OF
INSULATING COUPLING

NOTE: INTERNAL
PIPING MUST NOT
MAKE A METALLIC
CONNECTION
WITH THE HULL

BRONZE SEACOCK

STAINLESS
STEEL
BOLTS OR
RIVETS

BOLTS OR CAP
SCREWS OF
BRONZE TO BE
RECESSED TO
AVOID METALLIC
CONTACT

MICARTA, OR
SIMILAR DURABLE
INSULATING
MATERIAL

ALUMINUM

BRONZE THRU-HULL FITTING

Fig. 13-5 Sketch shows suggested method of attaching bronze seacock to an aluminum hull to minimize corrosion. The fitting is insulated from the hull.

under nor overprotected, whereas other metals can be over-protected and suffer little harm.

For aluminum boats, experts suggest aluminum or zinc anodes. "Magnesium anodes," says the ABYC, "should be used only when the cathodic protection system has been reviewed by a qualified corrosion engineer." The underlying idea is that magnesium, improperly applied, may overprotect the aluminum hull and damage it.

Underwater parts of bronze or of other metal more noble than aluminum must be well insulated from electrical contact with the aluminum hull; otherwise the hull will be sacrificed to the hardware. Insulation of bronze parts minimizes galvanic activity between hull and hardware. Through-hull fittings such as seacocks may be mounted through insulating ferrules or washers of nonconducting material. Shafts and rudder posts should be insulated from the hull; then these may be protected separately from the aluminum hull.

Impressed Current Systems

Protective systems of the kind described, using metal anodes, generate their own current, and in a sense are passive. These systems work well, within limits, provided the anodes are replaced regularly and are kept clean.

Impressed current systems, as the name implies, use an outside source of current, doing the same or a better job, and requiring no anode replacement. Engelhard's CAPAC system is typical of the impressed current system frequently used on metal hull boats.

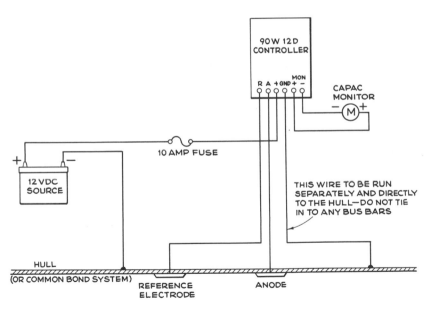

Fig. 13-6 Englehard's Capac system uses battery voltage to protect hull and hardware against corrosion. Reference electrode senses current amplitude for protection. In response, controller applies positive voltage to the anode, making hull and hardware cathodic, immune from rust and corrosion. The monitor indicates system condition.

One, two, or even more anodes are attached to the hull below the waterline. The anodes, however, instead of being easily corroded zinc or magnesium, are platinum coated. They are very noble, indeed, and do not corrode. The anode needs not be chemically active, and does not have to corrode, because the boat's battery raises its potential, more than simulating the activity of a freely corroding anode, and protecting the boat's hardware.

A typical impressed current system comprises three principal components: controller, anode, and reference sensor or electrode. Sensing corrosion potential in the water, the reference electrode transmits this information electrically to the controller. Then the controller, drawing power from the boat's battery applies required current to the anode. In response, current flows from the anode, through the water, to the otherwise unprotected underwater hardware, which is cathodic.

On boats of ordinary size, battery drain is all but negligible, being on the order of a few hundredths of an ampere. Anode corrosion is practically nil because of platinum's terrific corrosion resistance. Most impressed current systems are designed for negatively grounded boats because that is the standard grounding system. While the CAPAC system is for sizable inboard boats, in the main, several of the outboard and outdrive manufacturers are offering impressed current systems to protect the lower units of sterndrives and larger outboard motors.

Stray Current Corrosion

Referring to stray current corrosion, an engineer recently said, "It is a real hardware wrecker. It is the black beast that can ruin a boat from the waterline down, in nothing flat. A severe case of stray current corrosion makes ordinary galvanic corrosion look almost friendly."

Strong talk? Not really; because stray current corrosion is generated like this:

Through bad design or a mistake in electrical wiring, the boat's electrical system has its wires crossed. Impressed voltage on one piece of submerged hardware is higher than on another; and as a result, current flows through the water from one item to the other. If the circumstances are bad enough, currents can be several amperes, and an otherwise sturdy item of hardware ruined in a matter of days.

Stray current corrosion is scary; but fortunately it is usually easy to trouble-shoot and cure. If you have reason to suspect stray current activity in a boat, corrosion can be arrested immediately if you will simply disconnect the boat's batteries and disconnect the shore plug from its receptacle. This will kill the stray currents and give you time to plan your trouble-shooting program.

Crossed grounds, voltage drop in a circuit, and alternating current leakage from the "housecurrent system" to ground are the most frequent offenders causing stray current corrosion.

Consider crossed direct current grounds first; Suppose that a boat has two bilge pumps, one forward, another aft. One pump

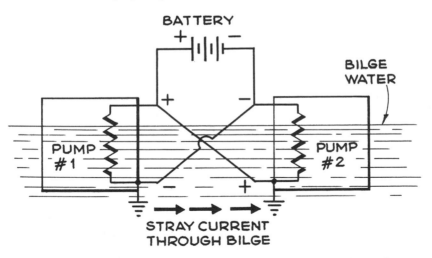

Fig. 13-7 Crossed grounds, giving opposite polarity to the grounded frames, forces stray current through the bilge water separating pump #1 from pump #2. Severe corrosion results.

is grounded in the standard negative ground polarity; the other, alas, is grounded to the positive side of the system: This spells trouble. Current will flow from one pump frame to the other; and the resulting electrolytic corrosion will surely wreck one pump.

Another example: Consider a bilge pump and a bait tank permanently installed: Assume that the bait tank is wired properly and grounded to your boat's negative ground; but assume that the pump has positive ground, which is backward. This spells trouble. Current is going to flow from one to the other; and the resulting corrosion will ruin one of the items.

Don't Cross Grounds

Watch polarity. Always ground accessories to the same polarity. Make sure there is one continuous, integral, heavy ground conductor serving all appliances; and be sure all electrical accessories are connected tightly to this system.

Watch New Installations

When installing new d.c. appliances or checking old ones, make sure that switches, circuit breakers or fuses are in the hot (positive, as standard) side of the line. The ground side must never have a switch or fuse, because if that side of the line opens electrically, current will flow through water or dampness from appliance to battery, and corrosion will be invited to do its worst.

Check on Voltage Drop

Loss of voltage between battery and accessory is termed line voltage drop, and is a cause of stray current corrosion. For example: Assume that battery voltage is 12.6 volts. But there is a drop of 0.6 volts in the ground wire feeding the radio transmitter. If the radiophone is tied directly to its ground plate, the plate, in the water, will take on a voltage 0.6 volts lower than

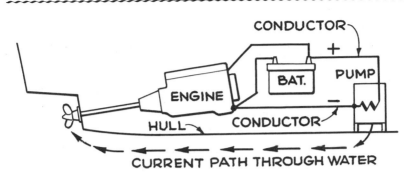

Fig. 13-8 Where conductors to the pump are insufficiently heavy, the pump will be at a different voltage than the engine and its propeller. Current will travel through the water between pump and prop, inviting corrosion.

that of the battery and its negative ground system. The prop shaft and propeller are electrically tied to the ground system; therefore, these will be 0.6 volts positive with respect to the radio ground plate. They will corrode.

The remedy for this is to electrically connect the radiotelephone's ground plate to the boat's common ground point, which is usually close to the battery. The radiotelephone system is then tied to the same ground point, and the underwater metals are at the same potential, with corrosion stopped.

This same technique, that of tying all accessory grounds by individual heavy wire to the common ground point, is an important step toward eliminating stray current corrosion.

Well designed modern boats usually have electrical systems with a common ground point close to the battery or batteries. In the interest of reducing corrosion, the following are usually connected to this common ground:

- Negative battery strap.
- Bonding system conductor.
- Main switchboard ground return conductor.
- Radio ground plate lead.
- Auxiliary generator ground.

227

Bonding is Important

A tight bonding system is definitely needed on inboard powered boats. As a matter of fact, it is *required* on boats meeting ABYC standards. Bonding is discussed in some depth in Chapter 5, and the reader may want to review the chapter, noting the importance of bonding in corrosion prevention. One of the prime objects of bonding in a boat is to provide a low resistance electrical path between otherwise isolated metallic objects. This, to reduce the possibility of electrolytic corrosion due to stray currents.

Corrosion from Shore Power

When plugging into the pier receptacle to bring 60 Hertz a.c. housepower aboard, you may unknowingly bring an uninvited guest as well: stray current corrosion. Aboard a boat with a well designed a.c. system it is not likely, but on a craft with haywire circuits, it is a good possibility.

Make dead sure there is no electrical connection of any kind between the black or white current-carrying wires and the boat's ground. That is a prime rule in preventing corrosion from the 60 Hz system. The entire housepower system must float at its own potential; because if power wires are connected to the boat's ground, current will flow from underwater appendages to earth: The current can be of considerable magnitude, and will cause severe corrosion.

The green or bare equipment grounding conductor in the a.c. system can be connected to the boat's common ground point. This conductor ties the boat's ground network to shore ground, bringing both to the same potential. However, only the equipment grounding conductor may be connected to the boat's ground. Never attach the white neutral wire to the boat ground, or you will have corrosion rampant should the shore plug be reversed, or if the local feeder is wired incorrectly, with the white wire hot, and the black neutral. Such things are known to happen.

Isolation Helps

The isolation transformer a.c. system, described in Chapter 4, helps greatly in blocking the cause of stray current corrosion. In this arrangement, land furnished current flows through the transformer's primary winding only. Transformer core and frame are insulated from the hull.

Shielded and insulated from the primary, the secondary winding furnishes a.c. power to the boat, and the boat's system floats completely free of shore current. Correctly designed and installed, the isolation transformer system completely eliminates a.c. stray current between boat and water, and is strongly recommended for steel and aluminum boats.

Frequent Causes

Three frequent causes of a.c. stray current corrosion are:

1. Leaky insulation on the hot (black or red) a.c. wire.
2. Defective battery chargers.
3. Shore power polarity devices.

Leaks from the Hot Wire

Damaging leakage currents are created by poorly insulated wires in wet locations, also in circuits in which the hot (black or red) wire is energized while the neutral (white) is open. Both wires should be switched on and off in a marine system, because if the shore plug is reversed in a system where only one wire is switched, it may be the neutral. That leaves the hot wire hot; and nowhere for the juice to go except to be a potential trouble maker.

Some older boats have switches in one wire only, supposedly the hot (black) conductor. If yours is such a system, always plug into the dock so that the black wire is hot. A quick check with a neon tester will tell you immediately if polarity is OK. Touched to an energized black wire and earth ground, it should glow. Touched to the white wire and ground, it should remain extinguished.

Battery Chargers

A few garage type battery chargers are built around autotransformers and are not suited to marine work. An autotransformer is one where the primary and secondary windings are electrically connected, usually being one winding with taps. This kind of transformer offers no true isolation of a.c. power line and the d.c. charging circuit. It can create strong stray currents.

You can check your charger for stray leakage with this simple test: Clip a low watt, 12 volt, automobile light bulb in series between one battery clip and a good ground, such as a water pipe. Energize the charger; and the bulb must not glow. Reverse the power cord; again, the bulb must not glow. Repeat the two tests on the other battery clip. If the bulb remains cold, the charger is OK.

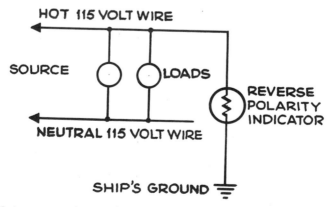

Fig. 13-9 A reverse polarity indicator, where used, must have very high resistance or it will leak current to the boat's ground, generating corrosion.

Polarity Devices

Some shore power polarity indicators or polarity reversing devices cause mild stray current corrosion because they have insufficient resistance between a.c. power connection and the boat's ground system. If you have a polarity device on board, it is a good idea to check its effective resistance from line to ground, which should be at least several thousand ohms. Incidentally, ABYC does not approve the use of polarity indicating devices because of the possibility of leakage.

SYNOPSIS

Electrolytic corrosion, incorrectly called electrolysis, eats away at underwater hardware which is not at the same electrical potential. Least noble metals are active and are eaten away when in contact with more noble ones. Some metals can galvanically corrode themselves. Corrosion is accelerated by higher temperature or salinity of the water, by close proximity of dissimilar metals, and by the extent to which the metals are dissimilar on the galvanic scale. Protection is provided by applying anodes, such as zinc, to hardware, by installing an active battery-powered system, by adequate bonding, and by eliminating stray currents which may come from the boat's electrical system.

CHAPTER XIV

How Shocking!

MOST READERS of this book realize that 115 or 230 volt alternating current "housepower" presents more of a shock hazard aboard the cruiser than in the home. The extension cord is also more of a potential killer on the damp pier and adjacent wet terrain than it is in the dry surroundings of the typical kitchen or bedroom. Electricity and wet locations mixed, spell danger.

No One is Safe

You face danger when standing on a wet deck, pier or on marina ground, using or touching an electric tool. If the appliance develops a fault internally, current can surge from it through you to ground; and the resulting shock can be lethal.

Current Does It

It is not voltage, but current, which kills people. Naturally, the two are related, and higher voltage can force more current through a man. But don't ever believe the foolhardy fellow who says 115 volt house current can't hurt. Properly (or improperly!) directed through your chest, it is lethal.

How Much Current?

According to medical experts, a healthy adult can be killed by a current as small as 0.06 ampere, 60 milliamperes, surging

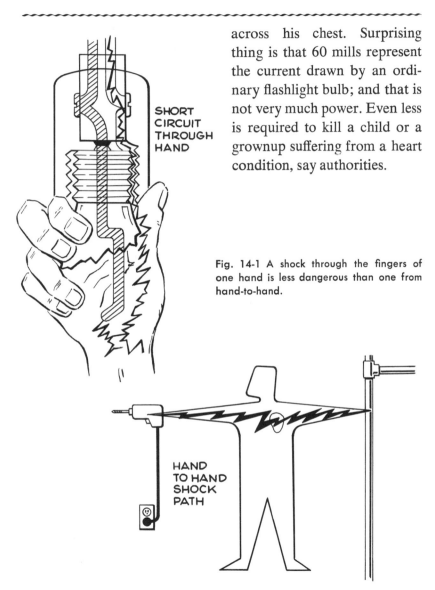

across his chest. Surprising thing is that 60 mills represent the current drawn by an ordinary flashlight bulb; and that is not very much power. Even less is required to kill a child or a grownup suffering from a heart condition, say authorities.

SHORT
CIRCUIT
THROUGH
HAND

Fig. 14-1 A shock through the fingers of one hand is less dangerous than one from hand-to-hand.

HAND
TO HAND
SHOCK
PATH

The Case of the Wet Sailor

Drenching wet with salt water, a boatman might have as little as a thousand ohms resistance between his hands or on other points across his body. Consequently, it appears that wires carrying as little as 60 volts may be dangerous; certainly those carrying twice that voltage *are to* be more than respected! Since dockside power runs from 110 to 125 volts above ground potential, it certainly can be classed as dangerous.

Electricity is Quick

Lethal shocks happen in mere seconds, often too fast for you to save yourself by dropping the offending wire. Technicians who've studied the matter say that in one second, less than a tenth of an amp can kill; and a third of an amp takes only a third of a second. That does not give you much time to take remedial action after you have grasped a hot conductor. What is worse, sometimes the current makes your grasp tighten in an involuntary vise-like grip. Then, unless help arrives *fast*, it may be curtains for you.

The Stage is Set

The standard shorepower 115/230 volt a.c. system was explained in Chapter 4. However, with emphasis on how shock hazard is created, we will review it here quickly:

Power is transmitted by a three-wire system wherein the conductors function as follows:

    1. A black coded wire is 115 volts "hot" above ground or earth potential.

    2. A white coded wire, called neutral, is at or close to safe ground or earth potential.

    3. A red coded wire, like the black, is 115 volts "hot" above ground.

Remember that the red and black wires are 115 volts hot relative to the white neutral, which is grounded in the manner of a lightning rod or water pipe. Should you touch the white conductor while simultaneously grasping the black or red, you'll get a nasty shock. Similarly, if you ground yourself, as by touching a water pipe or standing on a wet pier, while at the same time touching a live wire, you will be shocked.

Aboard a boat or in the dockside area, most electrical accidents occur when someone with wet hands completes a circuit between a hot conductor and damp grounded surface. Frequently, the accident is through no negligence on the part of the victim. It's not a bare wire, obviously dangerous, which he touches; it is a defective appliance, tool or badly wired receptacle.

A typical accident is where a diligent boatkeeper is working in a wet bilge. While handling an electric power tool, he grabs a through-hull fitting or other metal hardware connected to the bonding network which is grounded. The electrical tool has an internal fault, there being a connection between its motor's field winding and the aluminum frame. Completing the circuit between the tool's "hot" frame and ground, the worker gets a frightful shock.

Another typical accident happens in the galley where the cook reaches to the electric frying pan, at the same time touching the galley sink, which is electrically tied to ground. If the electric fryer has an internal fault, the cook will receive a jolting shock straight across the chest, where the danger is greatest.

There's Safety in the Green

The most basic prevention against electric shock is the green equipment grounding wire which runs through modern power cords. Terminating on the third, or middle, blade of newer appliance plugs, the green wire is a safety ground, specifically intended to eliminate or substantially reduce shock hazard. Attached to the appliance frame, outer casing, or exposed chassis, the green equipment grounding wire protects the appliance user from shock. It does so by diverting to ground most of the voltage surging in the item when it develops an internal fault. The most

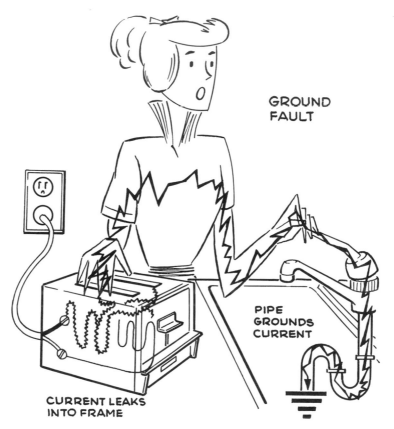

GROUND
FAULT

PIPE
GROUNDS
CURRENT

CURRENT LEAKS
INTO FRAME

Fig. 14-2 If its green equipment grounding wire is missing or defective, a galley toaster can be a lethal instrument.

typical fault is where the hot wire in the power cord touches the frame internally.

But Even the Green Can Fail

It is apparent from the above that the green equipment grounding wire improves tool and appliance safety manyfold. But unfortunately it does not offer completely foolproof protection, as pointed up by the following examples:

236

• Sometimes, unknown to the appliance user, there is a defective connection, or high resistance in the equipment grounding conductor. The electrical connection may be defective in the appliance or at the plug, or the plug's grounding blade may be corroded. The receptacle may be wired incorrectly, or wired without the grounding conductor. Possibly the marina or yard's feeder wiring is improperly arranged, with the grounding conductor missing, designed with high resistance, or simply not grounded. Worst of all, the supposed equipment grounding wire may even be hot: This is rare, but has been known to happen.

• Older, non-grounding receptacles will not accept the modern three-prong ground plug. Here the green wire in the appliance cord is rendered inert unless an adapter is inserted between the equipment power cord and receptacle. The catch is that the user will frequently neglect to screw the pigtail grounding wire to the receptacle plate to complete the ground. Alas, even when he does, he must pray blindly that the old receptacle plate is grounded.

• Well grounded, as when touching a galley faucet, the sailor is an excellent current conductor. In the event he handles a faulty appliance while grounded, and if the green coductor offers even a moderate resistance, he may be shocked: The high-fault current can divide, with most flowing through the green wire, but the remainder surging through the human. Contrary to popular belief, current in conductors does not *all* flow through the easiest path. It divides, most going through the easy path, but the remainder going through the higher resistance, in proportion (see the equation for parallel resistance on age 334).

Breakers Don't Protect You

Circuit breakers and fuses in the a.c. wiring protect the conductors and appliances against harm due to overcurrent; but they in no way offer protection against shock hazard. Circuit protective devices are rated at much too high a current to reduce shock. In the housepower a.c. circuits, typical circuit breakers are sized to trip at from 5 to 20 amperes. However, we have seen that it takes but a fraction of an ampere to kill; therefore, fuses and breakers offer no protection against electrocution.

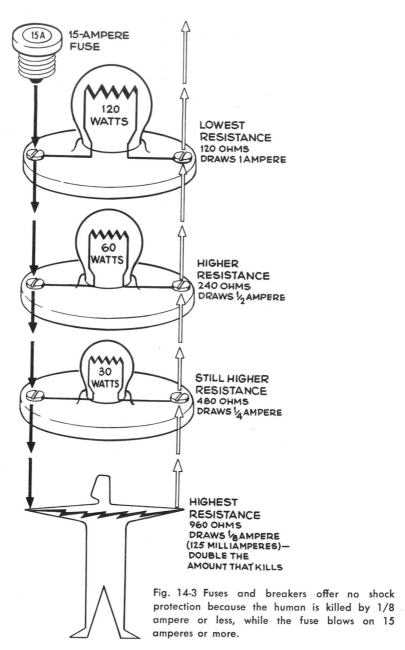

Fig. 14-3 Fuses and breakers offer no shock protection because the human is killed by 1/8 ampere or less, while the fuse blows on 15 amperes or more.

How about changing to circuit breakers or fuses sized small enough to offer protection against shock hazard? This approach will not work: Breakers or fuses sensitive enough to protect against shock danger would be far too delicate to energize even the tinest bulb or motor.

Additional Protection

Two electrical devices offer themselves as additional protection against shock hazard in damp locations:

- The isolation transformer.
- The ground fault circuit interrupter.

Each has its advantages and limitations, as explained below:

Isolation Helps

The on-board isolation system is explained and illustrated in Chapter 4, starting on Page 65. The transformer, in isolating shore power from the on-board system, enhances safety by reducing shock hazard. Since the on-board system is "floating" free of ground, almost like the electrical system on an airplane, a person may touch either of the 115 volt a.c. wires, simultaneously touching ground, and he will not be shocked. Should he touch *both* wires, he'll receive a shock, because there is voltage between them; but on touching one or the other and ground, he'll be safe.

Since the majority of shocks, and the most dangerous ones, result from contact with a hot conductor and ground, the isolation transformer offers considerable protection.

To do its shock protection job well, the isolation transformer should preferably be made specifically for the marine job to which it is assigned. Autotransformers are strictly no good. The on-board isolation unit must have high resistance between the primary (shore side) winding and secondary (boat side) one. A capacity shield between windings is desirable; and there should be convenient means for connecting the iron core to the shore grounding conductor. That, incidentally, is the only point where the system is grounded in any manner.

The isolation transformer's secondary winding may be tapped up to provide on-board voltage slightly higher than provided at dockside. The idea is to compensate for sagging voltage at the end of the pier and power cord. The feature does not detract from the unit's main purpose.

A disadvantage of the isolation system is that the transformer is heavy and bulky, and is usually located low in the boat where it is subject to rust. An obvious minor drawback is its cost which, for a 5,000 volt-ampere (approximately 5,000 watts) unit, is about $150. A partial drawback is that, because of inevitable slight electrical leakage, isolation may not be absolute. And in the event of a serious internal fault inside the transformer, isolation will be completely lost.

Searching for Leaks

It is simple to search for loss of transformer isolation. A sensitive test is to connect a neon test light between either of the secondary winding connections (the boat's wiring) and ground. In this case, ground is represented by the boat's engine, or other component attached to the grounded bonding system and underwater hardware. Thus connected, when contacting either of the boat's a.c. conductors, the neon test light should not glow.

Even in a relatively secure isolation system, a sensitive miniature light may glow slightly, but the system might still be safe since many glow lamps will indicate current as slight as 2 to 3 milliamperes (0.003 ampere) and this magnitude of current is relatively safe from the shock standpoint.

A less sensitive test is made with an ordinary 115 volt parallel strung Christmas tree lamp of the indoor tree variety. These bulbs will glow dimly on a current of 20 to 30 milliamperes, and shine at full brilliance, passing about 60 milliamperes. Consequently, when connected between ground and either of the boat's power wires, if the Christmas tree lamp glows, the system is too "leaky" to be safe.

The two tests described, one with neon, the other with a miniature incandescent bulb, are not infallible. The results depend to some extent upon where the electrical leak is located. If it is a short circuit between one power wire and ground, voltage between that wire and ground will be zero; between the other and ground it will be 115 volts. If the leak or short is at the center of the isolation transformer's secondary winding, voltage from each of the boat's two power wires to ground will be half of circuit voltage, and measured leakage current from each will be the same.

If there is serious worry about current leakage, it can be measured from each circuit wire to ground with an a.c. ammeter, and the readings will help determine the nature of the trouble. Only difficulty is that sensitive a.c. ammeters are expensive and not readily available.

One point for safety: Test lamps, meters, or other leakage-to-ground devices should be removed from the circuits after tests are made. Left in place, they constitute a leak themselves, partially destroying the very safety they are intended to reveal.

The GFCI

Old in theory, but newly popularized through the use of modern electrical components, the *ground fault circuit interrupter* is a safety device which can replace the isolation transformer in some instances. It can also do some jobs that the isolation unit can't; and in many versions it is light and portable.

About the size of a small adding machine, the portable ground-fault circuit interrupter instantly and automatically opens the a.c. circuit when a grownup or child touches a hot conductor or the frame of an appliance having an internal fault. Working almost magically, the GFCI is such a life saver that is is required in certain hazardous locations by safety codes. For example, the National Electrical Code requires the installation of ground fault circuit interrupters on feeders serving receptacles placed within 10 feet of a swimming pool.

Inside the GFCI

Connected in the circuit between source and appliance, or between source and receptacle, the ground-fault interrupter, in a sensitive circuit, compares the exact current flowing in both the hot wire and neutral. When both currents are indentical, indicating an "all's well" balance, the interrupter leaves its gate open, allowing juice to flow to the load.

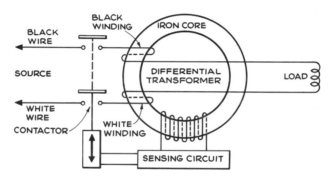

Fig. 14-4 When the load pulls more current through black winding than white, sensing circuit trips the contactor, opening the circuit in mere milliseconds.

Upon sensing even a slight unbalance in current between the hot and netural wires, the GFCI flips to alarm condition. Immediately, it chops off the flow of current to its protected circuit. In effect, the GFCI's brain has told it that someone or something is connected between the hot wire and ground. "Shut off the switch!" it says. And that is just what the interrupter does. Promptly.

Fast and Sensitive

Acting with incredible speed, a typical ground fault circuit interrupter will trip as fast as 0.025 second after sensing a fault. And so sensitive is it that it will trip upon detecting a fault as tiny as 0.005 ampere, which is only 5 milliamperes, current far less than that required to hurt a normal human, or even a frail child.

Limitations of the GFCI

When a person touches *both* the conductors in an extension cord coming from the GFCI, the device cannot protect him. Fortunately, this kind of shock poses less danger than the kind received when that person touches the hot wire with one hand while completing the circuit to ground with his other hand or feet or both.

When a child sticks his finger in a light socket, the little digit completes a circuit between shell and center conductor. The kid yells bloody murder. His finger burns; but no current has flowed through his chest area, and he is unharmed except for lost pride, which his mother can restore. However, when the little future sailor stands in water, or sits in a bath, and then grabs a "hot" appliance or live wire, he receives a jolt across his body which may be lethal.

It's that kind of body shock that the GFCI protects against.

Using the GFCI

At the present state-of-the-art, the best GFCI around boat and pier is the portable variety. Aboard your boat you may protect yourself by using the fault interrupter when working with electric tools in damp locations. In the galley, plug appliances into it. In the head, use it to power hair driers, electric razors, and

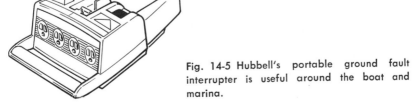

Fig. 14-5 Hubbell's portable ground fault interrupter is useful around the boat and marina.

243

space heaters. Always keep it between your hand-held tools and the power source when working around the pier or in the boat-yard. You simply plug the power cord from the portable inter-rupter into any 115 volt a.c. receptacle; then plug the appliance into the GFCI. You are safe from shock.

GFCI Limitations

Plugged into dockside, and feeding all the boat's a.c. receptacles, the GFCI usually flunks out. In theory, it should be able to pro-tect the entire boat against ground fault; but actually it can't make the grade. Boat environment, including the wiring, is so damp and electrically leaky that the current leakage to ground through the hull appears to the GFCI's brain as a dangerous fault. Not being able to tell whether the leakage is through some-thing inert, or a human, the instrument transfers to alarm con-dition, shutting off the power.

It is feasible to protect individual appliances or a limited number of cabin receptacles with one GFCI. But, because of extensive electrical leakage, it is impractical to guard the en-tire boat with one instrument.

Not for Overcurrent

The GFCI must not be relied upon as an overcurrent protective device, replacing circuit breakers. It is not intended as a working current limiter, and should be used in addition to ordinary over-current protection, not in place of it.

Where to Buy

GFCI's are increasing in popularity; and better electrical supply houses carry them, particularly suppliers in areas having swimming pools and boats. One popular GFCI is named *Circuit Guard*. It's a portable, compact interrupter made by Harvey Hubbell, Inc., Model GFP-221, with four receptacles, rated 20 amps at 120 volts, trips to safe condition on detecting a fault current of 5 milliamperes. List price, at this writing, is about $192. Hubbell has a smaller model rated 15 amps which simply plugs into a wall socket, fitting over the existing receptacle plate. Price is just under $70.

An extensive line of fault interrupters is offered by Pass and Seymour, Inc., which manufacturers units rated from 15 to 100 amperes. Model 91 is of interest to yachtsmen. Priced at about $134, its current rating is 30 amps at 120 volts, and trip current is five milliamperes.

The Square D Company has introduced a new series of circuit breakers incorporating ground-fault protection. Selling under $50 list price at this writing, the breakers named "Quick-Gard," are available in 15, 20, 25, and 30 ampere ratings for 115 volt service. They fit Square D QO load centers or NQO panel boards, directly interchangeable with ordinary breakers. Rated fault trip current is five milliamperes, assuring that the breakers comply with National Electrical Code requirements.

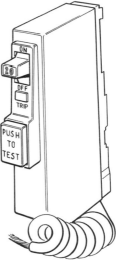

Fig. 14-6 Square D company now offers its Quik-Gard series of circuit breakers, incorporating a ground fault interrupter.

SYNOPSIS

Dockside "housepower" of 115/230 volts is definitely a serious shock hazard, more so around damp boating locations than about the house or apartment. As little as six hundredths of an ampere can kill in less than a second.

Suggested means of protection against shock hazard are:

- Make sure only three-blade, approved, grounding receptacles are used onboard and on the pier.
- Fit the boat with an isolation transformer "floating" system, making sure it is as "leak free" as possible.
- Use a ground-fault circuit interrupter to feed tools and appliances in wet locations.

CHAPTER XV

Protect Your Boat
Against Lightning

IN OTHER CHAPTERS we have seen how to secure the boat against fire and persons against shock created by relatively tame a.c. and d.c. on-board voltages. Now we turn our attention to protection against the very real dangers created by high voltage from outside the boat—hazards created by lightning bolts.

Bonded and correctly wired, with attention to the squelching of lightning strikes, your boat is a safe, secure place to be during a thunderstorm. Statistics bear this out. Rare, indeed, are cases where boatmen have been hurt by lightning striking a boat which is properly protected as described in this chapter.

Securing your boat against lightning is not difficult; we will be specific about how to do it in a moment. But first a few words about lightning itself. Understanding the frightening phenomenon helps make clear the reasons for the steps we will take.

What is Lightning?

Many years ago, Ben Franklin theorized and then proved that lightning is ultra high voltage electricity. In later years, scientists learned that there is always a space charge over the earth; but that during storms the charge increases in voltage until there is arc-over between earth and sky, or between clouds of opposite potential.

The earth is negatively charged, the upper atmosphere positively charged. Thus, say experts, the earth, the atmosphere, and the ionosphere form a vast capacitor, through the dielectric of which there is a constant leakage resulting from ionization. What maintains the charge against the leakage is not well understood. Apparently, magnetic phenomena, radiation, and bombardment from space keep the atmosphere charged, counteracting the electron leakage from earth to sky.

During a Storm

Even during the early stages of a lightning storm, the space charge increases; voltage difference between clouds and ground rises. Leakage current multiplies by several orders of magnitude, and becomes measurable on ordinary instruments. As a storm approaches, a voltmeter connected between a high antenna and earth will indicate an erratic, rising potential. And sometimes, when the storm is near, voltage gradients between earth and sky become so intense that sharp points, as at the top of a mast, glow with an eerie flame-like corona.

During a violent storm accompanied by rapid vertical build-up, theory states that clouds become charged positive at the top, negative below. Some experts say that charging results from the differential falling rate of large and small water drops.

Falling through rapidly rising air currents, larger water droplets acquire a positive electric charge, smaller ones take a negative charge. At the tops of rising air currents, great thunderclouds form. In the clouds, large drops, falling through the rapid upward currents, split upon reaching a critical size, and an electrical as well as physical separation takes place: Large drops take a positive charge while continuing to fall; smaller particles assume a negative charge, and are carried upward by the vertical wind. Particles may unite again, then drop and reseparate; consequently, charging is a continuing process.

Lightning

The great clouds we have described operate as an enormous electric generator, increasing the potential until something just *has* to give. Finally, a lightning bolt flashes out, temporarily reducing voltage and relieving the stress. The lightning may jump between two surfaces in the same cloud, may flash between two clouds, or between clouds and the earth below.

The arc between cloud and earth is sometimes more than a mile long, packing many millions of volts. According to some experts, lightning between clouds may be as much as twenty miles long! However, discharges between clouds do not worry boatmen. But lightning between clouds and earth is dangerous; and that is the variety against which we must protect our boats.

Security

We take several relatively simple steps to secure our yacht against the ravages of lightning. All measures are designed to intercept the lightning bolt, conducting its massive voltage to ground with as little electrical resistance as possible. The two principal steps in marine lightning protection are to short circuit the high voltage before it can do harm, and to bond the boat together so all parts will be safe. Bonding was discussed earlier in this book; but its lightning squelching aspects will be amplified here.

Guidelines

The American Boat and Yacht Council offers recommendations and sets standards for marine lightning protection. It is upon ABYC standards that our suggestions are based.

A Safety Check

Inspect your boat, checking point by point, reassuring yourself that she is fully protected from lightning. If you find equipment or wiring not to your liking, have corrections made in accordance with the recommendations that follow:

The Grounded Mast

Primary lightning protection is a well grounded vertical conductor, a mast, serving as a high-rise lightning rod. A conducting mast or rod attracts to itself direct lightning hits which might otherwise strike within a cone shaped space. The apex of this cone is the top of the rod or mast; and the base is a circle at the surface of the water, the circle having a radius approximately twice mast height.

The Circle of Protection

Lightning authorities say that protection is 99% for the 60 degree angle shown in Figure 15-1. They also say that the probability of protection can be increased to 99.9% by extending the

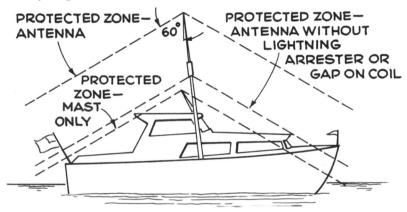

Fig. 15-1 An invisible umbrella of lightning protection is offered by a properly grounded and bonded mast or antenna.

mast height sufficient to reduce the 60 degree angle to 45 degrees. This means that if you have a good conducting rod or mast located about equidistant from bow and stern, and if it has a height about half the boat's length, you are extremely safe. This points up that the conventional sailboat having a well grounded aluminum mast, enjoys an excellent cone of protection, which should bring justifiable peace of mind to her skipper.

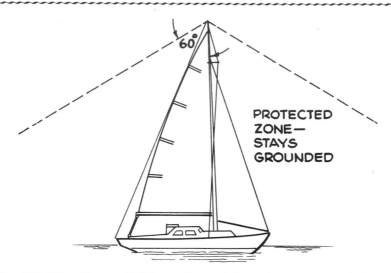

60°

PROTECTED
ZONE—
STAYS
GROUNDED

Fig. 15-2 This sailboat, with lofty, well-grounded metal mast, is particularly well-protected against lightning strikes.

Securing the Mast

The lightning arrester or protective mast is bonded from top to ground with #8 gauge or heavier copper wire. When doing this job, keep the conductor as straight as possible, because sometimes a lightning strike will leap from a sharply bent conductor to an adjacent surface. A sailboat's aluminum mast need not be fitted with a heavy copper conductor since aluminum has splendid electrical conductivity. However, the aluminum mast together with its rigging must be electrically connected to ground as described in the following paragraphs.

Large Metal Objects

Avoid placing bulky metal objects close to the grounding conductor if you can possibly make other arrangements. There is a strong tendency for sparks or side flashes of lightning to leap from the grounding conductor to adjacent metal objects. A method of preventing damage from such side flashes is by electrically bonding large metal objects to the grounding conductor.

Using heavy wire, electrically interconnect large metal masses within the hull. This would include stoves, machinery, refrigerators, and the like. Connect these masses electrically to the lightning protective system and to the boat's bonding network which was described in Chapter 5. Proper interconnection will prevent the objects from "attracting" side flashes of lightning.

Workmanship

Don't skimp on the mechanical construction of a protective system; and make all electrical connections tight. Use noncorroding materials and heavy conductors. You will expect your lightning grounding system to remain effective for many years, yet you are likely to give it little attention after it is installed.

Use the Antenna

You may use your boat's radio antenna as a lightning protective mast, provided it is fitted with a transmitter type lightning arrester or means for grounding it during a lightning storm. Experts say that the grounding of metal rod radio antennas is sufficient protection for wood or fiberglass boats which have no other masts or spars, provided the following conditions are met:

1. All conductors in the antenna grounding circuit must be be at least #8 AWG copper or equivalent.

2. A line drawn from the top of the antenna to the water at an angle of 60 degrees to the vertical must not intercept any part of the boat.

3. Antennas with loading coils are considered to end at a point immediately below the loading coil unless this coil is provided with a suitable gap for by-passing the lightning current.

4. Non-conducting antenna masts having spirally wrapped conductors are not suitable lightning protection.

Where your radiotelephone antenna is relied upon for lightning protection, the above four points are important. Remember that the bottom of the loading coil is considered the top of "rod" unless the coil has a gap provided for by-passing lightning. However, newer VHF FM antennas usually have no loading coil, and no gap is required.

Corrosion Resistance

Your lightning protective system must use materials that are highly corrosion resistant. Never use a combination of metals that are basically different and form a galvanic couple in the presence of moisture. Always use copper for a conductor except for conducting materials which are otherwise part of the boat (rigging and spars, for example).

Conductor Defined

The American Boat and Yacht Council advises the following in regard to copper conductor used in the lightning arresting system:

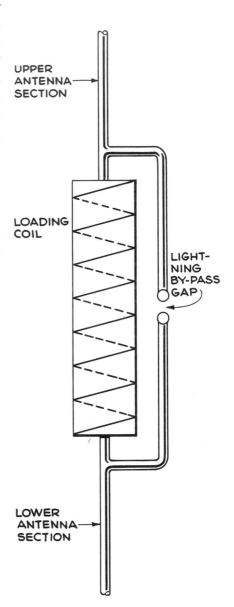

UPPER ANTENNA SECTION →

LOADING COIL

LIGHTNING BY-PASS GAP

LOWER ANTENNA SECTION →

Fig. 15-3 As a lightning protective mast, the transmitting antenna ends at the bottom of the loading coil, unless the coil is by-passed by a gap.

252

Copper conductor should weigh at least 50 pounds per thousand feet. Cable conductors should be of a diameter not less than #8 AWG. The size of any individual wire strand in a cable should be not less than #17 AWG. Thickness of any copper ribbon or strip should be not less than #20 AWG (0.032″). Where other materials than copper are used, the gauge should be large enough to give conductivity equal to or greater than #8 AWG copper cable."

Connections and joints in the lightning squelching system must be mechanically strong and made so they have no measurable electrical resistance. The reason for using heavy electrical conductors and for making perfect connections in the lightning grounding system is that powerful electric currents flow at the instant of a direct strike. Should the conductor be too small, it may fuse. Fire could result from the arc-over. Connections must be excellent because high resistance junctions will heat up, or may fuse, flash, and start a fire.

Electrical Togetherness

It is particularly important to tie your boat together electrically. Interconnection is part of the lightning protection plan devised by engineers in the ultra high voltage field. All sizeable metal objects are made a part of the lightning conductor system through interconnection with it. An alternate plan, where tying together is impractical, is to independently ground each large metal mass. As mentioned earlier, the object of tying all major parts firmly to ground is to prevent side flashes.

Both interior and exterior metal bodies are interconnected in the network. Such masses as horizontal hand rails on decks and cabin tops, vents and stacks from heaters or galley stoves, dinghy davits, metal masts, and the like, must be electrically "welded" together. An air-conditioner, extending through the cabin wall, must not be neglected.

Sizeable inboard metal objects should be electrically interconnected; aboard a well-designed boat, the basic bonding system (described in Chapter 5) will suffice. However, be safe: Inspect your boat. Bonded together with heavy conductor should be the engine, water and gasoline tanks, auxiliary generator and, if used, the control rods serving clutch and rudder. There is little need to ground small metal objects such as clocks, instruments, medicine chests, or compasses, but you can do so if you are inclined.

Pointed Objects

Metal projections through the boat's deck, cabin top, or sides above the sheer line should receive your attention. Be sure to bond these items to the nearest bonding conductor. Where possible, also ground them at their lower extreme ends within the boat. Be particularly careful to ground spotlights and other projecting hardware that can be touched by the crew.

Ground Revisited

Ben Franklin grounded his early lightning rods directly to Mother Earth; but you cannot do that aboard your boat, obviously. Consequently, you "ground" the entire lightning conductor system to the water in which the boat floats. According to lightning rod men, final ground can be almost any metal surface which is normally submerged in the water, and has an area of at least one square foot. Metal rudders, propellers, and keels may be used for grounding. Incidentally, the ground plate required by the Federal Communications Commission for medium frequency transmitters is usually adequate. Obviously, if the boat has a metal hull, its bottom presents a superior grounding surface, and no further ground need be provided.

Sailboats

Adequate protection is offered by a sailboat's wood mast *provided* it has metal standing rigging with all rigging well grounded. Simply depending upon the shroud's partly sub-merged chain plates is not enough for a safe ground. There must be at least a full square foot of grounding surface in the water: This, regardless of heel angle. In addition, experts say that all stays, sail tracks, and other metal rigging should be grounded.

Dinghys

Dinks, canoes, launches, and the like can be made safe by a temporary lightning protective mast which may be rigged before an electric storm. The mast, unless of sturdy metal, must be fitted with a heavy conductor all the way to the top. Grounding may be a heavy gauge, flexible, copper wire attached to a sub-merged metal ground plate one square foot in area or larger. A metal centerboard might serve as a good ground plate on a small sailboat so equipped, provided the board is down in sailing position.

Protect Yourself

Safety people suggest you do the following to protect yourself during an electric storm:

1. Remain in the cabin of a closed boat when at all possible.
2. Don't swim. Stay out of the water until the storm passes.
3. Avoid contact with any components connected to a lightning conductive system. Never act as a bridge between items. For example, don't touch the clutch lever and spotlight control handle simultaneously.
4. If you're caught on the beach, exposed and lacking pro-tection, lie low. Remain close to the ground until the worst of the electric storm passes.
5. Do not touch radio receiving or transmitting antennas or lead-in wires during a storm. Avoid touching on-board electri-cal appliances.

After a Close Shave

Protected as described in this chapter, a boat will come through any number of strikes with complete safety. However, if your boat is struck, and you are aware of it, give the electrical system an inspection, and also swing the compass, re-correcting it for deviation if necessary. Lightning strikes on a boat have been known to alter the magnetic characteristics of a boat and its machinery.

SYNOPSIS

Lightning is a bolt of ultra high voltage lashing from sky to earth; and to protect against its ravages, we direct it to a first class electrical ground before it can cause trouble. On the boat, the greatest protection comes from a grounded conducting mast, while secondary effects are suppressed by bonding of all metal on the craft. Heavy conductors are used for all lightning protection work, and sharp bends are avoided in all the related wiring.

CHAPTER XVI

Electric Motors
Aboard the Boat

THIS CHAPTER concerns electric motors both large and small, so commonly found aboard the cruiser, houseboat, or larger auxiliary. These busy little armature spinners range all the way from the miniature unit of a windshield wiper to the big jobs found in anchor winches and refrigerators.

Basic Types

Both direct-current and alternating-current motors are found aboard most cruisers. Looking much alike, they perform similar tasks; but internally they are quite different, both physically and electrically. Direct-current motors incorporate brushes, a commutator, and wire-wound rotor. Most a.c. motors, on the other hand, lack brushes, and have a simple inert looking rotor.

A.C. Motors

Usually operating on 115 volt, 60 Hertz power, alternating-current motors draw their energy from dockside or an on-board a.c. generating set. An induction motor, the kind commonly used on refrigerators and most fans, simply has no urge to rotate when connected to direct current, even though the voltage be appropriate. Occasionally, small a.c. motors are operated from d.c. to a.c. inverters which derive their power from the boat's batteries; but here, the motors see a.c., not d.c.

Refrigerators, air-conditioners, power tools, galley appliances, clocks, and tape recorders comprise just a few of the applications for a.c. motors. On-board a.c. motors range from 1/300 hp for clocks and timers, to several horsepower for large air-conditioners.

D.C. Motors

Aboard moderate sized boats, direct-current motors are 12 volt, drawing power from the craft's storage battery. Some types of d.c. motor will operate reasonably well on alternating current provided voltage is matched to the motor; but others will be ruined by a.c. Popular applications for d.c. motors are in engine starters, windshield wipers, fans and blowers, bilge pumps, power tilt for outdrives, pressure water systems, electric toilets and winches. Powers range from over a horsepower for engine starters and winches down to perhaps 1/50 hp for small fans.

Special Motors

The universal type motor is special in that it will run satisfactorily on either a.c. or d.c. Electric hand tools and vacuum cleaners usually use this kind of inherently high speed motor, where armature speed is from 5,000 to 25,000 rpm. Contrast this speed to that of the induction motor, the most common variety of which spins 1,750 rpm!

Universal motors will run on either kind of juice; however, in order to do their rated work, they must be connected to the correct voltage. They are universal as to frequency, but not as to voltage; and a 115-volt universal motor will barely rotate on 12 volts. Reduced voltage will not damage the universal motor, however, whereas prolonged low voltage applied to an induction motor, as used in a refrigerator, may burn it out.

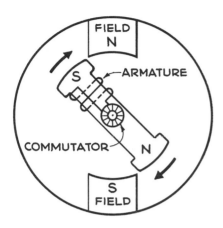

Fig. 16-1 The commutator feeds current to rotating armature poles so they are magnetically attracted to field poles. When rotating poles align with fixed ones, they are de-energized, and a following set are energized. The function is repeated many times for each revolution of the armature. Only two rotating poles are shown; actually there are many.

Inside the D.C. Motor

Fastened to the inside of the cylindrical motor frame and placed 180 degress apart are two wire-wound electromagnets. These are the fixed-field poles in a two-pole motor. On the motor's rotating member is another group of electromagnetic windings, usually numbering between four and 30, depending upon motor design. The stationary electromagnets or poles comprise the field structure, the rotating ones are the armature; and it is the armature which delivers the useful work.

How it Works

Immediately the d.c. motor is switched on, the field magnets become steadily energized by a flow of current from the source, such as the battery. However, the rotating electromagnets on the armature are energized only in timed sequence, determined by their angular relationship to the field magnets. Each rotating pole is momentarily energized and attracted to a field magnet just forward of it in its rotational path. Magnetic attraction pulls the armature magnet ahead in orbit. Then, when it is pulled around into alignment with the field magnet, the armature magnet is deenergized. Immediately, the pole following behind it is energized, and so on, in rapid succession.

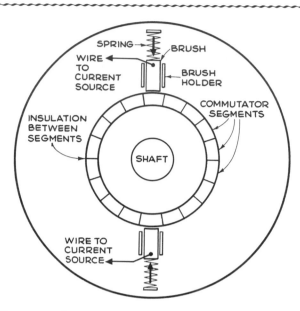

Fig. 16-2 Springs gently urge conducting brushes against commutator segments, transmitting current to armature windings sequentially as the shaft rotates.

The Commutator

The radially arranged spinning armature electromagnets or poles are electrically connected to a matching radial series of copper contacts. These constitute the commutator. Fixed to the motor frame, insulated, and sliding against the commutator segments are spring-loaded, current-carrying brushes, usually two, sometimes four. The brushes are graphite or metallic bars forming electrical contacts that energize the appropriate armature poles in correct sequence as the armature rotates.

Series D.C. Motors

Field and armature windings are series connected (like series Christmas tree lights) in a series-wound motor. Direct current flows through one field winding, across a brush and commutator, through the armature windings, then through the other brush to

260

the opposite field winding and back to the source. Very high speed characterizes this motor, rpm of from 5,000 to 20,000 being common.

The series-wound d.c. motor has indeterminate speed regulation: unlike most other kinds of electric motors, its rpm does not inherently level off at some relatively moderate speed; the series motor's armature spins increasingly faster as load decreases. In fact, on full voltage, some series motors will centrifugally throw their armature windings if operated load free.

Shunt Motors

Windings in the armature and field are parallel connected in a shunt-wound motor, each set of coils being fed from a common pair of terminals. Applied voltage flows directly across the field

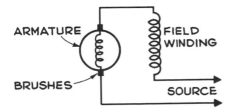

Fig. 16-3 Arrangement of armature and field windings in a series motor is shown. The type is characterized by high rpm and a wide range of speed, which is sensitive to load.

windings, which are attached to the motor terminals. The brushes are also direct connected to the terminals, energizing the armature through the commutator.

Characteristically, the shunt-wound motor has better speed regulation and operates more slowly than the series motor; and it will not run away if operated without load. The shunt type is typically found on marine engine starters, anchor winches, and some direct-current refrigerators.

Fig. 16-4 Armature and field windings are paralleled in a shunt motor. Relatively constant speed is typical of this type, but rpm is not as fixed as in a.c. induction motor.

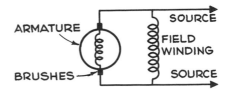

261

Compound Motors

Something of a hybrid between the series and shunt motor, the compound type has two sets of field windings. One set, through the brushes, is in series with the armature coils; the other set is connected directly to the motor terminals. Frequently designed for a specific application, the motor has good speed characteristics, and is sometimes found on direct-current appliances rated between 1/8 hp and 1/2 hp.

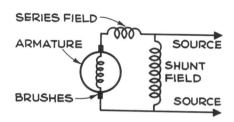

Fig. 16-5 The compound motor has speed characteristics between the series and shunt type. It will speed up on light load, but not run away.

Permanent Magnet D.C. Motors

A relative newcomer to the motor family, the permanent magnet variety owes its growing popularity to the recent development of super power permanent magnets. Made of new alloys, these magnets pack a terrifically strong field into small space, permitting compact, powerful motors to be designed around

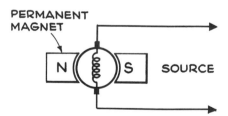

Fig. 16-6 Field coils are replaced by permanent magnets in the permagnet motor. Correctly applied, it shows very high efficiency.

them. The perm-mag motor is characteristically efficient because it has no field winding with attendant resistive losses. The rotating armature is conventional, but the field poles are permanent magnets; therefore, current flows via brushes through the the armature only.

Originally manufactured in flea sizes only, for toy and small instrument application, the perm-mag motor is growing constantly. One manufacturer announces he will soon introduce 1/6, 1/4, and possibly 1/3 horsepower units in the very near future. This kind of motor apparently has a bright future aboard ship, particularly because of its inherently high efficiency.

Reversing D. C. Motors

The easiest motor to reverse is the permanent magnet one. To reverse it, you simply interchange battery connections to opposite polarity at its terminals. Because the magnetic polarity of the field poles is fixed, reversing the polarity of supply voltage to the armature, through the brushes, inverts armature polarity, making the motor run backward.

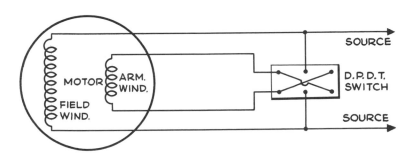

Fig. 16-7 Schematic shows switch arrangement used to reverse direct current motor. Switch is double pole, double throw. Note that the switch reverses the motor, but does not shut it off. A separate switch is required for shut-down.

The majority of conventional direct-current motors can be reversed, operating satisfactorily with right or left-hand rotation. But this is not true of all motors: If the manufacturer wants his motor to be field-reversible, he brings four numbered leads to the connection box. Two leads come from the brushes, and two from the field windings. To reverse the motor, the two field conductors are left in position while the two armature leads are interchanged. This reverses the polarity relationship between the two internal circuits, and the motor rotates in the opposite direction.

Shaft Bearings

Plain sleeve bearings are used a great deal on intermittent duty motors, and on some constant duty units. Heavy or long duty motors often have ball bearings, needing little or no lubrication. If the reader plans on buying a motor for continuous duty, or if it is to be installed in an inaccessible location, it is wise to buy a ball bearing motor. Such a motor is also best if the motor is mounted with its shaft vertical, or if there is an imposed end thrust load.

How Much On-Time?

Some d.c. motors are intended strictly for intermittent duty. An example is the marine engine starter motor, many of which are designed for a duty cycle of 15 to 30 seconds on, followed by several minutes off, during which to cool. A heavily loaded starter motor will roast if operated more than a few minutes without a following lengthy cooling off period.

Of course, there are d.c. motors designed for continuous duty; others are designed for continuous duty only when used in fan service where they are externally cooled. In buying a motor for some specific service, you must always consult the nameplate for ratings, or refer to the technical bulletin describing the motor.

D.C. Current Demand

The size conductor you must use when wiring a new d.c. motor depends on its current demand. Textbook theory states that a motor will demand 746 watts per theoretical horsepower. That assumes 100% efficiency. But because of losses, and for added safety, it is better to compute current assuming about 1,800 watts per horse for small, low voltage motors. To determine approximate motor watt demand of small motors, multiply hp times 1,800. To derive amperes, divide watts by supply voltage.

Example

A 12-volt, 1/8 hp, direct-current motor will consume about 225 watts, with current demand just under 19 amps. Therefore, if the motor is fed by 20 feet of wire, the conductor size should be a pair of #10 AWG, assuming a 10% voltage drop is acceptable. See Figure 3-7 on Page 58 for required wire sizes for given currents and voltage drops.

Effect of Light Load

The above example assumed the d.c. motor to be fully loaded. However, if the motor is lightly loaded, it will draw less than full rated current. Current diminution, however, will not be proportional to load reduction, because the motor loses efficiency as its load is reduced. Simply "fanning the breeze" at no load, the motor still draws enough current to overcome friction, windage, and electrical losses.

Speed Control

Direct-current motors, particularly those driving windshield wipers, fans, and blowers, can have their speed varied by a variable resistance in the hot conductor. A rheostat or stepped resistance is usually used; and one is selected that will cut motor current to about half: This will reduce motor output to one quarter of full power, usually sufficient reduction.

Calculating a Rheostat

No great precision is required in selecting a rheostat to control the speed of a simple appliance such as, for example, a windshield wiper or blower: The following method will come close enough:

1. Energize the subject motor with full voltage and, using a d.c. ammeter, measure the current demand. For this example, assume it is 4 amperes. Also assume the voltage is 12.

2. Divide the voltage 12 by current 4 to obtain resistance 3 ohms. $R = \dfrac{E}{I}$. This resistance will cut current in half to 2 amps, and motor power to about a quarter. Consequently, you will buy a rheostate having resistance span from 0 to 3 ohms or thereabouts.

3. Rheostats are generally sized according to watts dissipation. To determine the wattage you will require, square the "cut" or reduced amperes 2, obtaining 4. Multiply rheostat resistance 3 by squared current 4 (I^2R), obtaining watts 12. You will buy a rheostat rated 12 watts or higher: The higher the wattage rating of the control, the cooler it will operate.

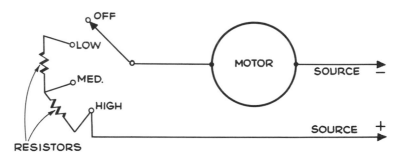

Fig. 16-8 Two resistors and four-position tap switch offer three speeds and "off."

It is well to buy a rheostat of larger than theoretical wattage not only for cool operation, but to assure the slider can handle maximum current. When you turn the control to high motor speed position, the rheostat winding need dissipate little wattage, but the slider will be carrying close to full motor current. For this reason, you may want to purchase your rheostat by specifying overall resistance and maximum current, rather than wattage.

Another approach, one eliminating the rheostat slider, is shown in Figure 16-8. Several resistances are wired in series; and a switch selectively energizes the motor with full battery voltage, or with one or more resistors, in series. The switch must, of course, be capable of handling full motor current.

Approximate H.P.	Amperes Original Current	Ohms External Resistance
1/4	38	0.31
1/8	19	0.63
1/10	15	0.8
1/25	6	2.0
1/50	3	4.0
1/100	1.5	8.0

Fig. 16-9 External resistance required to reduce motor (or lamp) output to one quarter of original value. Table is for 12 volt circuits. Currents shown for motor horsepowers are very approximate since current demand varies with motor type.

Figure 16-9 tabulates the resistance required to reduce 12-volt d.c. motor power to ¼ of full value, and indicates the wattage size of rheostat to use. The tabulated values can be used for dimming lights, also, where light current is substituted for motor current.

Watch for Voltage Drop

It is obvious that since a rheostat of few ohms will reduce motor power markedly, resistance in the boat's wiring will do the same thing. This emphasizes the importance of heavy d.c. wiring in motor circuits. Inadequate wiring not only causes power-robbing voltage drop, but may also be dangerous, since undersize conductors get hot due to resistance losses.

Two-Position Drop Test

Using a d.c. voltmeter, you can easily test motor circuits for

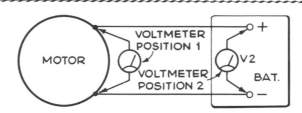

Fig. 16-10 With motor operating at load, voltage is measured at the motor terminals, then at battery posts. Voltage difference indicates circuit voltage drop.

voltage drop, as shown in Figure 16-10. First, run the motor with its normal load, then carefully measure the voltage immediately at its terminals while the motor operates. Then, with the motor still operating, measure voltage at the battery terminals. The difference in voltage is the line drop. It should not exceed 10%, because even a 10% potential drop causes 20% loss of motor power.

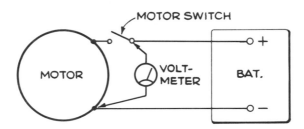

Fig. 16-11 Closing of motor switch causes voltage drop; and voltmeter indicates effect of circuit resistance, including that in the battery.

One-Position Drop Test

A simple but slightly less accurate method of measuring line drop to the motor may be used without significant error on small motors: The connections are shown in Figure 16-11. Energize the motor; run it with normal load; measure the voltage at its terminals. With the voltmeter still connected, close to the motor terminals but on the hot side of the switch, shut off the motor. Watch the voltage rise. Difference between "on" and "off" voltages is the drop. The reason this method is less accurate than the first is that it includes the battery's voltage with and without load. However, on a small motor, that change should be slight, particularly if there are other loads simultaneously on the battery.

Direct-Drop Test

A third method measures drop directly, and it is shown in Figure 16-12. This method is good where current is very heavy, and where you do not want to leave the motor running for more than a relatively few seconds. Typical application is to measure the voltage drop to an engine starter, eliminating the effect of battery voltage drop, which will be considerable.

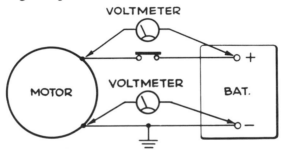

Fig. 16-12 Connected direct from motor terminal to battery post, the voltmeter will read voltage drop in the cable which it shunts. Switch must not be opened in test, or full battery potential will appear across the voltmeter in the hot cable.

Use a voltmeter with full-scale calibration less than motor voltage. For example, on a 12-volt system, use a meter scale of something like 3 to 5 volts. Proceed as follows:

1. Energize the motor.
2. Measure the voltage between positive battery post and positive motor terminal.
3. Remove the meter from the circuit.
4. Shut off the motor.
5. Repeat the procedure in the negative conductor.

The reason for taking the voltmeter out of the circuit *before* opening the motor switch, is that if the switch is between meter connections, the meter will see full battery voltage; that would be hard on the instrument unless its full scale matched or exceeded battery voltage. However, a high reading voltmeter makes the test less sensitive since such a meter has less resolution.

Inside the A.C. Motor

We have explored the d.c. motor; now let us look into the a.c. motors aboard the boat.

Although the theory of its internal modus operandi is fraught with mystery, the common a.c. induction motor is electrically and mechanically simple. Many induction motors, such as those used on blowers and other appliances, have but a single moving part, the armature. Modern induction motors have no armature windings, brushes, or commutator; some have starting switches or external capacitors, but all are simple.

Poles vs. Speed

In the a.c. machine, the stator or field windings are arranged around the motor frame, much as in a d.c. motor. Motors rated 3,450 rpm or thereabouts have two poles; motors of approximately 1,725 rpm have four poles, and motors rated around

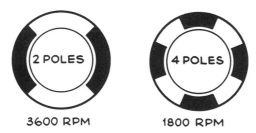

Fig. 16-13 60 Herz induction motors seek a synchronous speed of 3,600 rpm if two-pole, and 1,800 rpm if four-pole. However, the motors operate slightly slower than the synchronous speed.

1,150 rpm have six poles. Speed on 60 Hertz usually equals a little less than 7,200 divided by the number of poles, and within the motor's load rating is fairly independent of that load.

Stator "run" windings are connected directly across the 115 or 230 volt a.c. power source. As the alternating current surges 60 times a second through the pole windings, magnetic fields follow suit, rising and falling rhythmically inside the motor.

The Armature

Called a squirrel cage rotor, the induction motor's armature is similar in general appearance to that in a d.c. motor; but the squirrel cage rotor is simpler: Instead of windings, it has simple, straight individual copper bars buried in slots parallel to the motor shaft. Each bar is short circuited to the others at its ends, and there is no commutator, hence the motor has no brushes.

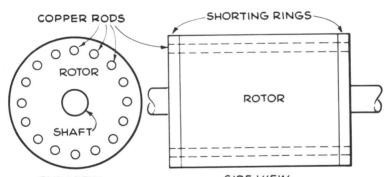

Fig. 16-14 An induction motor is simple, having no commutator. The rotor is comprised of iron laminations encasing lengthwise copper bars, and the bars are short-circuited at each end by metal rings.

Since there are no brushes, how does the rotor become energized? As follows: Magnetic fields are induced in the armature through induction, similar to the way one transformer winding induces current in another winding. As the undulating magnetic lines of force from the stator windings surge across the rotor's copper bar conductors, they induce strong currents therein. In turn, the induced currents create new magnetic fields, and these, acting with the stator magnets, give the rotor its torque.

No Inherent Starting Torque

Unlike the direct-current motor, the a.c. induction motor has no starting torque unless separate electrical means are provided to "get it going." As long as the rotor remains stationary in the pulsating magnetic field, it feels no urge to rotate. Think of it as compared to a surfboard, sitting still in the water, allowing waves to pass under. But once the rotor is nudged to rotate, however slowly, it is urged by the magnetic waves to follow, just as the surfboard, once started, is carried shoreward by the waves.

Good Speed Regulation

Because the induction motor's armature "rides" the electromagnetic waves created by the 60 Hertz electricity, it has superior speed regulation. It cannot go faster than the waves, and unless it is overloaded, it will not fall far behind. Therefore, line frequency, usually 60 Hertz, and number of poles, as explained on Page 270, determine the motor's speed. Special motors have provision for speed variation through switching the number of effective poles, or varying the amount of "slip" behind the waves. But the majority of induction motors are pretty well married to their one design speed.

Synchronous AC Motors

Synchronous motors are a special breed that run at *exactly* one speed, commonly 1,800 rpm. Properly loaded, the synchronous motor's rotor locks in on power line frequency and stays there with zero slip. Most common use is for clock and timer power. Some of these have a permanent magnet armature shaped like a star wheel, and the magnets spin around like wagon spokes following the magnetic field as it chases around the many-pole stator.

Getting the Motor Started

It was explained earlier that the armature, stalled in the pulsating magnetic field, generates no torque. But once urged in either direction, quickly accelerates to normal speed, continuing in the direction which it was started. Alternating-current motors are frequently classed by the means giving them their starting impulse.

Resistance Starting

Commonly called a "split-phase" motor, this variety is probably the most common a.c. type of all, and because it is inexpensive, it is used on numerous appliances not requiring high starting torque. A centrifugal pump often uses a resistance split-phase motor.

If two groups of waves or "phases" chase themselves around the motor stator, the armature will try to follow; and making the phases revolve is how the split-phase motor is given its starting torque. A set of "phase" windings is added to the "run" windings on the stator. The phase or starting windings are displaced ninety degrees from the run windings, and are wound with higher electrical resistance—more ohms.

The start or phase windings generate a second magnetic field, displaced from the run winding field because of higher resistance. Now, there are two phases of waves chasing in a definite direction around the motor; and the rotor is pulled around with the phases.

The Starter Switch

Start or phase windings are energized only during the brief moments that the a.c. motor accelerates to speed. As it approaches rated rpm, a starter switch deenergizes the start wind-

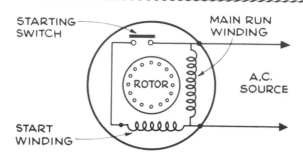

Fig. 16-15 In most induction motors, the starting switch is centrifugally operated, cutting out the starting winding as the motor approaches speed. In hermetically sealed galley refrigerator motors, the switch may be operated by a current-sensing coil.

ings with a click. In some motors the switch is internal, being actuated centrifugally by governor weights. On other units, particularly hermetically sealed galley refrigerator motors, the switch is actuated by a current sensing coil. In series with the power feed wires, the sensing coil is part of a relay, and when it feels the current decrease, as the motor reaches speed, it releases the contacts which feed the start windings.

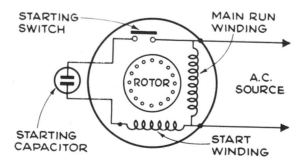

Fig. 16-16 In the capacitor-start motor, a high value capacitor is switched in series with the starting winding until the motor approaches running speed.

Capacitor Starting

Resistance starting and capacitor starting are almost the same. The important difference is that the phase or start windings are energized during the start interval via an electrolytic capacitor in series between starter switch and winding. Electrical size of the capacitor is typically between 50 and 160 microfarads, and physically it is often seen as a black cylinder mounted on or near the motor.

The capacitor creates better phase shift than simple resistance start windings, increasing the motor's starting ability while reducing its starting current for a given torque. Its reduced current demand and increased efficiency make the capacitor start motor attractive for on-board appliances, such as galley refrigerators, because getting enough current from the shore power cord is always a problem. Where the skipper has a choice between ordinary "split phase" or capacitor start motor, he should always choose the later.

Two-Capacitor Motor

Starting of the two-capacitor motor is as described for the capacitor start unit. The difference is that after the high value electrolytic capacitor has started the motor and been switched out of the circuit, a capacitor of smaller electrical value, typically 10 to 30 MFD, continues to energize the start windings. As long as the motor continues operating, the "run" capacitor keeps feeding a moderate current to the start windings. This improves efficiency while reducing hum. The two-capacitor motor approaches the polyphase industrial unit in smoothness and ability to hang on to a load. One might compare it to a plain resistance start motor as comparing a diesel to a gas engine.

Permanent Capacitor Motor

On board the boat, this simple, efficient a.c. motor is fine for easy starting loads such as fans, blowers and centrifugal pumps.

It has no starting switch, a single moderate size capacitor being permanently wired in the phase or start windings. With a capacitor sized somewhere between one and 15 microfarads, the unit is sometimes provided with special tapped stator windings, allowing its speed to be externally varied within the limits. The tapped stator capacitor motor is used a great deal on blowers.

Shaded Pole Motor

Extremely popular for cabin fans, blowers, and other light duties, requiring to perhaps $\frac{1}{10}$ hp, the shaded pole motor virtually sweeps the board in the flypower category. The motor is simple, inexpensive, and not particularly efficient; but efficiency is of secondary importance in very small a.c. motors and simplicity has its blessings. This type motor has the usual run windings of two or four poles, and each pole has a shading winding biased to one side of the pole piece. The shading winding is a single turn of heavy bus bar or copper strap, and is short circuited. Current induced in the shading coil creates a secondary magnetic field displaced in phase from the main field. This acts as a phase winding, giving the motor its urge to rotate. No starter switch, capacitor or current relay is required since the shading coil remains active whenever the motor is energized.

Reversing

Except for the shaded-pole motor, all the types of a.c. motors described are potentially reversible. To reverse the motor, you interchange connections of the start winding leads with respect to the run windings. Motors intended to be reversed have all four leads led to a terminal box.

How Much Current?

Figure 16-17 shows the values of full load motor current for induction motors running at usual speeds and motors of normal torque characteristics. Specific motor current may vary from the given values, but for planning purposes, these figures are most

Horsepower	115 V.	230 V.
1/6	4.4	2.2
1/4	5.8	2.9
1/3	7.2	3.6
1/2	9.8	4.9
3/4	13.8	6.9
1	16	8
1 1/2	20	10
2	24	12

Fig. 16-17 Full load currents in amperes for alternating current motors are shown in this table.

useful. Some hermetically sealed refrigeration motors demand much more current than indicated in the table. These are electrically of low efficiency, depending upon refrigerant for cooling. However, the appliance nameplate will indicate current rating.

Effect of Light Load

Induction motors draw somewhat less than full load current when lightly loaded; but the decrease in current demand is not proportional to the reduction of load. This is true in the a.c. motor to a greater extent than in the d.c. machine. For example, one split-phase motor which draws 10 amps at full load, demands 8.7 amps at half load; and will still soak up eight amps with no load at all.

Because current demand of an a.c. motor decreases less than linearly with load reduction, it is unwise on board a boat to be overconservative in sizing a motor to a load. A ⅙ hp motor working full load, draws much less than a ⅓ hp motor loafing at half load. The picture can be improved somewhat with power factor correction, as explained in Chapter 17, but it is still best to select on-board induction motors sized to work hard rather than motors too big for the assigned job.

Speed Control

The a.c. induction motor is by nature a constant speed animal, and controlling its speed over a wide range is all but impossible. Unless the motor is designed for external speed changing, it should be operated at nameplate rpm. Note that this does not apply to the universal motor which, with its wound armature, commutator, and brushes, closely resembles the d.c. motor. Speed of the universal motor, commonly found in hand drills, may be varied by reduced voltage from transformer or rheostat, or may be controlled by a "light dimming" Triac or Powerstat.

Some a.c. fan motors are wound so that a different number of poles may be switched in and out of the circuit, giving two or more finite speed ranges. For example, when switched to four poles, fan speed is about 1,725, but when six poles are switched in, speed drops to about 1,100 rpm.

Watch the Voltage

Induction motors are sometimes damaged by dropping voltage from the shore power cord. Because they are constant speed devices, they will hang onto the load as long as they can, despite low voltage. Finally, however, if supply voltage sags too low, the motor will "stall" off its run windings and fall back on the start windings. After a short interval, the machine will either burn out or trip a protective device.

Sometimes an a.c. induction motor, such as one driving a pump, will cycle on and off in response to low voltage. Here, a thermal protector, sensing that the motor has fallen back to its start windings and is drawing excessive current, "pulls the switch." After the motor cools, the protector reenergizes it, and the struggle is repeated, until finally the motor roasts for good.

Voltage at the Pier

Aboard a boat having an a.c. appliance such as a refrigerator, supply voltage measured at the appliance cord, with the motor running should be 105 volts or more *minimum*. Otherwise, the motor may not be able to carry its load. In addition, during a brief interval when the motor starts, voltage must not drop lower than 95 volts; otherwise, there may be trouble ahead. Where voltage is low due to excess demand at the marina, current demand may be reduced by some of the means suggested in Chapter 17.

SYNOPSIS

Direct and alternating-current motors are outwardly similar, but electrically quite different. The d.c. motor has a wound rotor, commutator, and brushes. The a.c. induction motor has a simple "shorting bar" rotor, with no brushes or commutator. The universal motor, operating on either a.c. or d.c., closely resembles the standard d.c. motor, and operated at very high speed. Direct-current permanent magnet motors are highly efficient and are commonly found in small fractional horsepower units. The synchronous motor, operating on a.c., runs at exactly one speed, is used to power clocks and timers. Many motors both a.c. and d.c. are reversible by interchange of external leads. Motors draw less current when lightly loaded, but current reduction is not proportional to load reduction. This is particularly true of a.c. induction motors.

~~~~~~

CHAPTER XVII

Hold Down
That Current Demand

GONE ARE THE DAYS when metropolitan power companies, such as Con Ed in New York, advertised the beauties of heating homes by electricity, and "living totally by electricity." Now is the day of the blackout, brownout, and plea to turn off the air-conditioner.

The honeymoon of unlimited electric power appears to be cooling.

Reasons for Conservation

Aboard the boat tied to the marina's pier, there is another good reason for conserving watts and reducing current demand. Watts and current, as we shall see, are closely related, but aren't the same thing, even at the same a.c. voltage. Conservation on the boat is more important than in house or apartment because the entire marine supply system is generally weaker.

Consider a typical older marina and its a.c. power system. Piers have been added in the past few years; the electrical system has been extended, but not necessarily beefed up. By the time a.c. power leaves the pole transformer and is distributed over the yard's sprawling network, there's little reserve at the last receptacle down the line.

Another thing: With more families week-ending aboard the boat in its slip, and with the boat wife demanding all the conveniences to which she is accustomed, power demand has been amplified. Electric stoves, space heaters, air-conditioners, refrigerators, and deep freezers take a lot of power from the line. And the more power that's taken, the lower the voltage drops, until, at best, appliances refuse to operate properly, and, at worst, something burns.

Yet another reason for being careful about on-board current demand is that in many installations the power cord or boat's wiring, or both, are inadequate. This is particularly true on older boats on which the electrical system has grown haphazardly.

Four Ways to Conserve

To cool the fevered cord connecting boat to pier, and to ease the load on the marina's system, four approaches come to mind. Used individually or together, they work wonders toward chopping down current sucked through the power cord.

1. Use existing equipment with care.
2. Choose new appliances wisely.
3. Generate power with an on-board generator set.
4. Improve power factor of a.c. appliances.

Use Equipment with Care

Follow the old fashioned advice, "Turn it off when you're not using it." This applies to lights as well as appliances. Why burn a 200 watt reading lamp in one cabin, sucking almost two amps from the system, while you are elsewhere watching the TV, drawing another three amps? By killing the unneeded light, you've cut current demand by 40%. At home it may not mean much; but aboard the boat, saving two amperes might help a lot.

When possible, select "low" or moderate heat when cooking on an electric galley stove which is energized by dock power.

Try to use one burner at a time, and, of course, use the oven as little as possible. A plan used by some boat wives is to do the heavy cooking at home, then use the boat stove for reheating. Smart girls use pressure cookers, too, because with this kind of utensil, less electric energy is required to cook anything from a simple vegtable to a complete meal.

Keep electric refrigerators and deep freezers closed as much as possible. Use moderate settings for both. Don't turn them as cold as they will go. Also, if either the refrigerator or freezer seems to cycle on and off with unwarranted frequency, have it checked by a refrigeration mechanic: Starting current for these devices is five times greater than running current, and each time one starts, it loads the line something awful.

Choose New Gear Wisely

Where a 60 watt bulb is perfectly adequate, don't install a 100. If a little two-slice toaster takes care of breakfast, don't be tempted to set up to a four holer. Rough it a little; leave the electric hair drier off the boat. Want TV aboard? Then buy one of the new all (or nearly all) transistorized sets. They draw less current, and heat the cabin less than the tube models.

You plan to air-condition the cabin. This takes a lot of juice, so don't overdo it. Buy the smallest that will do an adequate job. You might also favor an air-conditioner incorporating a water-cooled condensing unit. For equal cooling capacity, it should draw less current than one with air-cooled condenser, and in many instances it will be quieter, since it needs no condenser fan or blower.

For on-board use, a top-opening deep freeze is much better than a front-opening one since the top-opening freezer does not lose its volume of icy air each time the door is opened. Holding its cold air better, the top-opener uses less electricity. It also is less liable to dump its contents on the cabin deck in a seaway.

The smallest electric refrigerator that will handle your needs comfortably is the best from a conservation standpoint. Its location can effect the refrigerator and its relative on-time. If the box has an integral condensing unit machinery compartment, the entire unit must be installed where there is adequate ventilation behind and around the cabinet. Otherwise, the condenser coil can't shed its heat; compressor head pressure will be excessive; the motor will work harder; and the refrigerator will be "on" more than required. This wastes power.

The same theory applies to boxes having remote condensing units connected to the cabinet by tubing. Either the condensing unit should be water cooled, or if air cooled, must be well ventilated so it can get rid of its heat.

Electric space heaters are nice to have aboard, breaking the chill on brisk mornings and cool fall evenings. But electric heaters draw lots of current: When buying one, look at the nameplate rating; you will find that most heaters are rated between 1,200 and 1,700 watts, which on 115 volts, means they draw from 10 to 15 amperes, admittedly a lot of current by boat standards.

Choose an electric cabin heater which has two "speeds" or a thermostat or both. With this unit, you can conserve by selecting the lower heat after initial heat-up, and can hold down total demand by adjusting the thermostat to the lowest setting commensurate with reasonable comfort.

Generate Your Own

On board the boat of, say, 33 feet or more, there is a lot to recommend an on-board a.c. generating set, where the a.c. demand is great. With your own little powerhouse, you're free forever from the dock's supply of power, except perhaps for battery charging while you're away from the boat.

With your own engine-driven generating set, you can cruise where and how you like, and still have all the a.c. power demanded by the crew. The generator makes it possible to anchor in remote places, far from the apartment house atmosphere of the crowded marina. The set, properly selected, and wired, also assures you of almost unlimited power for electric ranges, heaters, and other power sucking devices.

For example, a 12,000 watt a.c. generating plant, powered by a modest four-cylinder motor of 12 to 20 hp, can deliver 100 amperes of juice at 115 volts. That's a lot of current. How many marinas can you waltz into, plug in, and blithely demand 100 amperes? Mighty few! Their facilities simply can't handle it, and, in addition, the dockside power cord would have to be the size of a fire hose.

A discussion of a.c. power plants is found in Chapter 8.

Improve the Power Factor

Power factor is a slightly mysterious parameter affecting the current demand of many a.c. power consuming accessories. It forces the item to draw more current from the line than indicated by wattage. In extreme cases, for example, an appliance with exceptionally low power factor, running on 115 volts, and rated 100 watts will draw 2 amps rather than 0.87 amps. The lower figure is that expected when power factor does not enter the picture.

It is apparent, then, that if you can improve power factor of certain accessories, you will reduce a.c. current demand.

A Little Theory

In direct-current circuits, volts times amps equals watts. But in a.c. circuits, volts times amps times power factor equals watts. If P.F. is 100%, as in an incandescent light bulb, then a.c. volts times amps equals watts. But if power factor is 50%, as in many flourescent fixtures, then watts equals volts times amperes times P.F., and instead of drawing, say, 1 amp from the line, the fixture will draw 2 amps.

The Villains

Low power factor electrical items found aboard the cruiser include appliances driven by induction motors, transformers, fluorescent lights, and battery chargers. Depending upon motor loading, voltage, and design, power factor of the named accessories will fall somewhere between 40% and 80%, indicating that they demand 60% to 20% more current than indicated by their wattage rating. These are inductive components.

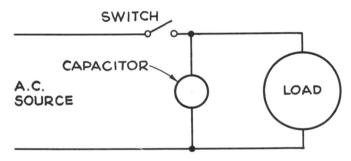

Fig. 17-1 The capacitor is wired in parallel with the load on load side of switch.

The Heroes

Toasters, hair driers, space heaters, galley stoves, water heaters, and incandescent lights are resistive loads, have high power factor, and require no correction. These are resistive (not inductive) components.

How to Correct

Connecting the correct value of capacitor across the power input terminals of low power factor components will raise P.F. and reduce current demand. If the exact value of capacitor (sometimes called a condenser) is connected across the appliance terminals, power facor may be raised to a hundred percent. To automatically switch the capacitor across the line at the same time as the inductive load, the capacitor is connected to the load side of the switch. This is shown in Figure 17-1.

Determining Capacity

How many microfarads of capacity are required to reduce current to its lowest value? The simplest way to determine is as follows: Run the appliance without correction, measuring its current demand. Start connecting capacitors across the line, incrementally increasing the number of units in parallel until current is brought to a minimum.

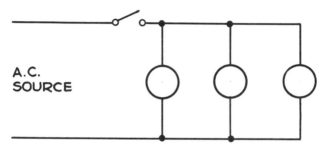

Fig. 17-2 For increased capacity, units may be connected in parallel across line.

It will be obvious when enough capacity has been stacked across the line. When you reach optimum capacity, additional capacity will have an adverse affect, increasing, rather than decreasing current. Because capacitors are expensive, it is customary to slightly undercorrect the P.F., picking a capacitor of the nearest handy lower value.

Typical Results

Figure 17-2 shows the effects of power factor correction on a sampling of typical on-board appliances. Except for the big 230 volt cabin air-conditioner, all are 115 volt. The examples are given only to indicate the magnitude of improvement possible through P.F. correction. The reader must not automatically assume that the same capacity will be required for similar units. As described earlier, the best way to determine the microfarads for correction is by experiment.

Appliance	Uncorrected Current Amperes	Corrected Current Amperes	Current Reduction	Required Capacity MFD
1/6 hp split phase motor running light	2.5	0.7	72%	55
1/25 hp fan motor running light	1.2	0.5	58%	20
Cabin fan	0.56	0.4	29%	8
Fluorescent light	1.1	0.54	51%	17
Battery charger light load	0.82	0.35	57%	18
Cabin dehumidifier	3.5	1.9	46%	60
230 volt cabin air conditioner	5.5	3.8	31%	48

Fig. 17-3 Table shows reduction in current demand with power factor correction.

Capacitor Specifics

Not every kind of capacitor will perform satisfactorily in power correction work. The kind that do the job, lasting for years, are impregnated film, oil filled, with names such as Dykanol, Askarel, Clorinol, and maufactured by Sprague, General Electric, Dayton, and Cornell Dubilier. When you buy capacitors, specify that they are for continued across-the-line application: These are the type used for motor *run* capacitors. Electrolytic

TYPE KT

Fig. 17-4 This oval case capacitor is typical of the kind used for power factor correction.

capacitors used for motor *start* are no good for correction work. Electrolytics will fail after a few moments of across-the-line connection.

Where to Buy Them

Electrical supply houses, lighting contractor suppliers, and industrial electronic mail-order suppliers, as well as electric motor repair shops are sources of capacitors for P.F. correction. If you need help in finding a source, look in the Yellow Pages.

Suitable capacitors are found in catalogs from electronic supply houses such as Allied and Lafayette. One such catalog lists Cornell Dubilier hermetically sealed a.c. Dykanol capacitors in drawn oval steel cases, and having 370 volt rating. The rating is adequate for any possible on-board use. An idea of capacitor prices, based on these units, is given by the following list prices:

Microfarads	Price
4	$3.21
10	5.21
15	6.71
25	10.04

If you can manage to buy capacitors through wholesale supply houses, such as W. W. Granger, the prices will be some 30% less than those indicated above.

How do you Measure Current?

Ordinary volt-ohm meters do not have a scale for measuring a.c. amperes; and the best instrument is a clip-on a.c. ammeter, opened like a pincher, and snapped around one insulated conductor. There is no contact with the conductor, current being measured magnetically, by transformer action.

The reader seriously interested in general a.c. system maintenance and power factor correction will do well to get a snap-on

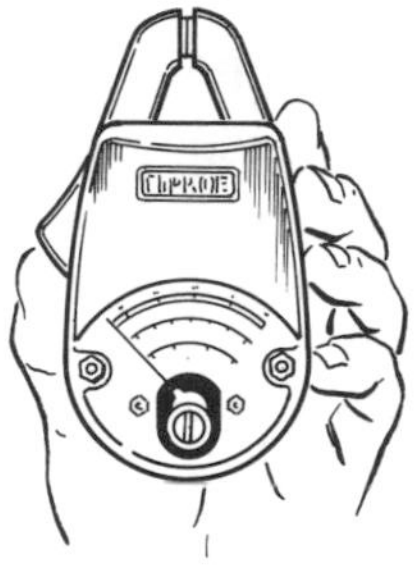

Fig. 17-5 The Amprobe is typical of good snap-on a.c. ammeters so useful for measuring appliance current demand.

ammeter. If not abused, it will last a lifetime. Amprobe is a well known a.c. ammeter, and the junior model sells for under $30.

Correction Strategy

With a limited number of capacitors, it is possible to make parallel combinations yielding many values of effective capacity. Using jumpers and clips, combinations of capacitors can be connected across the line to determine the capacity necessary to make the desired degree of P.F. correction. Suggested values to buy are the following, expressed in microfarads: two, four, eight, 16, and 32. Figure 17-6 shows the values of effective capacity that can be obtained by paralleling these. Should you want to extend the test possibilities to 126 microfarads in the same two step sequence, add one 64 MFD capacitor to the kit.

Desired Microfarads	Parallel Combination	Desired Microfarads	Parallel Combination
2	2	34	32-2
4	4	36	32-4
6	4-2	38	32-4-2
8	8	40	32-8
10	8-2	42	32-8-2
12	8-4	44	32-8-4
14	8-4-2	46	32-8-4-2
16	16	48	32-16
18	16-2	50	32-16-2
20	16-4	52	32-16-4
22	16-4-2	54	32-16-4-2
24	16-8	56	32-16-8
26	16-8-2	58	32-16-8-2
28	16-8-4	60	32-16-8-4
30	16-8-4-2	62	32-16-8-4-2
32	32		

Fig. 17-6 Five selected capacitors can be arranged in parallel combinations yielding 31 equivalent values.

Make up a dozen test leads, about a foot long, with alligator clips on each end. Using these and your snap-on a.c. ammeter, you can experimentally determine how much capacity is required for each accessory; it's really an interesting and educational project. After noting the required value for each, make permanent, neat capacitor installations using the test capacitors and additional ones as required.

You will have one of the few cruisers in the world with power factor correction.

Safety Precautions

Don't ever put your fingers across capacitor terminals after disconnecting from the power line. The highly efficient kind of capacitor you are using can store a shocking amount of energy, and can release it like lightning, giving you a nasty jolt, and perhaps a burn.

Avoid leaving charged capacitors around where children might play with them. After using one experimentally, discharge the capacitor through a light bulb to tame it. Otherwise it may sit innocently for several hours, still packing a punch.

Whether or not the capacitor will be charged depends upon the split second it was removed from the line. Occasionally, you will happen to remove it at "zero voltage crossover" during the cycle. Then it will be discharged. But if you remove it from the 115-volt line at exactly the "wrong" instant, it may be charged to as much as 160 volts.

Do not discharge a charged capacitor with a screwdriver or other metal tool. Doing so is hard on both the tool and capacitor. Use a light bulb with test prods, or a resistor of several hundred ohms.

SYNOPSIS

Current conservation aboard the boat is far more important than in home or shop because on the boat the source is limited unless an on-board generating plant is installed. Ways to conserve are to use existing equipment with care, choose new appliances wisely, and improve power factor on some appliances.

Power factor is improved through capacitors connected in the circuit and energized when the appliance is switched on. Typical items requiring correction are refrigerators, pumps with induction motors, deep freezers, chargers, and fluorescent lights. Required capacity is determined by experiment, current being measured with a snap-on ammeter.

~~~~~~

CHAPTER XVIII

Saving Soaked Equipment

ON-BOARD electrical gear sometimes gets thoroughly soaked, either by being drowned in sea water (or lake, or river water) or by being left out in a downpour. Of the two varieties of soaking, immersion is the worst, because flotation water carries dirt, silt and muck into the accessory. Furthermore, if the water is saline, it impregnates the item's innards with salt, an enemy of all electrical equipment.

Salt, the Foe

When you're cleaning up a drowned electrical assembly, it is particularly important to get out all salt, because remaining salt will cause future trouble in two ways: It is hygroscopic, attracting moisture from the air, causing corrosion. Furthermore, it converts virtually nonconductive, clear dew point or atmospheric moisture into highly conductive electrolyte, causing all kinds of internal faults in electrical machinery. Even the trace of salts in brackish or fresh lake water can do this.

Salvation is Universal

Almost any kind of electrical accessory can be saved after a dunking. No matter how sad it looks after you have recovered it, there is a strong possibility you can restore the appliance to service. In his shop, the author has recovered items as diverse as an air conditioner, pump, hair drier, electric drill, toaster, battery charger, distributor, generator, and starter.

Patience is Important

Drying, cleaning, and refurbishing drenched equipment, and putting it back into service involves a simple technique; but it requires patience. The prime rule is: Don't apply power to it until you are sure it's bone dry. The higher the operating voltage, the more applicable the rule. Obviously, the insulation resistance in damp 115-volt fiber insulator is more severely stressed than that on one handling only 12 volts.

Should you plug in a unit, such as a 115-volt motor, while it is still soaked, current will flow across moisture paths where it shouldn't go. Soon, the electricity heats the wet insulation; and that material chars, quickly losing resistance. Current increases through the fault; and finally the entire circuit burns up.

Equipment

Simple kitchen and home workshop equipment is adequate for drying and cleaning drowned marine gear:

- A gas or electric baking oven with a thermostat that is reasonably trustworthy, and a thermometer. The thermometer can be the familiar meat-cooking kind.
- A ladies hair drier, or electric bathroom heater with blower.
- Spray can of CRC or other moisture inhibitor.
- Oil can.
- Plenty of clean fresh water.
- Patience.

Not commonly available, but most useful, is a supply of compressed air. High velocity air, blowing from a compressed air gun, has a fast drying effect in tough-to-get-at labyrinthian passages inside the electrical equipment. The air's low dew point, combined with its speed, does a fast drying job which can then be topped off with a little heat. Small compressed air rigs intended for paint spraying are readily available from tool rental houses. You might consider leasing one of those for your next drying out session.

Take it Home

Where at all possible, take the soaked electrical equipment from the boat and transport it to your home or shop. Granted, you cannot easily remove fixed wiring and switchboards; these must be dried in place. Motors, generators, heaters, electric tools, and appliances, however, should be taken ashore for drying.

Rinse it Well

In a tub, laundry sink, or any available watering place, rinse the accessory thoroughly with warm, clean, fresh water. Use a little soap, if you desire. The bath will flush out silt, dirt, and salt; and the rinse is obviously more important if the accessory was immersed in salt water than in fresh.

After washing and rinsing the motor, or whatever it is you are recovering, shake it out. Position it every which way; and if you have a compressed air source, blow out as much water as possible. The exhaust blown from a vacuum cleaner is of help, because its air stream is warm and dry. Set the item down on a table in front of an electric fan for a while, as an alternate. If possible, do this out in the sunshine.

Bake It

Warm the electric or gas baking oven to about 185°F, and allow the temperature to stabilize. Many ovens overshoot to temperature hotter than thermostat setpoint when first started; and such heat might damage your item. So, check temperature with an oven thermometer before baking out the electrical widget on which you are operating.

Place the electrical item on an open grid shelf, and bake it gently. Shift its position occasionally; and give it plenty of time.

On an ordinary starter motor, for example, two to three hours at 185°F is satisfactory. But at all costs, avoid trying to speed the process with higher temperature which might damage the insulation or a plastic feedthrough bushing.

Spray It

After you are sure the accessory is bone dry, use hot pads, unload it from the oven, and let it cool. When it is just a little warmer than room temperature, spray its insides with a mist of moisture inhibitor such as CRC. If the item has rotating parts, oil or grease its bearings.

Try It

After cleaning, rinsing, baking and spraying, you are ready to give the components a try. Hook it up to its normal power supply and run it a while. If it looks, sounds and smells okay, put it back in service.

On-Board Components

It is all but impossible to remove some components from the boat, short of doing a rebuilding job. How about drying out those things which must remain on board? Here, you must bring the required tools and equipment to dockside: fans, heaters, heat lamps, blowers, hair driers, moisture repellent, and, when available, a rented compressed air source with blow gun.

Clean It

Using a fresh water hose, watering can or bucket, rinse out the item. Drive out as much of the silt, salt, and dirt as you possibly can.

Dry It

If you have a compressed air supply, put it to work blasting air through all the waterlogged passages and starting to dry out the innards. If you do not have compressed air, try a vacuum cleaner with hose reversed. Then aim electric heaters at the component to start dehydrating it. Help the electric heater with a fan to keep the air moving and assist the drying. Be careful, however: Watch the temperature; and never leave the make-shift rig unattended. You don't want to ruin the accessory or start a fire. Repeatedly feel the thing you're drying. When it feels too hot to hold, move the heat source farther away, or reduce heating power.

Maintain the item good and warm all day. If it is a motor that you are reclaiming, rotate the shaft occasionally. Move the heater to different angles, too, making the bake-out as uniform as possible. When you are sure things are completely dry, allow the temperature to return just warmer than ambient; then spray with moisture repellent. Now, the equipment is ready to try.

Tricks of the Trade

Alternating current induction motors can be dried slowly through the application of low voltage d.c. to the windings. The author has had success with this method, using a 12-volt battery charger with adjustable output. The motor is first washed, rinsed, and blown clear of as much water as possible. Then, on a typical quarter horsepower a.c. motor, about six amps d.c. is flowed through the windings via the motor's power cord. After a few hours, the motor frame will become uncomfortably warm to the touch, and current may have to be reduced. If the charger has but one fixed rate, current can be cut back through the insertion of a resistance in the leads.

Low voltage direct current applied all day will do no harm to the motor's insulation, but will dry it out. Moderate voltage d.c. can force appreciable amperage through the windings in an induction motor because the motor's a.c. reactance does not impede direct current.

It is a good idea to remove the capacitor from a capacitor-start motor before baking it. And it is not a bad idea to replace a start capacitor that has been submerged any length of time; because even though it functions at first, internal seepage may condemn it to failure after a few days.

Resistance heater elements often found in toasters and electric space heaters, usually gather grass, weed, or bilge dirt after a dunking. Such resistance elements need brushing, blowing and cleaning while being dried. If they are left contaminated, the remnants may catch fire when the heater is first energized.

Heater banks positioned by ceramic ferrules must be especially well dried before the elements are energized to full heat. If you attempt drying them with their own heat at full power, the wet ceramics will crack. However, you can dry this kind of heater assembly by applying greatly reduced voltage for a prolonged period.

Testing

As pointed out in Chapter 1, an ohmmeter is a most useful electrical trouble-shooting tool. You can make use of it here, testing for short circuits or electrical faults to ground in appliance or motors.

When you believe the accessory is well dried and ready to use, test it: Set your ohmmeter on the X100 scale, and measure the resistance between the unit's terminals and its frame. The resistance should be close to infinity. If it is not, and if additional drying does not bring resistance up, the appliance may be risky to put back in service.

SYNOPSIS

Most drowned electrical gear can be saved through a program of cleaning, rinsing, air drying, and baking, followed by a spray of inhibitor and a resistance test. Bake-drying should be at moderate temperature; and no electrical item should be placed back in service until it is thoroughly dried.

~~~~~~

CHAPTER XIX

Shooting Faults
With a Dual-Purpose Light

THE TROUBLE LIGHT and the methods of using it described here, will help you a great deal in finding trouble in the 115-volt a.c. system and the d.c. system on board.

A trouble light, particularly the two-mode, self-powered type used in this chapter, is just about the most useful, practical electrical tool you can have on the boat. It can be used almost anywhere, at any time; and when its signals are understood, it is a gem of a trouble spotter. For some trouble-shooting work, this test light is equal to or even more useful than a voltmeter or ohmmeter because:

- The light is cheap, rugged, and requires no adjustment.
- Its indication is instantly apparent.
- The light is electrically less sensitive than a voltmeter or ohmmeter. It places a small but useful load on the circuit under scrutiny, and is less likely to give false readings. This is particularly true when it is used to test the diodes in an alternator.
- The test light refuses to glow to full brightness unless the circuit has at least reasonable integrity and low resistance. An ohmmeter, on the other hand, deflects measurably on stray leakage currents through the damp hull or poor insulation.
- Having its own battery power, the test light will quickly check out components which are disconnected from their circuits. It

will glow if they have continuity, remain dark if they are open circuited.

The Test Light

If your boat has a 12-volt direct-current system, you can construct your dual purpose tester from readily available, inexpensive parts. Use some kind of box or case, a single-pole double-throw switch, eight flashlight batteries in series, a small 12-volt bulb and socket, and a pair of test leads, preferably terminated with small alligator clips.

Suitable for the tester, and available in most gas stations, a GE #57 bulb, (or equivalent) is the miniature instrument dashboard type. It draws about one-quarter of an ampere at 12 volts, which is just about right for your purpose. Naturally, if your boat has the old 6-volt system, you will use a small six-volt bulb and four flashlight cells rather than eight.

Wiring Arrangement

Figure 19-1 shows how the components are wired. As arranged, when the test prods are touched together, they make a circuit through the batteries and switch to the bulb; that's the arrangement in "internal" mode. In "external" mode, the test leads make a circuit through the switch directly to the bulb. In this configuration, the test prods energize the bulb only when touched to a live 12-volt source, such as the boat's battery.

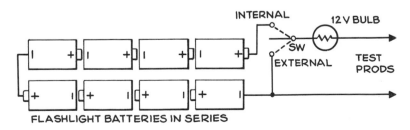

Fig. 19-1 Switch SW selects internal or external mode for trouble light.

Longevity

With the suggested GE #57 bulb and a set of fresh flashlight cells, the batteries should last a full season. This is especially true since you only energize the bulb for brief periods while trouble-shooting or testing. When storing the instrument, always throw the selector switch to "external." Then, if the test prods accidentally are in contact while the light rig is stored, the cells will not be discharged.

Usable on 115-Volt Circuits

An attractive feature of this type light is that it can be used to wring out 115-volt a.c. circuits as well as battery voltage ones. When used for work on a.c. housepower, the circuits are deenergized during the tests.

Be Careful about Selection

When trouble-shooting, do not throw the selector switch to "internal" while touching the test clips to a 12 volt live circuit. If you touch the leads with one polarity, no harm, the light won't light. But if you connect with opposite polarity, the bulb will be subjected to double voltage, and may burn out. A close look at the electrical schematic in Figure 19-2 will show why.

The following are tests you can make on specific accessories, components, and systems:

Boat's 115-Volt Standard System

Select "internal."

Make certain that every switch in the 115-volt a.c. system is open, and that non-switched items such as electric clocks and refrigerators are unplugged. All fuses should be intact and in place. Unplug the dockside power cord, and carry out the tests on the cord's plug blades. When the test light is hooked as indicated, you should have the following response:

300

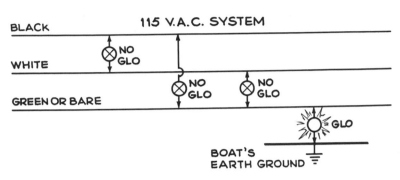

Fig. 19-2 Desired test light responses on standard 115 volt a.c. system un-plugged from shore power.

    a. Black wire to white wire: No glow.

    b. Black wire to green wire: No glow.

    c. White wire to green wire: No glow.

    d. Either black or white to boat's common ground: No glow.

    e. Green wire to boat's common ground: Glow.

If the test bulb glows when it should not, in (a.) to (d.) above, or if it does not glow, in (e.), here's what is signaled:

    a. Continuity between black and white (hot and neutral) indicates a load on one of the circuits, or a bad insulation leak between wires. You can locate the offending circuit, by pulling all branch circuit fuses, or opening all circuit breakers. Then close one breaker or fuse at a time, testing until you find the loaded circuit.

    b. There should never be continuity between the black (hot) and green (grounding) wire. Conductance here indicates a dangerous condition, and you must trace individual circuits until you locate and correct the fault. Glowing of the light on black to green connection indicates a shock hazard.

    c. A current path from white (neutral) to green (grounding) wires aboard the boat defeats the safety feature of the grounding conductor. Both of these wires should be grounded at some place *on shore*, but not on your boat. If your light tells that they are connected on the boat, find out where and untie them. Only the green or bare wire can be earthed on the boat.

d. Test d. is made touching one test light clip to an earthed metal such as the engine block. Glowing of the light indicates there is a ground fault. It should be traced and eliminated since such a fault can cause severe electrolytic corrosion.

e. In the standard system, the green (grounding) wire is tied to the boat's common ground. Failure of the light to glow tells that this connection has not been made. However, note the remarks under "Isolation System" below.

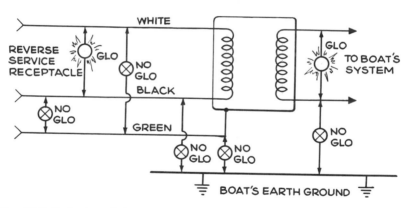

Fig. 19-3 Desired test light responses on 115 volt isolation system un-plugged from shore power.

115-Volt Isolation System

Select "internal."

Where the boat's shore power cord terminates at an isolation transformer aboard the boat, the test light should indicate as follows when hooked to the shore power cord plug in various blade combinations:

a. Black wire to white wire: Glow.

b. Black wire to green wire: No glow.

   c. White wire to green wire: No glow.

   d. Either black or white to common ground: No glow.

   e. Green wire to boat's common ground: No glow.

Here, the light's response is different from that on the standard system: Test (a.) shows continuity through the isolation transformer's primary winding; and test (e.) tells that the grounding conductor is not tied to the boat's common ground.

230-Volt Standard System

Select "internal."

Tests are the same as for the 115-volt standard system with additional checks on the plug blade attached to the red wire. Correct responses are:

   a. Black to red: No glow.

   b. White to red: No glow.

   c. Green to red: No glow.

   d. Red to boat's common ground: No glow.

230-Volt Isolation System

Select "internal."

Here again, the red wire enters the picture; and all is okay if the test light responds as follows:

   a. Black to red: Glow.

   b. White to red: Glow.

   c. Green to red: No glow.

   d. Red to boat's common ground: No glow.

When making test measurements on red, white, and black conductors in an isolation transformer system, you may notice the light is slightly less bright than when the test prods are short circuited. This simply indicates the resistance in the transformer's primary winding. One other point: When manipulating the test clips on the shore power plug from the isolation transformer, handle the thing gingerly. If your fingers are across the blades when you break the test connection, the inductive kick from the transformer may give you a startling bite.

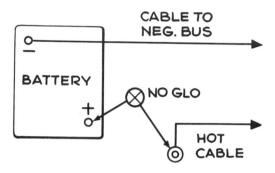

Fig. 19-4 With boat circuits turned off, test light in "external" mode must not glow when connected between hot battery post and its disconnected cable clamp.

12-Volt D.C. System

Select "external."

Open all the switches in the boat; but have all d.c. breakers and fuses closed and intact. Leave the battery ground strap connected, but remove the hot cable. Be sure the master switch is closed. Connect the test light between the battery's hot post and the disconnected clamp. The light should remain out. If the light glows, connected as described, current is leaking from the battery to some circuit or other in the boat, or to ground. If there is a leak to ground, corrosion is invited, and in any event the current leak is a drain on the battery.

To locate the direct current leak, leave the light connected between battery post and cable clamp. Then disconnect one circuit after another throughout the boat until the light extinguishes. You will have located the culprit, and can make repairs as needed.

Bonding System

Select "internal."

Clip one test lead to the common bonding conductor, or to some accessory known to be well connected thereto. One at a time, touch the other test lead to all other items which should be bonded. The light should glow, indicating continuity. Try the engine, ground bus, major accessories, refrigerator, fuel and water tanks, radio ground, and lightning protective mast.

Appliances

Select "internal."

Test 115 volt toasters, electric tools, refrigerators, hair driers, and the like for shock hazard. Clip one test lead to the appliance's outer frame or shell. Touch the other lead alternately to one blade, then the other of the appliance power cord plug. The light must not glow. If it does, the item is dangerous and must be repaired. Leave one test clip on the frame. Touch the other lead to the third plug blade found on modern plugs. This is the grounding blade, attached to green wire, and should make the light glow.

Direct-Current Motors

Select "internal."

Connect the test leads to the motor's terminals; and the light should glow. If it does not, rotate the motor shaft. If manual rotation causes the light to blink on and off hesitatingly, it may be signaling badly worn brushes or commutator.

Connect one test prod to the motor frame. Touch the other prod alternately to one, then the other of the motor's terminals. The light must not glow. If it does glow, it is saying that the motor has an internal fault to the frame. Granted, on 12 volts there is no shock hazard, but leakage due to this kind of fault can cause electrolytic corrosion if the motor is used in a damp location. (This test does not apply to an engine starter motor in which the frame is the ground return conductor.)

YOUR BOAT'S ELECTRICAL SYSTEM

Alternating-Current Motors

Select "internal."

The same tests as described for direct-current motors may be performed on a.c. motors. However, manual shaft rotation will have no effect on the continuity response of induction motors. Those are the kind having no commutator or brushes, as opposed to universal motors found in vacuum cleaners and hand tools, which do have brushes.

Fuses

Select "internal."

Connect the two test leads to the fuse, one to each of its terminations. A good fuse will make the light glow; a blown one will leave the light dark.

Circuit Breakers

Select "internal."

Make connections as on a fuse. A tripped breaker will leave the light dark; a closed one will make it glow.

Conductors

Select "internal."

Where the test prods can be brought to the terminations, any wire or other conductor can be checked for continuity. A good conductor makes the light glow; an open circuit leaves it cold.

Condensers

Select "internal."

Ignition condensers and other capacitors are checked by touching one test clip to the pigtail lead, the other to the shell. The light should remain cold. If it glows, the capacitor is internally shorted. Connections to motor start or motor run capacitors are to the two terminals. If the value of capacitance is large, and your bulb small, a good capacitor may make the bulb glow for

306

an instant when you first make contact; but it should then quickly extinguish.

Ignition Ballast Resistor

Select "internal."

Clip the test leads to the resistor terminals; and the light should glow. Designed ballast resistance is insufficient to observably reduce the brightness of your small bulb. Supplementary ballast tests are found on Page 210.

Breaker Points

Select "external."

Turn the ignition on. Clip one test lead to the engine block, the other to the ignition coil terminal which is connected to the

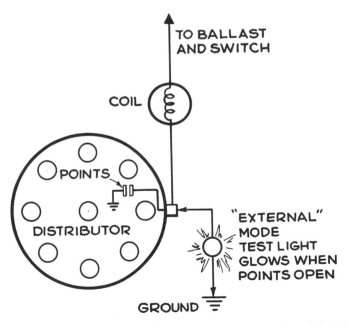

Fig. 19-5 Connected as shown, in "external" mode, glowing of test light indicates that points are open. The hook-up is useful for initial timing adjustments.

distributor. This is the low voltage primary winding terminal. Electrically, you are now connected across the breaker points, in series with ignition coil and ballast.

Crank the engine. The light must blink on and off cleanly. With points open it must be bright; with them closed it must turn off. If it fails to respond in this way, see additional trouble-shooting information in Chapter 12.

Engine Timing

Select "external."

Attach the test clips as described in "Breaker Points" above. Crank the engine ever so slowly until number one cylinder is on compression stroke and the timing marks are approaching alignment. Just as the specified marks match up, the test bulb should glow, indicating that the points have opened.

If the light glows before the moving mark reaches the stationary one, ignition is early. If it does not glow until after the moving mark passes the stationary one, spark is late. Adjustment is made by slight rotation of the distributor body in the direction required for correction. Additional details on timing using a high speed strobe light are found in Chapter 11.

Alternator

The following are test light responses on a negative ground Leece-Neville alternator with a star-connected stator. The results are typical for alternators of this kind, where stator windings terminate at a neutral terminal.

Select "internal."

a. Test light's negative lead clipped to alternator ground:
Responses:
Rotor (FLD) to ground: Glow.
Neutral terminal to ground: No glow.
Output (B plus) terminal to ground: No glow.
b. Test light's positive lead clipped to alternator ground:

Responses:
Rotor (FLD) to ground: Glow.
Neutral terminal to ground: Glow.
Output (B plus) terminal to ground: Glow.

Where the reader is in doubt as to internal connections on his particular alternator, he can clear his doubts by performing trouble light tests on a unit of known integrity. He will then know the correct responses on his own. The skipper with foresight might make tests on his alternator when it is functioning properly, jotting down his findings. Such information is invaluable during a trouble-shooting session.

One reminder: Make all tests on the alternator, as on other accessories, with the unit disconnected from its control and output wiring.

Generator

Assuming the generator has conventional negative ground, make your tests with the light's negative clip grounded to the frame of the unit. Doing so will prevent your reversing the magnetic field. If you should inadvertently hook up with reversed polarity, flash the generator's field with correct polarity as explained in "Flashing The Field," Chapter 6.

Select "internal."

Connected between field terminal and ground, the light should glow. Between output terminal and ground it should glow. While it is connected between ground and output, manually rotate the drive pulley: The light may flicker slightly as the commutator slides under the brushes. But if the flicker is pronounced, you may suspect dirty or worn commutator, brushes, or both.

When connected between field and ground, the light may be slightly dimmer than when between output and ground. This simply indicates higher resistance in the field windings than in the armature. No problem.

309

SYNOPSIS

The dual mode, self-powered trouble light is an extremely useful trouble-shooting and tune-up tool, applicable to both the d.c. and a.c. circuits aboard the boat. Easily built, it can test almost every kind of component. The instrument flows a moderate current through the circuit under test, thus minimizing false readings as might be offered by a sensitive voltmeter or ohmmeter. Fuses, breakers, conductors, insulators, capacitors, breaker points, and complete circuits are among components which can be tested with the light.

CHAPTER XX

~~~~~~

Keeping Electrical Noise
Out of the Electronics

ELECTRICAL NOISE generated in the boat's electric circuits can bother electronic equipment in diverse ways. It causes static on radio receivers, fools depth sounders into reporting incorrect depths, takes the fidelity out of sound equipment, and reduces the accuracy of direction finding equipment. It also forces the TV picture to roll or tear.

Some varieties of interference are so cantankerous that even the expert electronic technician has difficulty in tracking them down and effecting a cure. But other sources of noise are common to most power boats. It is those common sources with which we are concerned here, and which can be quieted by simple techniques.

Many radiotelephone receivers incorporate a noise limiter circuit which suppresses sharp noise peaks, both those coming from the boat's electrical circuits, and those generated in the atmosphere. Unfortunately, the receiver cannot differentiate between a radio signal and electrical noise. Similarly, depth finders have filters to clean up the returning signal, but here again the circuit cannot always discriminate between a returning blip and noise which has similar characteristics.

There is little trouble when the logic signal is considerably stronger than the noise. However, if the noise is the stronger of the two, the receiver, depth finder, or other device will transduce and amplify it despite internal filtering. Even the sharpest circuits have a hard time seeking signals mired in a swamp of electrical noise.

Different kinds of man-made electrical noise generated aboard the boat can deteriorate performance of radiophones, portable radios, direction finders, depth sounders, and TV sets. Common on-board creators of electrical noise are:

1. Engine ignition
2. Generators and alternators
3. Voltage regulators
4. Propeller shafts

Each component requires its own kind of noise suppression, to be discussed in the following paragraphs.

A Useful Search Coil

A handy radio noise sniffing coil is a useful tool, helping you locate the source of radio frequency electrical disturbance. There is nothing critical about this search coil's design; and you can make it yourself.

Wind about 50 turns of insulated magnet wire, any gauge such as 16, 18, or 20, on a short cardboard or wood form about 2½ inches diameter. Or, if you prefer, you can simply wind the wire into a trim hank, securing it into a neat coil with strips of tape. Connect the ends of the coil to several feet of television antenna twin lead, preferably making a soldered connection. Attach the other end of the twin lead to a radio receiver's input terminals, one wire to the antenna post, and the other to ground.

Turn on the radio, tuning it between two stations. If it has an automatic volume control switch (AVC) turn it off. Carry the search coil from place to place, putting it close to accessories which you suspect of generating radio noise. As it approaches

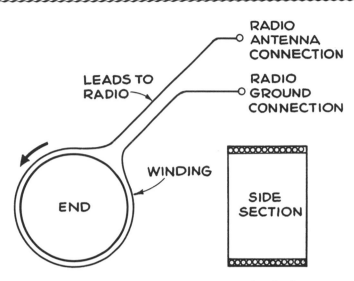

Fig. 20-1 This simple search coil helps locate sources of radio frequency static.

close to an item which is generating hash, you will hear the volume of that interference increase on the radio.

Junior's low fidelity pocket size transistor radio can be a help as a radio noise sniffer, too. Using it as such, tune it between stations, and move it around like a geiger counter, placing it alternately near one suspected component, then another. Keep the volume control low. When the little set comes close to an accessory which is radiating static, you will hear the fuss on the radio speaker.

Ignition Noise

Interference from ignition is easy to identify since it has that characteristic sharp snap, pop, noise each time a plug fires, the staccato keeping time with engine revolutions. As a first step in silencing this, install a suppressor resistor in the high voltage wire between coil and distributor cap.

Install a 1 MFD 200 volt capacitor between the ignition coil's hot primary terminal and ground, the best ground in this case

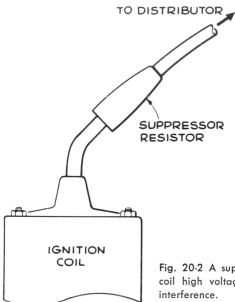

TO DISTRIBUTOR

SUPPRESSOR
RESISTOR

IGNITION
COIL

Fig. 20-2 A suppressor resistor in the ignition coil high voltage cable often reduces radio interference.

being the engine block. It is important that you connect the capacitor to the terminal wired to the ignition key, not the terminal connected to the distributor. Connecting to the wrong coil terminal will do little good toward noise suppression, and may deteriorate engine performance.

If ignition noise is still bothersome, install resistor type spark plugs or, alternately, replace the copper high voltage wiring with suppression resistance wire. It is available at auto parts stores.

Should the above steps fail to reduce ignition noise to a tolerable level, you may have to resort to shielding. Shielding kits are available for many ignition systems from marine electronic shops. Encasing the entire high voltage system including spark plugs, the distributor and coil, the conductive shielding effectively grounds radio frequency signals before they can be radiated from the system.

In lieu of shielding around the ignition components, screening can be tried, although it is usually not as effective. Here, the engine hatch is screened in with copper mesh, and the screen is grounded to the craft's bonding system. In such an arrangement, it is important that the hatch above the engine also be screened and flexibly bonded.

Noisy Spark Plugs

An occasional engine will be found fitted with Champion "U" type spark plugs, one such plug being UJ6. It is all but impossible to eliminate noise caused by these plugs because they have a spark gap near the top of the porcelain; and this gap radiates strong spatter over a wide RF spectrum.

Replace type "U" plugs with resistor types such as Champion XJ6, XJ8 and equivalent. Investigate all spark plug wires for continuity and also that they are making good contact in the distributor cap and at the spark plug terminals. High voltage discontinuities which cause visible spark are a potential source of radio frequency noise.

Ignition Coil Location

The coil must be mounted on the engine—not on a bulkhead; and its metal container must make good electrical contact with the engine head or block. A few coils are plastic cased rather than being encapsulated in a metal can. Plastic types often radiate excessively, and should be replaced with metal units, or shielded.

Generator Whine

The whine and snarl often associated with the conventional generator can be softened or eliminated as follows: Connect a 1 MFD 200 volt capacitor between the armature (battery) terminal and ground—ground in this case being the generator frame. Do not install the capacitor on the field (control) terminal; doing so may alter regulator characteristics.

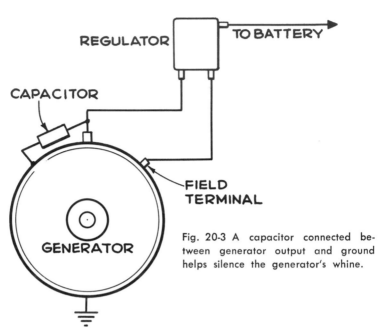

Fig. 20-3 A capacitor connected between generator output and ground helps silence the generator's whine.

In very bad cases of generator whine, install a 1 MFD 200 volt capacitor on each carbon brush holder to ground, using short, stubby leads. This suppresses brush spark and electrical noise close to its source, and is reported especially effective on 32 or 115 volt direct-current generators.

Alternator Hiss

The alternator is inherently quieter than the conventional armature-and-brush generator, its high frequency noise being quieted by an internal capacitor. Most remaining alternator noises can be eliminated or greatly minimized by a 1 MFD 200 volt capacitor between the alternator's output (battery) terminal and ground.

Regulator Noise

Generator and alternator voltage regulators generate various kinds of radio frequency noise. Often, the noise is similar to that

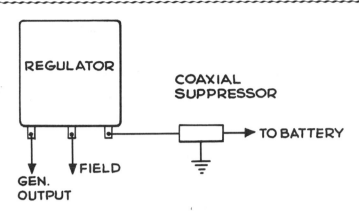

Fig. 20-4 Connected in the lead between the regulator and battery, the coaxial suppressor reduces noise originating in the regulator.

coming from spark plugs; and popping noises are common. In some cases the popping stops as engine speed is reduced to idle.

When suppressing the regulator, put a 1 MFD 200 volt capacitor between the regulator's battery connection to ground. Keep all leads short. If the by-pass capacitor reduces the noise, but not enough to satisfy you, purchase a coaxial suppressor capacitor, wiring it in series with the battery lead. You can get a coax suppressor in an electronic parts store.

Electric Motor Noise

Direct-current motors such as those on pumps, fans, and windshield wipers, and also universal a.c. motors, such as on hand tools, can be filtered. Connect a 1 MFD 200 volt capacitor across the line close to the motor. If the motor is still electrically noisy, install a capacitor on each commutating brush holder, connecting the other end of the capacitor to the grounded motor frame. Keep all pigtail leads as short as possible.

Propeller Shaft

Should you hear steady noise bursts on the radio when the prop shaft is spinning, but notice that the noises disappear when

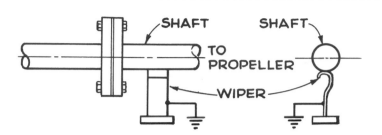

Fig 20-5 A metal wiper or brush conductively bearing on the propeller shaft is connected to the boat's bonding network for radio noise reduction.

the clutch is thrown to neutral with the engine still running, the prop shaft may be generating static. You can eliminate this source of disturbance by installing a bronze finger or brush that wipes the shaft while maintaining electrical contact with it. Electrically connect this finger or wiper to the boat's common bonding system, using heavy wire.

Electric Tachometer

Some electrical tachometers, those connected to the ignition system, cause electrical noise which can be detected by electronic equipment. If you suspect that interference may be coming from your electric tach, perform a test by disconnecting it while listening for improvement.

One remedy is to shield all the wires associated with the ta-chometer, and ground the shielding. Also enclose the sending unit in a shielded box, and ground that.

Sailboat Shrouds

An eerie electrical whine may sometimes be heard on sailboat radios despite all other electrical equipment being turned off. This mysterious interference sounds as though an invisible giant is running a knife blade along the antenna wire; it's a static-like noise with no specific pattern.

Such noise is caused by turnbuckles on stays and shrouds. You can eliminate the trouble by installing shorting jumpers across the turnbuckles. The best method is to drill small holes in each half of the turnbuckle, fastening a wire to each half with small screws. Then wrap the entire turnbuckle neatly with plastic tape to protect the connections.

Grounding and Bonding

Many facets of bonding and grounding were explored in Chapter 5; but the noise reduction aspect is worth reiterating here. Good grounds help minimize electrical noise. When grounding any accessory, use heavy wire or cable, connecting metal enclosures and chassis to the boat's bonding. Don't allow equipment to share one ground wire; and provide an individual grounding conductor for each piece of electrical gear.

VHF Radiotelephone Precautions

Raytheon Company, in its instructions for installing the RAY-45 VHF/FM Marine Radiotelephone, cautions as follows about bonding:

"All unbonded metalwork in the vicinity of the antenna, such as hand rails, steering cables permanent halyards, windshield frame, or plumbing can affect the performance of the radio. It is good practice to bond these together and ground to the engine with a heavy conductor and suitable clamps. In some cases, this bonding will be essential, since any unbonded metalwork may act as a parasitic absorber or re-radiator of the antenna transmit signal. These parasitic elements may severely distort an otherwise excellent antenna pattern. *Bond all metalwork!*" (Emphasis is Raytheon's.)

SYNOPSIS

The boat's electrical and mechanical machinery generates radio frequency noise which can be searched out and suppressed.

Ignition crackle can be suppressed or shielded, while the noise from generators, alternators, and motors can be softened by capacitors or shielding. Prop shaft noise can be grounded; and all electrical machinery is less likely to radiate hash when well grounded and bonded.

CHAPTER XXI

Electricity and Your Compass

SINCE a current-carrying conductor is encircled by a magnetic field, and since the compass responds to such fields, a conductor close to the compass will deviate the instrument. The stronger the current, the greater the disturbing influence; and the closer the wire is to the binnacle, the greater the effect.

In the spring of 1972, the author conducted a series of experiments to demonstrate the practical effects of boat wiring on compass accuracy; and the results appeared in *Motor Boating & Sailing*. Results of the tests highlight the disturbing effects of conducting wires and electronic equipment on the magnetic compass.

The Method

In the experiments, we placed several types of compass in the center of a turntable, the lazy-susan simulating a boat, able to head in any direction. Sequentially, a current-carrying wire was placed fore-and-aft, then athwartship, at compass level, then above and below the compass.

At each relationship, the wire was dressed at several measured distances from compass center. Then at each of these measured distances, several values of current were sent through the con-

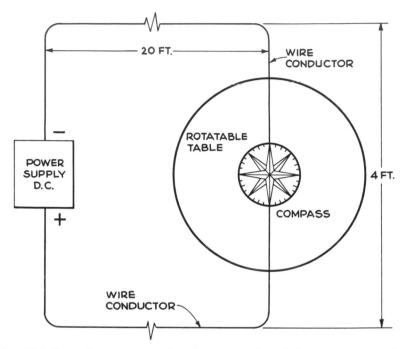

Fig. 21-1 General arrangement of rig for testing effect of electric currents on the magnetic compass.

ductor. The wire was 12 gauge. Four feet comprised the straight test length arranged near the compass, the balance being dressed away at right angles, running to the power supply 20 feet away. The power source was kept this distance to make its magnetic effect negligible. The test arrangement is shown in Figure 21-1.

Effect of Latitude

The described experiments were conducted at latitude north 40° 34′. We mentioned latitude because farther north, close to the earth's magnetic poles, the effect of stray currents would be worse. This is because at high latitudes the earth's horizontal magnetic component is weaker. Had the experiments been conducted closer to the equator, the deviating effects of our electric wires would have been less.

Effect of Compass Type

Several yacht compasses and a surveyor's needle type instrument were tested and each seemed to respond about the same. Regardless of damping, each compass would settle, pointing at the magnetic vector resulting from earth's attraction and the field encircling the conductor.

Current is the Enemy

Direct current flowing in a wire close to the compass induces deflection, and the magnitude of deviation is proportional to current intensity. Thus, eight amperes has twice the effect of 4 amperes. *Current*, not voltage, is the important parameter. A wire several hundred volts above ground potential, but carrying no current, bothers the compass not, even though in close proximity to it.

Alternating Current

Wires carrying alternating current have no effect on the directional readout of the compass unless they are carrying exceptionally powerful currents and are very close. In that case they cause the compass magnets to vibrate; and it is conceivable that high density a.c. currents might damage the compass. But in practical application there seems to be little to fear from a.c. circuits.

Twisted Pairs

Direct-current wires dressed close to the compass in twisted pairs have little or no effect on the compass, causing no perceptible deviation. This is because the magnetic field around one wire is clockwise, around the other is counter-clockwise, and the two fields cancel. Conversely, the worst situation is where the wires, far from being closely twisted, are actually dressed apart, the positive conductor on one side, the negative on the other side of the binnacle. Here, the two fields, rather than cancelling, double their deviating effect on the compass.

Horizontal Wires

Direct-current wires in the horizontal plane exactly at the level of the compass magnets have no deviating effect. However, as the wire is raised or lowered from the magnet's level, it deviates the compass clockwise at one level, counter-clockwise at the other, depending upon the direction of current in the conductor.

Horizontal direct-current wires running above or below the center of the compass deviate the card. Induced error is greatest when the wire is aligned north-south, and is essentially zero when alignment is east-west.

Vertical Wires

Direct-current conductors arranged vertically in proximity to the compass have a deviating effect. Deviation is greatest when the vertical wire is north or south of the compass needle, and is substantially zero when located east or west.

Effect of Roll and Pitch

Magnitude of deviation from the field around direct-current wires as the boat rolls, pitches, and heels. For example, a wire positioned horizontally athwartships at compass card level will deviate the card first clockwise, then counterclockwise as the boat pitches.

Effect of Boat's Heading

The boat's magnetic heading modifies the effect that live direct-current wires have on the compass. Consider a vertical conductor located forward of the compass lubber line. This wire will have maximum deviating effect when the boat heads north or south, will have little influence when the boat is on east or west courses.

Effect of Radios

Virtually all radio receivers, from tiny shirt pocket models to the largest shelf consoles, incorporate permanent magnet speakers. In recent years, technological advances in the magnet art have made these magnets more powerful. The result is that even a small radio in the compass's vicinity can have a profound effect on instrument readout; and, in fact, if the radio is close enough its magnet can even reverse the compass card. Small TV sets and most radio direction finders also have internal permanent magnet speakers, and these instruments can exert an evil influence on the compass, just as a radio receiver does.

The Experiments

The effects of various wire arrangements and of the relative positioning of radio speakers were determined in the experiments described in the following paragraphs. The specific distances and positioning of wires will convey an idea of what to expect from conductors carrying known currents on board your boat.

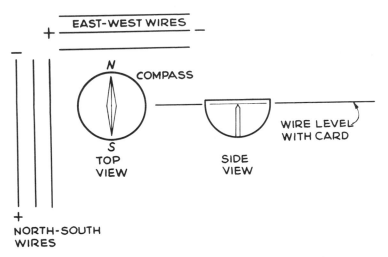

Fig. 21-2 Horizontal wires at compass card level do not deviate the instrument.

325

Wires at Compass Level

The experiments with direct-currect wires strung horizontally at compass card level are illustrated in Figure 21-2. Currents of 2.5, five, and 10 amps through the conductors at six, 12, 24, and 36 inches from the compass center generate no perceptible compass card movement. Immediately the north-south wires were displaced from the compass card plane; however, the compass was deflected. For the illustrated polarity, deviation was counterclockwise as the wire was elevated, clockwise as it was depressed below the compass magnet plane. The experiment demonstrates the effect of a boat rolling when on a northerly course, or pitching on a west course. It emphasises that dressing wires at card level will not prevent deviation on an actual boat.

Wires Under the Compass

The effect of a wire running directly under the compass is shown in Figure 21-3, where the wire is aligned north and south,

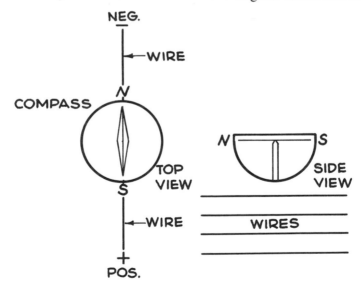

Fig. 21-3 A north-south current-carrying wire under or over the compass has considerable deviating effect.

parallel to the compass needle. The following table gives the deviation produced by different currents and wire distances from the compass card. With the polarities shown, the card deflects clockwise in response to current. Reversed polarity reverses the deviation.

Amperes	Distance From Compass			
	6"	12"	18"	36"
10	26°	14°	8°	4°
5	12.5°	7°	4°	2°
2.5	7°	3.5°	2°	1°

Deviation

Vertical Wires

Figure 21-4 demonstrates the effect of a wire running vertically, directly south of the compass; and the following table shows the effect of current and distance. With the polarities shown, the needle deflects clockwise when current flows. Reversed polarity

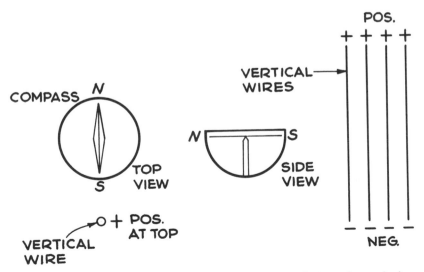

Fig. 21-4 A vertical wire north or south of the compass deviates the card when current flows.

gives reverse deviation; and when the wire is east or west of the compass, its effect is zero.

Amperes	Distance From Compass				
	6″	12″	18″	24″	36″
10	23°	10°	5.5°	3°	1°
5	13°	5°	2.5°	1°	
2.5	7°	2.5°	1.7°		

Deviation

Effect of Headings

An experiment simulating the effect of a conductor on the compass aboard a boat placed on several headings, is shown in Figure 21-5. The energized conductor is fore-and-aft, eight inches beneath the compass card. The wire is carrying five amperes, positive aft, negative forward, creating clockwise deviation with the boat on north headings. The boat's heading versus deviation is tallied in the following table:

Heading	Deviation
360°	14°
45°	12°
60°	9.5°
90°	0°

Specific Components

Wire-wound electrical components having external fields can amplify the deviating effect of direct currents. Such components are typified by relays, solenoids, and ignition coils. The point is illustrated by the following tests made with an ignition coil drawing three amperes, and placed due east or west of the compass:

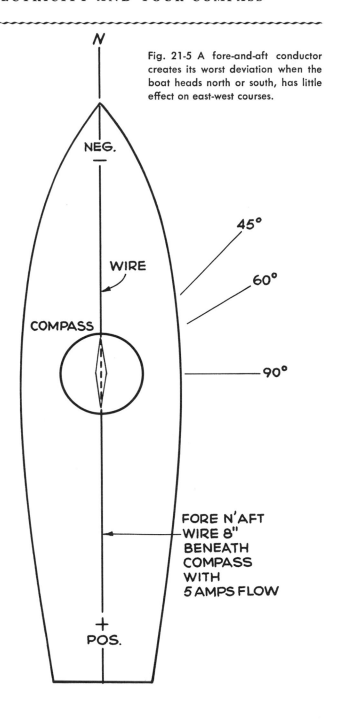

Fig. 21-5 A fore-and-aft conductor creates its worst deviation when the boat heads north or south, has little effect on east-west courses.

N

NEG.
−

WIRE

45°

60°

COMPASS

90°

FORE N' AFT
WIRE 8"
BENEATH
COMPASS
WITH
5 AMPS FLOW

+
POS.

Distance	Deviation
36″	2°
24″	4°
18″	10°
12″	30°

Radio Speakers

Earlier in the chapter the radio speaker was mentioned as a source of compass error. The following figures indicate just how bad an influence a speaker can be, and are based upon a little three inch portable radio speaker, having a magnet of but a few ounces. Orientation of speaker is due west of compass:

Distance Of Speaker To Compass	Deviation
6′	Trace
4′	2°
3′	4°
2′	13°
1′	50°

These figures show that any on-board radio with permanent magnet speaker should be in a fixed position if it is closer than some 5 feet from the compass. With the radio in a fixed location, the compass can be swung and adjusted; compensation will then include correction for the effect of the speaker.

Checking Your Boat for Deviation

If you would like to check the effect of your boat's electrical systems on the compass, perform this test in calm water: Set the boat on a north-south heading. Watch the compass closely while someone energizes and deenergizes each direct-current circuit. Watch for telltale compass deflection. Repeat the experiment on an east-west heading, and, if you wish, on several intercardinal headings.

Curing Deviation

If you locate a circuit which upsets the compass, you can take one of three tacks, of which the first is best:

1. Rewire any offending circuit, using twisted pairs of wires, and dressing all conductors as far from the compass as practicable. At all costs, avoid running one wire of a pair on one side of the compass, its mate on the other side.

2. If the deviating circuit is one which will be energized part time, as a light circuit, prepare two deviation cards. One will give compass correction with the circuit energized; the other will apply when the circuit is cold.

3. Have the compass swung and corrected with the circuit either energized or cold; thereafter, always navigate with the circuit in that state.

The experiments indicate that when you correct your compass, or have it adjusted by a professional, the boat's electrical circuits should be in the cruising state. Furthermore, the compass should be checked in the normal daytime electrical condition, lights off, and in the nighttime state, lights on. Cruising sailboats should try the compass with the auxiliary engine running, and shut off, and also with the boat reasonably heeled to simulate her attitude on both tacks.

After electrical alterations on the boat, and following the installation of new electrical or electronic equipment, reswing the compass to make sure the compass has not been affected. Also, when doing any wiring, pay particular attention to the dress of conductors in the helm area, assuring they are dressed in twisted pairs.

SYNOPSIS

The magnetic field surrounding direct-current conductors deviates the compass from its earth-induced heading, the error being modulated by the amplitude of current and distance of the conductor from the binnacle. The effect is more pronounced at high latitudes; and it is current, not voltage, which induces the error. Alternating current has little effect other than to make the compass vibrate. Both horizontal and vertical wires create error; but if the conductors are dressed in twisted pairs, the error is negligible. Roll, pitch, and boat heading modify the deviation caused by a given conductor; and the same applies to the effect of a magnetic radio speaker. Deviation can be measured and corrected on the boat; and correction tables can be prepared.

A Few Useful Formulas

Ohms Law

The most frequently used equations in electricity are those of Ohm's Law. These useful expressions are: $I = \dfrac{E}{R}$, $R = \dfrac{E}{I}$, $E = I\,R$. Where I is the current in amps; E is the potential in volts; and R is the resistance in ohms. Entering the equation with any two knowns, you may extract the unknown. Thus if the voltage is 12 and the resistance is six, the current is two. The serious electrical boatkeeper might want to memorize Ohm's Law.

Power

1. Watts equal volts times amperes in direct current circuits.
2. Watts equal volts times amperes times power factor in a.c. circuits.
3. The heating of a conductor, or resistance element, is I^2R, the result expressed in watts. Thus five amps flowing through 10 ohms equals 250 watts.
4. 746 watts equal one horsepower.

Resistors in Series

The total resistance of several resistive components in series is equal to the sum of the resistances. Thus if resistors of four, 10, and 15 ohms are wired in series, the total resistance will be 29 ohms: $R_1 + R_2 + R_3 + R_{etc} = R_{tot}$.

Two Resistors in Parallel

The equivalent resistance of two resistors in parallel is found as follows:

$$R_e = \frac{R_1 \times R_2}{R_1 + R_2}$$

Where: R_e is the equivalent resistance; R_1 and R_2 are the resistances in parallel. Thus resistances of four and 10 ohms in parallel equal 2.86 ohms equivalent resistance.

Three or More Resistances in Parallel

The equivalent resistance of several resistances in parallel is found as follows:

$$R_e = \frac{1}{\dfrac{1}{R_1} + \dfrac{1}{R_2} + \dfrac{1}{R_3} + \text{etc.}}$$

Thus if resistors of four, 10, and 15 ohms are wired in parallel, the equivalent resistance will be 2.4 ohms approximately. The equivalent resistance is always smaller than that of any resistor in the network.

Capacitors in Parallel

Several capacitors wired across the line, as for power factor correction or noise suppression, have total capacitance $C_1 + C_2 + C_3 + C_{etc}$. Thus capacitors of four, 10, and 15 microfarads in parallel equal 29 MFD.

Capacitors in Series

The same formula applies to capacitors in series as to resistors in parallel. Thus capacitors of four, 10, and 15 MFD in series have an equivalent capacitance of 2.4 MFD approximately.

334

Thoughts on Shop Practice

• Whenever at all possible, take electrical parts and accessories home or to a shore based shop for trouble-shooting and repair. It's much easier to work where you have elbow room, tools, and equipment.

• Use a muffin pan or a series of short jars to hold nuts, bolts, washers, and other small parts as they are disassembled from an accessory under repair. The receptacles can be grouped according to the section from which the parts were removed, preventing mixups when things go back together.

• When taking apart an intricate device, shoot Polaroid pictures of the assembly as it comes apart. These photographs will be a blessing as you reassemble things, reminding you of the order in which things go together.

• Try small spring clips, paper clips, and clothes pins to hold parts together when you are soldering or arranging delicate assemblies.

• Keep one hand in your pocket when working on conductors carrying a dangerous bite. Stand on a dry rubber mat.

• Solder electric joints using rosin core radio solder, never using acid fluxes, even those said to be non-corroding. Sandpaper the metal shiny bright; apply heat with a clean, tinned iron; then feed on a sparing length of small diameter solder. Heat the work, letting the work heat the solder. Don't apply the heat directly to the solder.

• After fastening cable clamps to the storage battery posts, apply a healthy coat of battery terminal compound. Viscous stuff, it is sold in auto supply stores, and does a better job of discouraging "acid toadstool" than does grease.

• When using a multi-meter, always set the selector switch on a scale higher than the voltage (or current) you think you're measuring. Then, after hooking up, click down to the correct scale. The practice may save you many a blown meter.

• Always, but always, look at the meter selector switch before touching the test prods to the work.

• Use your engine timing strobe light only as required for a good job. Unnecessary flash time shortens the length of tube life, which is rated in X number of flashes, expressed in hundreds of thousands.

• Slip lockwashers under nuts when attaching terminal lugs to studs. Boat vibrations have an uncanny way of backing off seemingly tight nuts.

• Be awfully careful when working around storage batteries with metal tools. A short circuit across the battery posts can trigger a frightful arc, welding the tool, and burning you painfully.

• Take frequent short breaks when doing tedious jobs. After a sip of tea, or a short chat with a fellow boatman, thorny things seem to go together much easier.

• Try to arrange for a helper on big jobs. Often, two boatkeepers can finish a job in a third the time required by one. Having a mate read a meter on the far side of a bulkhead can save hours of improvising and cussing when you're alone.

• Don't depend upon solder for strength in a connection. First, make a secure mechanical connection, then flow in solder to assure a perfect, noise-free electrical junction.

~~~~~~

On-Board Spare Parts
And Supplies

THE FARTHER the cruising man ventures from the pier, the more complete should be his stock of spare parts and electrical supplies. There are no electrical shops "out yonder" where she is most likely to break down. Below is a reminder list of spares and supplies; and the reader is urged to modify it to suit his individual needs:

- Set of spark plugs
- Set of ignition points
- Ignition condenser
- Distributor cap and rotor
- Ignition system ballast resistor
- Ignition coil
- Alternator V-belt
- Several of each size fuse on the boat
- One or more of each size light bulb, especially for navigation lights.
- Brushes for much used motors
- Roll of rosin core electrical solder
- Roll of electrical tape
- Spray can of moisture inhibitor
- Junque box of choice terminals, lugs, lengths of wire, screws, nuts, bolts, washers, cotters, and all the other stuff so dear to the heart of the electrical tinkerer.

~~~~~~

Useful Tools
For Electrical Work

IN ADDITION to the usual boatkeeping tools such as ordinary pliers, wrenches, vice-grips, and an assortment of screwdrivers, the Corinthian electrician will find the following tools and instruments of help in his electrical maintenance and trouble shooting:

- Electrician's combination cutter-plier
- Combination wire stripper and lug crimper
- Thin, long-nosed pliers
- Pair diagonal cutters
- Scout knife
- Ignition tool set with feeler gauges
- Flashlight
- Trouble-light
- Volt-ohm meter
- Snap-on alternating current ammeter
- Battery hydrometer
- Half dozen test leads with alligator clip each end
- Set of battery jumper cables
- Electric soldering iron or gun
- Plug-in polarity tester for a.c. receptacles
- Ignition timing light
- Dwell meter

APPENDIX D

Handy Addresses

American Boat and Yacht
    Council, Inc.
15 East 26th Street
New York, N.Y. 10010
(Safety information and standards)

Allied Radio & Electronics
2400 W. Washington Blvd.
Chicago, Ill. 60612
(Electrical parts, switches,
    capacitors, wire, tools)

Cole-Hersee Co.
20 Old Colony Avenue
Boston, Mass. 02127
(Heavy duty marine switches)

Engelhard Industries
850 Passaic Avenue
East Newark, N.J.
(Capac corrosion protection
    systems)

Heath Company
Benton Harbor, Mich. 49022
(Electronic kits, instruments, tools)

Hubbell Division
Harvey Hubbell, Inc.
Bridgeport, Conn. 06602
(Marine wiring devices and fixtures,
    ground fault interrupters)

James Bliss & Co., Inc.
Route 128
Dedham, Mass. 02026
(Marine electrical hardware and
    fixtures)

Kohler Company
Kohler, Wis. 54044
(Electric generating plants)

LaMarche Mfg. Co.
Route 2, Box 82C
Annapolis, Md. 21401
(Battery chargers)

Marine Development Corp.
P.O. Box 8675
Richmond, Va. 23226
(Battery chargers)

Mercantile Mfg. Co., Inc.
P.O. Box 895
Minden, Louisiana 71055
(Engine driven a.c. power plants)

National Fire Protection Assn.
60 Batterymarch St.
Boston, Mass. 02110
(Safety information and standards)

National Association of Engine
& Boat Manufacturers
537 Steamboat Road
Greenwich, Conn. 06830
(General boating information)

Onan
1400 73rd Ave. N.E.
Minneapolis, Minn. 55432
(Electric generating plants)

Pass & Seymour, Inc.
Syracuse, N.Y. 13209
(Ground fault interrupters)

Raritan Engineering Co.
1025 N. High St.
Millville, N.J. 08332
(Battery chargers)

Ratelco Inc.
610 Pontius Ave.
Seattle, Wash. 98109
(Battery chargers)

Research Enterprises, Inc.
P.O. Box 232
Nutley, N.J. 07110
(Approved type electric fuel
shut-off)

A. L. Rogers Development Corp.
107 Vanderbilt Ave.
W. Hartford, Conn. 06110
(Heavy battery switches)

Ray Jefferson
Main & Cotton Streets
Philadelphia, Pa. 19127
(Battery chargers)

Scott & Fetzer Co.
Adalet Div., 4801 W. 150th St.
Cleveland, Ohio 44135
(Power centers)

Sprague Electric Co.
North Adams, Mass. 01247
(Capacitors)

Starrett Corp.
4522 W. Ohio Ave.
P.O. Box 15497
Tampa, Fla. 33614

West Products
P.O. Box 707
Newark, N.J. 07101
(Marine electrical hardware &
switchboards)

Westerbeke Corp.
35 Tenean Street
Boston, Mass. 02122
(Electric generating plants)

Good Reading

Boatman's Handbook, Tom Bottomley, Motor Boating and Sailing Books, P.O. Box 2316, New York, N.Y. 10019

Electronic Corrosion Control for Boats, John D. Lenk, Howard Sams & Co., Inc., Indianapolis, Ind.

Fractional HP Motor & Control Handbook, Bodine Electric Co., 2500 W. Bradley Place, Chicago, Ill. 60618.

National Electrical Code, National Fire Protection Assn., 60 Batterymarch St., Boston, Mass. 02110.

Motor Craft, N.F.P.A. No. 302, National Fire Protection Assn.

Marinas and Boatyards, N.F.P.A. No. 303, National Fire Protection Assn.

Lightning Protection Code, N.F.P.A. No. 78, National Fire Protection Assn.

Safety Standards For Small Craft, American Boat and Yacht Council, Inc., 15 East 26th St., New York, N.Y. 10010.

Small Boat Engines, Conrad Miller, Sheridan House, New York

Basic Electricity Kit Course, Heath Co., Benton Harbor, Mich. 49022.

(This is a manual and kit to demonstrate electric theory, and the kit builds a d.c. volt-ohm-milliameter. Cost is about $25.) Kit EK-1.

Index

INDEX

INDEX